371.95 REN
Renzulli, Joseph S.
Light up your child's mind
:finding a unique pathway to
happiness and

P9-DOE-977

LIGHT UP YOUR CHILD'S MIND

LIGHT UP YOUR CHILD'S MIND

FINDING A UNIQUE PATHWAY
TO HAPPINESS AND SUCCESS

Joseph Renzulli, PhD, and Sally Reis, PhD

with Andrea Thompson

FOUNTAINDALE PUBLIC LIBRARY
300 West Briarcliff Road
Bolingbrook, IL 60440-2894
(630) 759-2102

LITTLE, BROWN AND COMPANY
NEW YORK   BOSTON   LONDON

Copyright © 2009 by Joseph S. Renzulli, MD, PhD, and Sally M. Reis, MD, PhD

All rights reserved. Except as permitted under the U.S. Copyright Act of 1976, no part of this publication may be reproduced, distributed, or transmitted in any form or by any means, or stored in a database or retrieval system, without the prior written permission of the publisher.

Little, Brown and Company
Hachette Book Group
237 Park Avenue, New York, NY 10017
Visit our Web site at www.HachetteBookGroup.com

First Edition: August 2009

Little, Brown and Company is a division of Hachette Book Group, Inc. The Little, Brown name and logo are trademarks of Hachette Book Group, Inc.

Library of Congress Cataloging-in-Publication Data
Renzulli, Joseph S.
    Light up your child's mind : finding a unique pathway to happiness and success / Joseph Renzulli and Sally Reis with Andrea Thompson. — 1st ed.
        p. cm.
    Includes bibliographical references and index.
    ISBN-13: 978-0-316-00398-8
    1. Gifted children — Education.   2. Gifted children.   3. Child rearing.   I. Reis, Sally M.   II. Thompson, Andrea (Andrea B.).   III. Title.
    LC3993.R465 2009
    371.95 — dc22   2008028505

10   9   8   7   6   5   4   3   2   1

RRD-IN

Book design by Meryl Sussman Levavi

Printed in the United States of America

To our children, Liza, Sara, Scott, and Mark,

who taught us to parent with love and humor.

We hope they will always follow their dreams.

Contents

PART THREE

SPECIAL CONSIDERATIONS

＊

Preface

The mind is not a vessel to be filled but a fire to be kindled.

— Plutarch

The twenty-first century is in many respects an astonishing time to be a child growing up and just beginning to understand life, and an equally astonishing time to be the parent of that young boy or girl. Soon enough, he will be moving into arenas — specifically, higher education and careers — that have been reshaped by profound changes that occurred in a generation or less. One American business leader says that the work world now urgently demands particular talents: "lateral thinking, courage, and an ability to see things, not the way they were but how they might be."

Consequently, never has there been a more pressing need for dynamic approaches and informed, sensitive attention to what children must acquire during their twelve or so initial years of "getting educated" if they are to meet the challenges ahead.

When you envision your child's future and what you want for him, perhaps words such as *happiness, health,* and *success* come to mind. When you consider how such desirable, understandable goals might be reached — that is, what your child needs in the way of informed, sensitive attention — you probably find yourself caught up in the stressful concerns of the here and now. You think about grades, test scores, how tough it is to be accepted into a top college, and what constitutes a useful area of study that will lead to a rewarding career.

In *Light Up Your Child's Mind,* we urge a different kind of focus, one that describes the path from a child's early school years to that happy, healthy, successful future as having less to do with good grades and the "right" colleges and "useful" subjects, and more to do with early experiences in creative thinking and productivity.

Albert Einstein wrote, "It is in fact nothing short of a miracle that the modern methods of instruction have not yet entirely strangled the holy curiosity of inquiry; for this delicate little plant, aside from stimulation, stands mainly in need of freedom." (About himself, Einstein insisted, "I have no special talents. I am only passionately curious.") Our work originates from the National Research Center on the Gifted and Talented. But our work — and this book — is not about the "gifted child," in the currently popular sense of the term. Your child, whether or not he has been officially labeled as gifted, has strengths and interests and a holy curiosity about the world that must be stimulated and allowed the freedom to grow.

In the chapters that follow, we describe dozens of ideas that encourage an investigative, or inquiry-oriented, approach to learning, rather than the one-size-fits-all, drill-and-practice approach that is common in most classrooms. These are workable ideas that you can use in the home to support your child's unique strengths and interests, or enthusiasms. Many of our strategies in the central how-to chapters in Part Two are highlighted in boxes — for example, conversations to have with your child, projects to help get started, suggestions on how to offer gentle guidance, and tips on how to recognize your child's preferred style of expression.

None of this is hard or tricky or hugely time-consuming. Our enrichment and talent-development tools are accessible and inviting to any typically time-pressured, stressed-out mom or dad. We believe that, more than ever, it is essential for involved parents to have these strategies at their fingertips. They are instrumental in helping children understand and develop empowering aspects about themselves that frequently are not taken into account in most school learning experiences. They nourish the "delicate little plant" that is your child's bright and curious mind.

Given such opportunities and self-discovery experiences, here's what can happen for your child:

- She realizes that learning is actually a lot of fun and incredibly exciting.
- Her self-confidence grows; she perceives herself as a potentially creative person with genuine talents.
- She acquires real problem-solving skills that are transferable to a variety of endeavors, in the present and in the future, rather than a mind simply filled with facts.
- She gains insights that can lead to smart choices about everything from extracurricular activities to college majors to career options.
- She may start doing a lot better in school — a huge added bonus.

And for you, the parent, there will be fewer worries over homework and grades and more joy and delight in watching your child blossom in ways uniquely his own. Of course, many factors influence what a youngster will become, but surely the uncontested role of parenting is key in guiding your child on a happy, healthy, successful path.

PART ONE

What Is This Thing Called Giftedness?

✳

CHAPTER 1

Beyond the Classroom

Looking for Gifts "Outside the Box"

School really ought to be an enjoyable place, a place your youngster looks forward to every day. More than that, or as part and parcel of it, school should help to prepare your child to live effectively in a complex world. The psychologist Jean Piaget once defined the principal goal of education as "creating men and women who are capable of doing new things, not simply repeating what other generations have done." To become capable of doing new things, your child must acquire skills that go beyond reading, writing, and arithmetic during his critical formative years. They include an ability to:

- analyze and select from various sources of information;
- approach the unpredictable with confidence;
- take appropriate chances — "safe risks" — in uncharted waters;
- confront, clarify, and act on situations imaginatively and constructively;
- apply the world's knowledge — today instantly accessible by logging on to the Internet — in ways that promote critical

thinking, infectious enthusiasm, self-motivation, and genuine problem solving; and

- cooperate with others while remaining true to an emerging personal system of attitudes, beliefs, and values.

Is what goes on in your child's classroom offering him sufficient opportunity to develop such skills? Maybe yes, maybe no. We would go so far as to guess, unfortunately, probably not. But a parent can provide opportunities that a school does not.

Without knowing your youngster personally, we will state with confidence some qualities he possesses:

- He has unique strengths and interests, perhaps still untapped or yet to be discovered.
- With a little guidance from you, he can be encouraged to engage in experiences that are fun, exciting, rewarding, and skill producing.
- Somewhere down the road, there exists for him a meaningful career path that will bring joy and deep satisfaction, and there's much to learn right now that will help prepare the way.

FROM THE MOUTHS OF PARENTS

Our work has brought us into contact with thousands of young people and their parents and teachers. We know the sounds, smells, and sights of classrooms. We know what kids — and their mothers and fathers — are up against as they navigate elementary school, middle school, and high school. And what we hear from concerned parents is often a litany of quiet — or not so quiet — frustration and worry as they consider their child's education:

"The teacher says my son doesn't pay attention."
"She's in a gifted program, but she doesn't seem to be doing much there."
*"There's an awful lot of drill work and routine stuff that my kid has
    to go through in class."*
"She gets all As in one area and Cs in everything else."

Sometimes, children develop an aversion to the very notion of
school. The mother of a second grader was upset to hear from her
son's teacher that the boy never talked in class. "This kid is a chatter-
box at home!" she said. "He's full of questions and observations, just
curious about everything, and he's a friendly, outgoing little guy. After
I heard that report at the parent-teacher meeting, I asked Will why
he's so quiet in school, and he said, 'Because school is dumb.'"

What's going on here?

It might be argued that at perhaps no other time in the recent past
has there been a greater focus on children, schools, and the educational process. Like all involved parents, you have probably read a
great deal about the overscheduled child, hothouse kids, underachievers, and children with learning disabilities or Attention Deficit Hy-
peractivity Disorder (ADHD). You are aware of the current testing
mania, the tutoring mania, the pros and cons of homework, and the
pressure on children to excel starting in preschool.

What you may not know is that very bright children with much to
offer are going through school without ever being given an opportunity to realize their unique talents. The classrooms in which most of
our children spend their time typically fail to inspire a true love of
learning and accomplishment. Even though you may not have read
about this, you may be keenly, painfully aware that your son or daughter could be doing more or doing better.

Many of those children who are bored or not living up to their
potential or amassing spotty academic records are amazing young

people capable of achieving amazing things. Many others who have no difficulty sailing through their early school years with top grades nevertheless find little that genuinely engages them, little that inspires them to stretch beyond their comfort levels in learning.

Over more than three decades, we have been involved in developing the talents and gifts of young people. Those efforts have been shaped by an attempt to answer for ourselves some simple-sounding but tough questions:

- Who has talents and gifts, and why do we think so?
- What causes a smart youngster to become excited about the process of learning?
- How can those smart youngsters be encouraged to use their strengths in creative and personally enjoyable ways?
- What is happening or failing to happen in the classroom that inhibits the development of excitement and creativity?

Our first clues came from children we knew.

CHILDREN WHO FLY UNDER THE RADAR

Ross, a middle school student we met years ago, was in danger of failing math, according to his teacher. He didn't complete homework assignments, didn't respond to offers of help, and once or twice a week actually fell asleep during class. Ross seemed to be turning away from mathematics and other academic areas early in his school career.

We hoped to gain insight into Ross's situation by reviewing the boy's permanent record. Maybe an unusually low and discrepant math test score would indicate that he had a learning disability. Perhaps a previous teacher or two had noted an apparent inability to deal with male instructors, such as his current teacher. Any evidence of difficulties might explain Ross's underwhelming performance and justify moving him to another class or arranging for remedial support. But, to our disappointment, nothing in the file indicated past problems that might shed light on his current troubles.

All this started us thinking about permanent records, those ferociously guarded school files that collectively contain thousands of teacher comments such as:

> *"Jack needs to practice his multiplication tables this summer."*
> *"Rosa should spend time reading aloud at home."*
> *"Clark must hand in homework more regularly."*

We were then struck by an aha moment: we too had been searching for Ross's *deficiencies,* looking for what was wrong. Maybe his trouble was related not to a deficiency but to the fact that insufficient attention had been paid to his strengths and talents, whatever they were, and that little had occurred in his school life to capitalize on them. Nowhere in the records could we find documentation related to the very *best* things that were known about the youngster. For that kind of information, it seemed the only person to turn to was Ross himself.

So we did. We simply asked Ross what interested him. For the next twenty minutes, he poured out his passion for trains and the railroad system that crisscrosses the United States. He knew he'd loved trains even as a small child because his mother told him he always reached for them in the toy box. Growing older, he read everything he could about the subject. His mother bought him games and construction materials related to trains, and recently Ross had purchased videos about railroads, which he watched repeatedly at home. His mom had also taken him to visit a nearby railroad switching station located under a bridge that spanned the Connecticut River.

He had a lot to tell us. We wondered if any of his teachers were aware of his enthusiasm. But Ross had never mentioned it in school, he said, because "no one ever asked me what I like to do." As to why he sometimes dozed off in class, he guessed that after staying up late watching his videos and studying train books, he was tired during the day.

We asked another question: "What can we do to make school meaningful for you?"

Ross had an immediate answer: "I'd really like to make a video about the switching station under the bridge, the trains that come in and out of the station, and the people who run them."

It was arranged. And that year, Ross went on to script, film, and edit his video, which he cleverly titled "Breaking Through," and ultimately presented it to the local chamber of commerce and the eastern division of Amtrak. Though he missed some class time because of his long hours at the railroad yard, he willingly made up the needed work. Here was the payoff: Ross's enthusiasm for school increased dramatically, his grades reflected that enthusiasm, and he was later accepted into a highly regarded university.

Here's another story, this one close to home:

Our son Mark was an obviously bright boy whose grades, nevertheless, fluctuated wildly year after year. He had high potential, everyone agreed, but was labeled an underachiever because of his inconsistent attitude toward school. Figuring out the situation wasn't hard. If Mark liked his teacher, he'd do well in that class. If Mark liked the content of the class but not the teacher, he'd do well enough to get by with Cs. If he didn't like the teacher or the content, or if the content was too simple, Mark usually failed or pulled through with a D. Though he typically excelled on most exams — and achieved a near-perfect score on the math portion of the SAT — he lost credit for every bit of homework and class work that he didn't complete.

This was not an idle kid. In fact, we usually had to plead with him to go to bed because he was up late reading books about artificial intelligence or building computer components, each an enthusiasm we wholeheartedly supported. Once or twice, Mark made an effort to negotiate with a teacher about substituting more challenging and enjoyable assignments, to no avail. He tried to show his teachers some of the work he was doing at home, but they expressed little interest. Mark just didn't fit the mold of the typical student, and was, in his teachers' words, an enigma. He flunked English and history and didn't graduate from high school.

That was about fifteen years ago, but there's a happy ending to the story. After holding various jobs for a while and searching for the right school program, Mark started college part-time — without a high school diploma. Eight years later, he had completed both his bachelor's and master's degrees in systems engineering and began a rewarding career in sophisticated software design. The change came about when he made up his mind that it was time to succeed academically and when he had a chance to pursue his passions. He didn't get top grades in every class, but he managed to put out enough effort to pass required courses not in his major area, which in turn enabled him to continue taking the subjects he loved.

A fascination with railroads and the desire to make a film about them, a determination to master complex computer problems — were these demonstrations of giftedness? School records for Ross and Mark would probably suggest no. But we would say yes. Countless other young people whom we met and tracked over the years in our continuing involvement with schools across the country lent support to our convictions about giftedness and how it is, or fails to be, displayed. Like Ross and Mark, many bright kids with great potential find little to support them academically. Often, their strengths fly right under the radar of educators who are so intent on looking for what's wrong about a youngster that they miss what's right.

Some children thrive in the classroom; some do not. Why that is may have to do with differing characteristics found in youngsters with academic gifts and those who are creatively gifted — or what we call the good consumers and the good producers. And it surely has to do with "the system," and what that system expects and requires of the children within it.

SCHOOLHOUSE GIFTEDNESS: THE STRAIGHT-A KIDS

Schoolhouse, or academic, giftedness is largely about test taking, lesson learning, and homework producing. This kind of education is mainly what your child receives during the day, and it's delivered via the "four-P" approach to instruction: lessons are *prescribed* by a teacher or textbook, *presented* to a student without giving her much opportunity to decide whether or not she wants to participate, have *predetermined pathways* to the solution of problems, and have *predetermined goals* (a correct answer, for example). We might add one more "P" and characterize this as *passive* learning.

In passive learning, the child is a consumer of information, and the kids who function most successfully at it generally score well on traditional intellectual or cognitive ability assessments, including IQ tests. Every child must be part consumer, of course, because every child should know how to read, write, spell, and deal with numbers. At the same time, schoolhouse learning and its emphasis on content rather than on process, combined with a school's inclination to seek out and attempt to correct deficiencies, has clear limitations.

For one thing, a great deal of the information a child takes in is acquired for the sake of repeating it back on a test. The information may or may not be personally interesting to the student. It may or may not "stick" or be transferable to other areas of endeavor. The kid who complains, "Why do I have to study [fill in the blank]? I'm never going to need it," might, indeed, have a valid point.

Think back for a moment to your own years as a student. What did you learn then that you can easily pull from memory today? Much — perhaps most — of that knowledge will fall into the areas of basic language and math skills. These, of course, are both useful and essential for successful adult living. They enable you to communicate effectively, balance your checkbook, and calculate a 15 percent tip after a meal at a restaurant. You may realize that you seldom need to summon the rest of the compartmentalized material you were required to remember as a student. The names of famous generals, the periodic table, the parts of a plant — all these you have probably forgotten or dredge up only occasionally while completing a crossword puzzle.

That's no crime, except that in the classroom setting the focus on a child's mastery of specific knowledge — and the time spent on it — can have the unfortunate effect of preventing a young person from acquiring ways of thinking that will serve her throughout her life.

For another thing, even academically gifted children can feel pressured to maintain good grades and high test scores, a pressure that trumps a genuine attraction to learning. One father related how shocked he was when his daughter, a fifth grader, expressed panic about her upcoming report card. This dad had always told his daughter that he wanted her to love reading and studying, and to explore interesting new things even if she was unsure how to go about it or how successful her exploration would be. "Why is my child now saying, 'I have to get into a competitive high school?' Who's telling her this? Is that the message we want to send our kids?"

Some children find it satisfactory to go with the flow, to turn in the expected performance and get the high grades, while not being particularly interested in any of it. A seventh grader at a prestigious school told us: "There's a bunch of kids in my class who are just really great at playing the game. They get all friendly with the teachers, but then away from school they could care less, and they call the teachers jerks." It can be tempting to play the game when you're smart and playing the game comes easily — and, perhaps, when you are primarily intent on keeping your eye on the prize (as the directors of one private school put it to their students): acceptance at a top-tier college.

It's critical to recognize when a bright child is unchallenged or underchallenged by what's expected of her in the classroom. For many of these youngsters, going to school is time spent rather than time engaged, by which we mean time spent actively stretching for ideas and results and working with enthusiasm. Kids are engaged when they get caught up in creative work of their own choosing.

CREATIVE-PRODUCTIVE LEARNING: ANOTHER KIND OF SMART

Creative-productive learning takes place when a youngster is intent on developing an original something, a product that he hopes will have a positive impact on an audience of some kind. We might also call it personalized learning by doing. In chapter 3, we will explain the notions of product and audience in greater detail, but the stories of Ross and Mark suggest elements of their meaning.

A young person pursues something that he's curious about, that amazes him, or that he falls in love with. He puts his abilities to work on a problem or area of study that has personal relevance to him and that can be escalated to more demanding levels of involvement. Along the way, he develops self-directed learning skills in the areas of planning, organizing, locating and using appropriate resources, managing his time, making decisions, and evaluating how he's doing.

Throughout this book, we will share many stories of creatively productive children. Some worked independently; some worked together in small groups. Here are a few examples:

- **A first grader became wildly excited about the possibility of writing her own short story and producing it as a pop-up book. She quickly learned this was no easy task and struggled through four or five drafts of the story before starting on the illustrations and the mechanics of making them pop.**

Her mother found her a how-to book, and that helped. The girl's work area was littered with the results of many attempts at folding paper and gluing before she proudly presented her completed, successfully popping-up book to the school library.

- A fourth grader became concerned about the fact that her mom was returning to school to become a lawyer and that pretty soon both her parents, for the first time, would be away from home for most of the day. She thought about how she might help herself adapt to this changed situation, and then she began to wonder what other kids thought about it or did when both parents worked long hours. Over a number of months, she surveyed many of her classmates as well as personnel at a local guidance center, gathering information and tips. The end result was a printed pamphlet called "When Both Parents Work" that explained a variety of typical feelings and useful coping strategies.

- A six-year-old Massachusetts boy participated in a school enrichment program on starting a business and came up with the idea of a company that designs and produces buttons, those cardboard pin-on-your-shirt decorative accessories. He learned some rudiments of the business world — borrowing a small amount of start-up money for supplies, getting his dad to purchase a simple button-making machine for him — and went to work.

Over the course of a year, he made and sold colorful buttons commemorating birthdays, holidays, and special community events and ended up with a profit of more than $250. He insisted on donating his earnings to a local charity that collected funds for gloves and hats for needy children in his town. (When we visited him to check out his button factory, he offered to give us one of his buttons, but if we wanted any more we'd have to buy them, he said, "because I've got a business to run.")

- Eight sixth-grade girls in a school in Maryland worried about the health of their town's lake and the ducks that lived there. After researching the situation, the girls concluded that a large part of the problem was the tendency of people strolling around the lake to feed the birds chunks of bread. Consequently, the ducks went after and ingested anything that looked like a chunk of bread, including pieces of Styrofoam and other harmful substances. In addition, uneaten bread that sank to the bottom of the lake was causing dangerous organic growth and polluting the water.

  Through T-shirts, brochures, and signs they designed, these kids set about educating people about the dangers of feeding bread to ducks. They even managed to have a number of cracked-corn dispensers installed around the lake (cracked corn being suitable feed for hungry ducks), a project that took about two years and involved meetings with city officials, contacts with humane offices, and some promotion in the local media. The Mighty Duck Savers, as the girls became known, received a commendation from their state senator and also won the 1996 President's Environmental Youth Award.

The stories of the button maker and the duck savers point to another common aspect of creative giftedness. Often, the efforts of a creatively gifted child do not take place in the classroom. Rather, they might occur in research laboratories, artist's studios, theaters, film and video production sets, business offices, restaurants, the family basement, the great outdoors, or almost anywhere that products, performances, and services are pursued.

In our programs for schools — developed following our School-wide Enrichment Model (SEM) — we call involvement in such activities higher-end learning, enrichment learning, or independent learning. The SEM engages all kids, not only the "gifted and talented," with enjoyable and challenging project-based experiences that are constructed around individual preferences. We might also call this dynamic learning, a path by which a youngster becomes not just a consumer of knowledge following the four-P style of instruction but also a producer of original work that is an outgrowth of his personal strengths and interests. The two kinds of learning are not incompatible, of course. Certainly, many young people earning top grades in school year after year are also capable of wonderfully innovative accomplishments. But many with less-than-stellar grades are too.

It's important to understand that IQ and test scores are inadequate measures of potential. Many IQ tests are less an indication of a child's pure "natural ability" than a measure of specific achievement — in vocabulary, reading comprehension, or math. The inexact correspondence of creativity with IQ makes sense after a brief and broad consideration of history, which suggests that the creative and productive people of the world — the producers, not the consumers, of knowledge — are the ones recognized as gifted individuals. History does not necessarily remember people who scored high on IQ tests and learned their lessons well.

Earlier, we asked, what is giftedness and how do we develop it? As our discussion so far suggests, the answer lies in looking not for a "gifted child" but for a child who displays or has the potential to display gifted behaviors. Our research over the years has clearly demonstrated that such behaviors emerge when three clusters of traits are present and interact with one another.

GIFTEDNESS: THE THREE-RING CONCEPTION

The traditional approach to the study of gifted children might lead one to believe that giftedness is magically bestowed on a child, a golden chromosome she does or does not have. Add to that the bandying about of such terms as *truly gifted, moderately gifted,* and *borderline gifted,* and we might be searching for silver and bronze chromosomes as well. To the contrary, studies show that giftedness is not an absolute or static state of being but a dynamic condition that can occur if an appropriate interaction takes place between a child and a particular area of human endeavor.

In our writings, we have often expressed this concept in a drawing — a Venn diagram — of three overlapping circles, emphasizing that the coming together of three attributes is what provides the fertile ground for the development of gifted behaviors. Those three attributes are above-average ability, task commitment, and creativity.

- **Above-average ability: A youngster who possesses above-average ability is, in a general sense, a child with basic smarts. She can reason fairly well, express herself fluently and coherently, think abstractly, remember things, process information appropriately — all indications of a fairly high, though not necessarily exceptional or superior, level of intelligence. Ability is generally stable. If your child is very good at math at the moment, for example, chances are she was good at math two months ago and will still be good at it two years from now. Such abilities can be measured fairly reliably through cognitive tests and homework grades, which is why educators feel comfortable using these rubrics to determine who is admitted to a "gifted" program and who is not.**

  Above-average ability might also be demonstrated in areas that are not possible to assess strictly in terms of

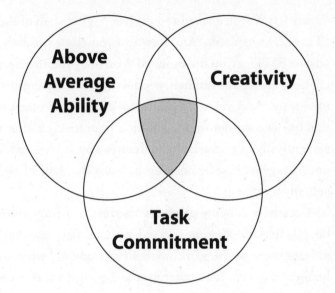

intelligence — for example, ballet, musical composition, sculpture, photography, and leadership.

- Task commitment: Call it motivation, perseverance, endurance, determination, hard work, or stick-to-it-iveness. The English scientist and writer Sir Francis Galton described "a nature which, when left to itself, will, urged by an inherent stimulus, climb the path that leads to eminence and has strength to reach the summit — on which, if hindered or thwarted, will fret and strive until the hindrance is overcome, and it is again free to follow its laboring instinct."

A child with a hearty laboring instinct shows a desire to find things out for herself, a laser-beam focus directed toward a goal that will be pursued until it is satisfactorily attained. The child, consequently, has an ability and willingness to put off completion or success until all avenues have been explored, until she's "got it right." Task commitment of this nature is typically demonstrated within the context of a particular and present problem or interest.

- **Creativity: We once asked a young boy, "What's half of eight?" "Three," he replied. "And how did you come up with that answer?" He wrote the numeral 8 on his paper with a pencil, then erased the left half, producing a 3. A wrong answer, obviously. And yet we might also think, how interesting; this boy is considering the solution figuratively rather than semantically or numerically, a creative approach — which is not to suggest that he need never learn that half of eight is actually four.**

  Creativity is being playful with ideas or being willing to be playful. It's kicking around possibilities, approaching at least some of the world with an attitude of "what would happen if . . . ?" It's sometimes going against convention and traditional ways of doing things, and being unafraid to challenge the status quo or the common modus operandi. Originality of thought, openness to experience, receptivity to that which is new and different or maybe even irrational, willingness to take risks in thought and action, sensitivity to the aesthetic characteristics of ideas and things — all these define creativity.

Unlike ability, task commitment and creativity cannot, obviously, be assessed through typical testing procedures. A child is not "creative" or "not creative" in the same way she is "good at math" or "not good at math." So we say that task commitment and creativity are variable rather than permanent.

Now, you may be thinking that our three-ring model oversimplifies the story of what accounts for gifted behaviors. And indeed, they do not exist in a vacuum. One mother explained her children's accomplishments in this way: "They're all smart, all good students. My son, the oldest, is serious and highly responsible — a supposedly typical first-born — and he's intent on becoming a doctor like his father, which, I have to say, pleases us to no end. He's outstanding in science. Our middle child is on the shy side. She's pursuing modern dance; that's the niche she's making for herself, partly, I think, because she believes her brother is the academic star. My youngest daughter is gregarious, flirty, a charmer. She's the social leader and organizer. So I think the way their gifts are emerging has a lot to do with their very different personalities and also with their attempts to kind of stake out separate territories for themselves within the family. I just think a lot of stuff goes into this."

She's undoubtedly right, and birth order or the dynamics that exist among several children in a family may be one aspect of that "stuff." Common sense, as well as hundreds of research studies, tells us that many factors probably contribute to any reasonable explanation of how and why some kids display gifted behaviors, while others do not. Aspects of personality (such as self-perception, character, temperament, a need for achievement, ego strength, "charisma") and aspects of the environment (parental expectations or personalities, siblings, the availability of role models, physical illness or well-being, money) all might be part of the picture.

Yet those aspects may come to bear in unpredictable or even counterintuitive ways. Each of us probably knows or can remember a young person who grew up with every seeming advantage — personal attractiveness, a good education, a stable childhood — but in adult life showed no evidence of creative productivity or perhaps even happiness. And we know or have heard about individuals whose early years were marked by deprivation, frustration, trauma, and lack of opportunity who nevertheless soared to worthy accomplishment or even greatness — and for whom, perhaps, those unfortunate early experiences were triggers for subsequent productivity.

But aside from the impossibility of mapping a path to success that accommodates the almost limitless number of combinations between and among the different potential factors, and the mysteries of human nature as well, there is a particular reason we have concentrated our talent-development efforts on the three rings. It's not difficult to see that many, if not most, of the variables of personality and environment in a young person's life exist beyond the realm of direct influence. Many are long-term developmental traits or genetically determined traits. Others are simply matters of chance. In contrast, our research has clearly shown that the attributes described in the three-ring conception of giftedness — particularly creativity and task commitment — are modifiable and can be influenced in a highly positive fashion by the right kinds of learning experiences.

The interaction of the three attributes is what leads to the display of a child's gifted behaviors, with the emphasis on interaction. A bright girl comes across something that stimulates her interest. She gets a creative idea relating to her interest and decides to do something about it or with it, and thus her commitment to a task begins to emerge. A deepening commitment, in turn, triggers the process of creative problem solving. Creativity and task commitment almost always feed off and energize each other.

Along the way, parents can set the stage for those right kinds of learning experiences by providing encouragement, opportunity, and appropriate resources.

SCHOOL-BASED GIFTED PROGRAMS

Fortunately, in recent years this whole matter of children's intelligence and how kids learn and thrive has dramatically advanced from earlier lockstep notions of who's smart and who's not. Developmental psychologist Howard Gardner identified "multiple intelligences" and called intelligence "the ability to solve problems, or create products, that are valued within one or more cultural settings." Psychologist Daniel Goleman termed "emotional intelligence" more important than IQ and proved the significance of characteristics such as self-motivation, self-confidence, and empathy as factors in eventual success. Pediatrician and learning expert Mel Levine has written that children learn in different ways and that every child can succeed.

All this is good. Nevertheless, our schools still routinely tend to identify the best and the brightest among their populations according to limited criteria. And kids typically selected for gifted programs are excellent test takers and lesson learners. Although the U.S. Department of Education sets forth a definition of gifted and talented children that includes several criteria aside from academic achievement — including personal recommendations and other more subjective factors — most school systems still focus on the more easily measured characteristics of cognitive intelligence, achievement, and aptitude. IQ, test scores, and grade point averages are key. In many districts, only the top 3 to 5 percent make the cut.

(A bit of perspective: Some years ago, a group of researchers conducted a comprehensive study aimed at estimating the IQs of 282 famous individuals from the past. Among those who would not have been accepted into a gifted program that established an IQ score of 130 as the cutoff were Cervantes, Copernicus, Raphael, Rembrandt, Martin Luther, Antoine Lavoisier, Henry Fielding, Ben Jonson, Joseph Haydn, Johann Sebastian Bach, Abraham Lincoln, Carolus Linnaeus, John Locke, and Jonathan Swift.)

Too many schools also overemphasize achievement in all content areas. A child typically must excel in every subject in order to be admitted to a gifted program or an enrichment program. This occurs despite the fact that many if not most innovators and leaders in the adult world would not claim to be well above average in math, science, reading, writing, social studies, and history all at once.

In any case, not all enrichment programs are created equal. What happens in many programs — adjuncts of the regular curriculum — often is not terribly challenging. The youngster is pulled out from her class to spend an hour or two weekly in a "resource room" with a random assortment of kits, puzzles, and other fun activities. And the child may be delighted. Kids consistently express great enthusiasm for special programs, which may be akin to their enthusiasm for recess. Certainly, it must be enjoyable for students to take a break from the more inflexible, testable work of the classroom and have some freedom to choose how they'll apply themselves for the next sixty minutes or so. It may also be enjoyable to sprawl on a rug on the floor rather than to sit at a desk or a table.

Getting away from prescribed textbook lessons and freedom to choose are precisely among the opportunities we urge on talented young people. But when there's not much evidence of continuity or systematic development of thinking and feeling processes in such programs, not enough is happening to lead a child into higher-end learning, or experiences that promote creativity, investigative study, and advanced thinking skills. Even some innovative adjunct programs tend to become, within a short time, overly structured and institutionalized in practice. A focus on creative thinking, with all the best intentions, easily slides into the kind of formulaic activity that characterizes the less enlightened curriculum.

The parent who remarked that her daughter didn't "seem to be doing much" in her gifted program was probably right about that. In too many cases, schools are merely keeping bright kids occupied with a prescribed curriculum, albeit at a more advanced level, rather than genuinely capitalizing on students' strengths.

PARENTS IN THE PICTURE

Now we must correct some erroneous impressions we may have inadvertently made.

Is there anything wrong with getting all As? If you are the parent of one of those academically gifted, straight-A girls or boys, should you be worried? Of course not. Pat your child on the back for earning an excellent report card.

Is there anything wrong with wanting (or wanting your child) to go to Harvard? Certainly not. Getting a degree from a widely admired college can mean getting an outstanding education — and it might also be a point of pride and a source of cachet for a lifetime.

Are schools and the people who teach in them the villains of this story? Not at all. Many of the examples of the creative-productive work of bright kids sprinkled throughout this book are based on the real-life accomplishments of successful school enrichment programs and dedicated teachers. But successes require determination on the part of those skilled teachers, and the support of inspired principals as well. It's not easy. The dismal reality is that many imaginative, deeply committed teachers are themselves unhappy and frustrated by local and federal mandates to raise schoolwide achievement levels. Adhering to curriculum guides and endless lists of standards that must be covered, teaching large numbers of students with diverse needs, and pressure to improve test scores can dim the lights of any dedicated educator. There's not enough time in the day, or sometimes money in reserve, to allow for more than the basics.

Here is the message we do want to convey: A lot of what goes on in school seeks to turn out a child who is an accomplished consumer and repeater of existing knowledge. Your child has plenty of opportunity to be a consumer. But she also needs dynamic learning environments to realize her strengths and to gain a sense of purpose. You can help to provide these environments.

Your child's gifted potential, curiosity, or interest in learning more about something, and ability to become engaged in challenging work related to it, come to the fore because of a combination of experiences:

1. Basic ability must be present, and any bright youngster has that. Gifted behaviors emerge when a level of drive and task commitment, coupled with creative spark, are added to ability. This is the "internal stuff" your child has to offer the world.
2. In order to thrive and blossom, she needs the right school support.
3. In order to thrive and blossom, she needs the right home support.

If she is one of the fortunate ones, your child is in a school that not only encourages accomplished schoolhouse results but that also helps her stretch and grow by engaging in the kind of higher-end learning we're talking about. If she is not so fortunate, there may not be much you can do to improve her classroom day (though in chapter 10, we offer some workable suggestions on how to involve yourself in the school and determine if and how some of your child's strengths and interests can be meaningfully incorporated in what is required of her there).

But what you can absolutely do is provide parental support through the enrichment strategies we describe in the following chapters.

DYNAMIC LEARNING: THE SHORT- AND LONG-TERM PAYOFFS

When children pursue their passions and set about creating something new, there are splendid payoffs. We've seen the effects through interviews with many young people and in our longitudinal research. They become genuinely engaged explorers and investigators. They show remarkable degrees of initiative and sheer enjoyment. Many experience heightened enthusiasm for learning in general. They do better in school.

But perhaps best of all, they gain a sense of their own power to make things happen, and the confidence to believe they will succeed and to pursue increasingly challenging levels of work. This is what noted psychologist Albert Bandura calls self-efficacy, a trait almost universally associated with highly successful people. Working on independent, personally selected projects promotes in a child the awareness that he can come up with more robust, more important results than he might have imagined.

What must take place, after all, in the mind and heart of a child who creates and sells buttons at age six, an age when the only other reward coming his way might be a gold star on a spelling test? Or in a child who sees she has been helpful, maybe comforting, to kids like herself whose parents are away from home all day? Such early-in-life success stories develop skills and competencies, but they also influence a child's self-perception. If successful young people articulated their feelings, they might say things like this:

"I can solve hard problems when I work at them."
"I can find another solution if the first one doesn't work."
"I'm good at sticking with something I started."
"I can locate what I need in order to accomplish what I want to do."
"I'm resourceful; I know how to handle new situations."

Bandura, the father of self-efficacy theory, writes: "People who regard themselves as highly efficacious act, think, and feel differently from those who perceive themselves as inefficacious. They produce their own future rather than simply foretell it."

See accomplishment in your child's future.

Celebrate as he begins to produce it.

※

CHAPTER 2

Dreamers, Challengers,
and One-Track Minds

The Child Who Stands Out from the Classroom Crowd

In our expanded conception of giftedness, we raise questions about the "gifted child" label, because our research has demonstrated that many children have the potential to display gifted behaviors at certain times and under certain conditions. This is not necessarily a widely held notion, and for years many studies have focused on identifying "the gifted."

This fascination is nothing new. Indeed, throughout recorded history, and probably before that, people have been curious about those who demonstrate superior talents, and what makes them tick. Much modern research has been concerned with how gifted kids look, sound, think, and act, largely in an effort to help educators better meet their needs in school and in supplemental programs. The conclusion: There *is* no one absolute profile. Gifted and talented learners are not a homogeneous group; rather, they are many, varied, unique, and diverse.

However, among youngsters in this population, studies do seem to indicate a number of common characteristics that are not shared by other learners. And so we *are* able to provide a few reliable and useful insights about children with high creativity, remarkable academic potential, and motivation to pursue challenging work. Some of those insights may be both surprising and reassuring. They may help to explain a few things.

Consider the phrase, "a child who stands out from the crowd." Some bright children distinguish themselves as classroom stars — obviously smart, willing to work, responsive. Teachers love them — and why wouldn't they? Other bright youngsters stand out for less appealing reasons. They attract the attention of educators who can't figure out how to "get through" to them. Or their peers find them annoying and distracting. Parents worry about the negative reports coming home.

Of particular interest, since it relates closely to the point of view we offer in this book, research findings lend credence to our theories about the distinction between schoolhouse learners and creative-productive learners. Creatively talented children may exhibit characteristics that differ not only from "average" learners but from academically gifted children as well.

The creatively gifted child tends to be an independent and original thinker, curious about many things, willing to take risks, and attracted to the novel and the complex. He will attack a topic of interest with energy and enthusiasm, showing a high tolerance for ambiguity and a willingness to surmount obstacles and persevere. He demonstrates what's called a *global mode* of information processing — thinking abstractly, generalizing, and extrapolating.

Many creatively talented kids have keen senses of humor. A first-grade teacher told a girl's mother that the youngster had a great capacity for mental playfulness and drollery. "I'll make a joke or use a pun," the teacher said, "and Emma is the only one in class who gets it." Some are genuinely clever humorists who can see witty and sometimes zany or whimsical connections in otherwise serious situations.

Creative kids tend to be aware of their own uniqueness. They may have a self-sense of "being different," and for the most part think being different isn't such a bad thing.

Along with these admirable, indeed enviable characteristics — and in fact, partly *because* of them — the creatively gifted may be prone to a number of seemingly "negative" traits, as we will describe below.

Our aim in this chapter is to help you better recognize why your child's strengths are possibly being overlooked, ignored, or blunted by certain behaviors he exhibits in school. We are not addressing the effects of learning disabilities or the problem of the gifted but seriously underachieving student, though some of the behaviors we describe here may be displayed by the learning disabled and the underachiever as well. (We'll discuss those subjects in greater detail in chapters 8 and 9.)

SOME TYPICAL TRAITS OF THE CREATIVELY GIFTED

Most parents recognize early on whether their son or daughter seems precocious or ahead on the developmental ladder relative to other children:

> *"She was talking in paragraphs by age two."*
> *"He was reading fourth-grade books by kindergarten."*
> *"She never went through a crawling stage at all but was walking and running by her first birthday."*

Parents sometimes take these achievements as indications that their child is gifted, and they may very well be right.

Still, in the early years, those parents might notice other qualities that seem to set their child apart from the crowd.

The mother of a four-year-old called her son "an old soul." Explaining further, she said, "He seems to understand people in a way that's surprising for such a little boy. He's very sensitive about things. If he sees someone unhappy or embarrassed, he recognizes that and he empathizes. I thought kids didn't really develop empathy until they were much older."

"She's very intense about her friendships," said the mother of a four-year-old girl, "very loyal, very generous. And if some little child she's befriended moves on to someone else or isn't so available one day, my daughter is just crushed. She takes these things hard. Whatever she's feeling, she feels it twice as hard as everybody else."

One parent described his son as "the Energizer Bunny when he gets interested in something, talking a mile a minute, waving his arms and hands describing what he wants you to know. It takes him a long time to settle down. He's like a dog with a bone. Very intense."

Such observations are common. Many creative youngsters seem to react with greater sensitivity and intensity than is typical; they are affected by a stimulus, what may even seem to be an extremely minor one, more deeply and for longer stretches of time than are their peers. Years ago, psychologist Kazimierz Dabrowski wrote that gifted children experience "overexcitabilities," perhaps related to central nervous system "wiring," and release their tension in five areas, or realms. Recent studies suggest his insights were spot-on. The types of overexcitability are:

- **Intellectual: Asking probing questions, concentrating intently or even obsessively, challenging authority, and jumping at logical problems and puzzles to be solved are all examples.**
- **Imaginational: Daydreaming, perceiving high drama or poetry in everyday events, and indulging in fantasies and "magical" thinking are typical.**
- **Psychomotor: This surplus of nervous energy might be seen in an enthusiastic child who talks a mile a minute while waving his arms, who acts impulsively, or who may be un-**

able to quiet his mind enough to relax or get to sleep; or it might be seen in one who's too much on the go to pay attention to small details or neatness in his schoolwork.

- **Sensory: Characterized by excessive reactions — great delight in or great dislike for sounds, smells, textures, and lights.**
- **Emotional: Concern for others, compassion, possible shyness or timidity, possible anxiety are common; this might be the "old soul."**

A gifted child may display some combination of these behaviors at various times, with perhaps one or two being dominant. In large part, they are what account for a child's charm and individuality, what define his personality. But extreme intensity, sensitivity, or other expressions of overexcitability may not help in the classroom, where there are established standards of conduct and all children are somehow expected to be interested in whatever is dished out to them. In a school setting, standing out in what are perceived to be negative ways doesn't make life easier.

CREATIVE MINDS GOING AGAINST THE CURRENT

Seven-year-old Adam was a chatty boy whose teacher complained about his inability to sit still, his constant interruptions of class with fantastic tales of superheroes and monsters, and his "inquisitiveness" — he was always looking at what other kids were doing, and listening in on private conversations between the teacher and other students. The only times he was quiet, Adam was "spacing out" in his chair. His parents worried: Did their son have ADHD? Sensory integration disorder? Clearly Adam was a compulsive storyteller. He liked anything that had some drama and human interest to it, but could he learn to follow classroom rules?

This seeming impasse was largely surmounted when together Adam's parents and teacher worked out a way to encourage his talents. He began to draw and write stories that the teacher allowed him to read to the class once a week. He still acted out, but he finished his work more often, was more involved in group activities, and by third grade had become a prolific writer and artist.

Adam was a creative boy who was largely indifferent to common conventions. When his mind was not engaged by what was being taught in class, he simply decided to make life more interesting for himself by moving around, interrupting people, and poking his nose in everyone else's business, oblivious to the fact that this kind of behavior did not go over well.

We might call him the distractor. Boys seem especially apt to engage in antsy, antic, or clowning behavior. But the class clown can also suddenly become serious and immersed in a particular area that intrigues him.

A review of a large number of studies listing personality traits of creative individuals identified several additional common "negative" characteristics or behaviors. These are the ones that parents and educators often find worrisome, difficult, or irritating.

Daydreaming

A student who "spaces out" is usually frustrating to teachers and vaguely detrimental to the overall mood of a classroom. The cause may be boredom, plain and simple. Interestingly — and alarmingly — *average* students report that they are bored in school about a third of the time. Extremely bright kids may be disenchanted even more frequently as they suffer through lessons they find relatively simple. But some youngsters with a tendency to be overly emotional may need to tune out for stretches of time, perhaps in reaction to interpersonal stresses with their classmates or with a teacher they find unsympathetic.

One teacher's report said that a third grader named Jenna was "dreamy," "seems to go off in her own little world," and had "an uneven attention span, though when working on a topic she feels enthusiastic about, she does well." She was also "timid," the teacher wrote, and "needs to feel more comfortable about speaking up." A psychological evaluation was recommended.

Jenna's mother thought that was a bit much but decided to follow through on it anyway and took her daughter for a day's testing with a child psychologist. "The upshot was that Jenna showed 'superior intellectual functioning,' had a high IQ, but was tuning out because of 'personal preoccupations' and 'a high level of inner tension.'" The psychologist's advice? Family counseling, which struck this mother as a misguided suggestion based on supposed psychological or relationship problems that were not really evident in other aspects of the girl's behavior. "She's a happy kid, really, though on the shy side." Instead, Jenna's parents made sure she had out-of-school activities she enjoyed and that she invited friends over to visit. Daydreaming didn't seem to be a problem the following year.

It's also the case that creative, imaginative kids, more than others, demonstrate a need for privacy and alone time. Sometimes the classroom and the playground, with their enforced togetherness and noise, may just be too much for them.

Questioning Rules and Authority

A fourth grader and her classmates were told to color in a coloring book, step by step, color by color, as instructed — in an effort to teach them how to follow written directions. The girl thought this assignment was beyond stupid and told her teacher as much.

Another child, age thirteen, "would just make confetti out of any teacher who wasn't very confident or something," said the boy's friend, who had observed several confetti-making scenes during their years in school. "He can basically outargue anybody. He's very intellectual, and if he thinks a teacher or another kid is on shaky ground, he'll just go in for the kill."

These youngsters often have little tolerance for toeing the line or accepting things because they're expected to. And some will go out of their way to make a point or to prove someone wrong, not hesitating to have a serious disagreement with a teacher or even a noted expert on a topic. They have no problem questioning rules and authority. Engaging in intellectual debate and even playing devil's advocate, of course, demonstrate a degree of courage and a lively mind. This tendency might not be admired, however, if carried out in a hostile manner or if certain rules really do have to be followed.

And occasionally, challenging and questioning can veer into stubbornness, a tendency to dig in one's heels. One experienced teacher said, "I have noticed over the years that sometimes these very creative, imaginative kids can become quite obstinate. They'll get on a kick about something, an argument about something, and they won't let it go. They can become doggedly persistent, even when it's clearly time to move on and sometimes even when they're wrong."

Carelessness and Disorganization

Nine-year-old Lexie said about herself: "I am a kid with perfect math in my head." She zipped through her assignments, took on more advanced work, and was the unofficial tutor for a couple of classmates who were struggling. It puzzled her parents that though her math workbooks were carefully completed, a similar precision wasn't evident in other areas. "She loves school," Lexie's mother said, "and she does okay in all her classes, though in math and science she's outstanding. But it's like she has a kind of hierarchy of what's important and what isn't. Unfortunately, one of the things she thinks isn't so important is expressing ideas in writing. She rushes through any kind of writing assignment. It looks like a mess. We have to sit on her a little, get her to do something over. She does know about spelling and punctuation. She just can't be bothered. She's got too much else she wants to do."

Lexie had "a dozen projects she's working on at any time," her mother said. Many creatively gifted young people become intensely involved in out-of-school activities, often more so than they are with schoolwork. Interestingly, research on the lives of people who, as adults, achieved great prominence in various areas shows that at early ages they developed interests in many more subjects than did their peers. They had extensive collections and serious hobbies, and conducted experiments, and in other ways were deeply committed to learning on their own terms.

Another parent said his son "is the perfect demonstration of the joke that he'd forget his head if it wasn't tied on. When he's into something, he has an enormous capacity to do very careful and detailed work. And then the rest of the time, he can be like the absentminded professor."

Obsessiveness

Children with singular enthusiasms tend to go above and beyond the call of duty in completing a particular assignment that provides an opportunity for creative expression. For example, Eliot, a fifth grader, loved nature and was especially fascinated by bees. As part of a homework assignment, he prepared a report that included drawing a simple picture of a bee, labeling the head, thorax, abdomen, antennae, stinger, and legs, and writing definitions of the queen, the worker, and the drone. But Eliot didn't stop there.

He went on to contrast life in the beehive with life in a factory, writing about bosses, managers, and workers. He made a series of panels showing how bees' eyes are different from human eyes and imagined what life would look like if humans had more than two eyes. He interviewed other kids about why they were afraid of bees and suggested a kind of sensitizing plan to educate readers about the worthiness of bees.

Clearly, this kind of exemplary work should be rewarded, and it was. With his teacher's support, Eliot pursued further independent investigations in the subject. He became so caught up in the world of bees that he talked about it constantly, which began to annoy his classmates. They started to find him boring and not much fun because he chose to stay indoors during recess to work on his projects.

Such passions are exactly what we look for when identifying appropriate enrichment activities — higher learning investigations — for talented kids. A child selects the same book or the same types of books again and again from the library. He's almost obsessed with a particular topic, theme, or area of study. He persists in asking questions about it, sometimes almost to the point of distraction. Such powerful demonstrations of interest can be the lead-in to independent creative work. But often there's not much way to accommodate them during the school day. And the child who has a hard time tempering his singular enthusiasm when around other kids — or sees no reason to — can be perceived as a bit of an oddball.

ADVANCING THE TALENTS OF THE CREATIVELY GIFTED

It's clear that standing out from the classroom crowd in some of these allegedly negative ways can blur a youngster's true capabilities in the minds of those responsible for educating her. It can also make school an occasionally unhappy place. Even so, it's not difficult to appreciate that some of the "negative" traits aren't all that negative. Challenging authority, sticking to one's guns, enjoying magnificent and productive obsessions, having an imaginatively lively mind — these are all qualities most admired and most desired in challenging worlds beyond the classroom. They should be admired at school too.

The conclusions from a recent summary produced by experts at our National Research Center on the Gifted and Talented, in association with our work with psychologists and educational researchers affiliated with the National Association for Gifted Children, are both reassuring and instructive. In brief, there is no research evidence to suggest that creatively gifted children are any less emotionally well adjusted than their peers. However, these highly able, talented youngsters can be more than typically vulnerable to risks in their social and emotional development. Some of these issues emerge from the internal mix of creativity, energy, intensity, sensitivity, and high aspirations. Some are related to a mismatch with educational environments that are not responsive to the pace and level of the learning and thinking of these children. And others occur because of unsupportive home environments.

The challenge is to channel all that intensity, sensitivity, and energy into constructive outlets, by, as one researcher put it, "encouraging playfulness, flexibility, and the production of wild and unusual ideas." We can recognize that the classroom does not provide the most fertile field in which these qualities can flourish. Aside from a possibly inadequate pace and level of teaching, bright kids — like the ones whose stories we've told in this chapter — must deal with the very real expectation that they follow the rules, produce neat work, pay attention, and not get too playful. All children must jump through essentially the same set of hoops. Parents to the rescue!

As an involved and concerned parent, you would not claim that your child's "learning" starts when she enters the classroom and stops when she comes home. You can probably list many ways you have contributed to her knowledge, awareness, and appreciation of the world around her — reading aloud to her from her earliest years, visiting the science museum and the aquarium, exposing her to a variety of interesting experiences. In the second part of this book, we describe a number of additional strategies for your parental repertoire.

They are designed to help your child get in touch with her own interests and concerns, so that she can then pursue activities that will unlock her talents and prompt the gifted behaviors that define creative productivity. First, we'll explain what we mean by creative-productive learning and why it has the power to light up your child's mind.

✳

CHAPTER 3

The Boy with the Lawnmower Shoes

Real Problems, Real Products, Real Success Stories

If creative-productive learning offers a lively antidote to unchalleng-ing schoolhouse learning, how can you provide the kind of environ-ment in which it might take place? The answer is simple: encourage your child to become involved in a real investigative activity that springs from a personal interest or passion. In our enrichment pro-grams, we emphasize the four elements behind that recommendation:

1. The problem
2. The process
3. The product
4. The audience

And now, a demonstration.

Some years ago, Bruce, a middle school student, had a passion for history and especially for stories of the American presidents, whose biographies he read voraciously. By the end of his first week of school that particular year, he'd finished reading his assigned textbook — all of it. At the suggestion of his social studies teacher, Bruce began poking into local history, and his teacher posed an intriguing question: Why was a nearby church called the Church of Presidents? It got its name, Bruce discovered, because this town on the New Jersey shore had been a favorite nineteenth-century summer resort for the nation's rich and famous. A number of presidents, including Ulysses S. Grant, Rutherford B. Hayes, Benjamin Harrison, and Woodrow Wilson, had worshipped at this particular church. James A. Garfield, the twentieth president, had as well. As Bruce continued his explorations, he found out that Garfield, who had been shot in Washington, D.C., by a disgruntled job-seeker, had died in a house across the street from the church. This intrigued the boy, who further learned that the injured Garfield had been brought to the town by train in the hope that sea air would revive him.

But the spot was lost to history — the house long ago destroyed, and the area carved into lots. Through town maps, old records, and building documents, Bruce was able to locate the exact site of the house in which Garfield had died and discovered that someone had in fact memorialized that event with a handwritten sign in a grimy garage window. Bruce thought that was an inadequate tribute to a murdered president and a missed opportunity to call attention to a matter of local historical interest, so he decided to act. He became a public advocate, causing a tiny piece of property to be deeded over from the owners to the state and a permanent marker to be erected. We should add that this four-year effort involved not only research but also fund-raising, overcoming indifference, and unraveling governmental red tape.

The boy had allowed his strong interest in history and American presidents to lead him along a unique path. We would say that Bruce found a real problem, pursued it through a demanding process, and came up with a final product of significance to an audience, albeit perhaps a limited one (not everyone will want to view the spot where President Garfield died).

Many children with this kind of potential possess that "inherent stimulus" we mentioned earlier in our discussion of task commitment, a predisposition to initiate and follow through on complicated types of investigative activity. Not all bright, talented kids will want to go that far, nor should they be expected to. When they do want to, however, quite remarkable results often occur, as a number of examples later on will illustrate.

In this chapter, we deconstruct some terms and suggest how our simple idea might provide the key to unlocking the gifted behaviors of which your child is capable. You may have questions or an objection or two to raise as you consider how all this talk about problems and products translates to enjoyable activity or how a parent fits into the mix. We hope to answer your questions and lay your objections to rest.

ABOUT THE PROBLEM: WHAT MAKES IT REAL?

Years ago, the philosopher and educator John Dewey wrote, "The whole process of education should thus be conceived as the process of learning to think through the solution of real problems."

That noble ideal is perhaps unrealistic or a bit too noble. Education inevitably includes routine elements that do not demand a great deal of "thinking through." The deductive model of learning, on which most schooling is based, seeks to place into children's repertoires the content and skills that are almost always delivered through prescribed, "taught" lessons. Your child needs to learn fundamentals such as spelling, sentence construction, multiplication tables, and so on. These problems have established answers, and the answers can and must be assimilated. No one can be creative on an empty brain.

Your child is familiar with math and spelling problems. She might also consider a homework assignment, such as a composition on the colonial settlements or on what a plant needs to grow, a problem. Solving it usually involves expending some effort to track down facts in reference materials and then writing about them. Kids often refer to such work as "doing research," though it is essentially reporting. Many educators miss the important distinction between the two. Reporting is simply repeating established knowledge about a topic; in research, established knowledge is used to draw conclusions or to discover underlying principles. Both learning activities may teach a child something. But looking up and reporting back does little to encourage a child to think through the solutions to real problems.

So, what makes a problem *real*? And what role does that play in promoting gifted behaviors?

- **A real problem has a personal frame of reference for the child who undertakes it.**

Her emotions are engaged; this is something she wants to dig into. No one else — whether teacher or parent or friend — can decide if it's real or not.

Now, it's easy to come up with a list of issues that most of us would agree constitute real problems in our world. We might cite global warming, cancer, or the lack of affordable housing for low income families. When such problems resonate with them personally, some young people willingly address them.

For example, Gregory lost a family member because of the actions of a drunk driver. When he entered fifth grade, Gregory turned crusader, figuring out how he could work with the city to identify businesses that might be serving too much liquor near closing time. Through the mayor's and the city planner's offices, Gregory acquired the necessary drunk driving data — arrest records, including times and frequency of arrests and locations — and coordinated it into an original program that plotted the intersections of those factors. This revealed about a dozen bars that Gregory suspected were overserving liquor, which in turn helped to trigger heightened police patrols.

Police did indeed find clusters of higher incidences of drunk driving in those areas. They cited the bar owners, and drunk driving declined. Gregory's crusade lasted more than a year and a half.

Gregory was deeply involved in his cause (later, he started a local chapter of Students Against Driving Drunk). He chose the problem, he "owned" the problem, and that in itself contributed to the task commitment that enabled him to work over a long stretch of time toward a specific and not easily realized goal. His teachers, neighbors, and best buddies would probably have all agreed that drunk driving is a problem, but it may not have been as "real" for them, in our sense of the term, as it was for Gregory.

- **A real problem does not have an existing solution; it lacks an established "right" answer.**

Real problems have an open-ended aspect. The child pursuing a real problem doesn't know what she's going to come up with or even how she will get there until she's well under way. She may not know exactly what kinds of information or resources will be relevant. She might find herself switching gears occasionally and considering alternative courses of action; or, after a false start, she may realize that she should probably adopt some new strategies and learn an additional skill or two to implement them, tactics shared by successful adult problem solvers. Jonas Salk, developer of the polio vaccine, said about his early work in medical science research: "You never have an idea of what you might accomplish. All that you do is you pursue a question. And see where it leads. . . . I learned what I needed to know in order to address those questions."

In these ways, true investigative activities differ significantly not only from schoolhouse learning, but even from the so-called guided-discovery methods that characterize many practices in gifted education.

Guided discovery — a colleague of ours calls it "sneaky telling" — has a child arriving at a fact, principle, or conclusion that the adults have determined she *should* reach and have arranged for her to reach by neatly laying out tidbits of information that lead to the desired end.

In contrast, a youngster seeking the solution to a real, "unguided" problem will come up with something new, something unique.

You may be asking yourself, "But how unique can a child's efforts be? How many new ideas are there in the world anyway?"

Here, we are using the word *new* not in an absolute or never-happened-before sense, but in a general sense. The results to a real problem can be new, for example, if they involve amassing local information. One group of children gathered, analyzed, and reported on statistics concerning how much television people in their town watched and what that meant for family dining habits, parental monitoring, and so on. Similar studies had been carried out in other communities, no doubt using similar techniques, but this was new to the children. Gregory, the boy who was determined to do something about drunk driving, did not invent data collection, but his conclusions were applied in a unique and specific context.

- **A real problem is approached by using the same tools, methodologies, and techniques typically favored by creative professionals in a particular field.**

For example, a child will do what a geologist, scenery designer, environmentalist, filmmaker, or newspaper reporter does, though obviously at a more junior level. Such an authentic approach lends itself to an end result that goes beyond what is possible with a report written after gleaning facts from encyclopedias, the Internet, or "all-about" books. Bruce, the American history enthusiast, did not simply read a history book about President Garfield. He *became* a real, live historian, albeit at a junior level, and something of a community activist as well.

If your child brings home a social studies book from school, flip through it, and you will probably find that it is more appealing than the textbooks you remember reading. Many newer books are attractively designed and visually inviting. Nevertheless, a history book is essentially a collection of facts. It does not convey any of the excitement or the joy of discovery experienced by a historian who tracks down materials that shed fresh light on the past. It also does not reveal the modus operandi of the historian: Which questions does the historian ask and of whom? Where does she look for evidence? What qualifies as a historical document? How does a historian move from raw data to conclusions?

The youngster who digs into a real problem, whatever it may be, starts by learning some of the methodology a professional would use to solve it.

- **A real problem requires a solution geared toward creating a real product for a real audience.**

All creatively productive individuals, in reality, go about their business with the goal of affecting other people. Creative work may be personally satisfying; it may even be an imperative that must be followed. But much of the satisfaction, and the driving force as well, comes from the possibility of affecting the human condition by contributing something original to the sciences, arts, humanities, or other areas of society and life.

The writer hopes that in sharing his perspective and insight, he will nudge his reader into understanding or feeling something new or something more; the scientist carries out research to add knowledge to her field. The artist creates work that will enrich the lives of those who see it. The composer writes symphonies for people who are interested in playing classical music or listening to it. The consumer advocate develops surveys in an effort to bring about legislative action or to change the public's buying habits. Even the philosopher, the abstract thinker, intends in time to come up with a theory that his peers in the philosophical community will study and maybe agree with or debate.

Other rewards — fame or admiration — might follow. And other factors might fuel productivity; the great impressionist painter Claude Monet, having eight children to feed, knew he had to keep turning out paintings and sell a lot of them. But creative folks are always motivated by a desire to inform, to entertain, or to influence the thinking or the feelings of a particular audience.

Our research has demonstrated that kids who get involved with real problems do their best independent work, and have the best time at it, when they intend to reach an audience other than the teacher.

The kind of learning that takes place while all of this is going on differs dramatically from schoolhouse learning. It might be characterized as the difference between learning in a natural environment and learning in an artificially structured environment. Starting with a personal and sincere interest or passion and a desire to act on it, a child works backward, in a sense, figuring out what she needs to know, acquire, or accomplish in order to take action. Depending on what she's after, she might absorb a great deal of collateral learning — maybe how to conduct a survey, arrange an interview with an important person, plan and sequence her activities, use time effectively, use the Internet and other resources wisely or economically, or a host of other factors necessary in real problem solving to get the job done.

How can you help your child achieve "realness"?

Start with what interests her. Does she enjoy some aspect of history? Does she think it would be great to make a film? Or to learn more about the world of puppetry? If you are not sure what she likes, or if she is not sure herself, chapters 4 and 5 cover a number of strategies, such as brainstorming together, focusing in, asking questions that prompt thought and self-reflection, to help the two of you come up with some good ideas. But first, we'll tell you a little more about methodology, product, and audience.

ABOUT THE PROCESS: GAINING "KNOWLEDGE HOW"

Early on in the development of our enrichment learning theories, we realized that an ideal model for encouraging gifted behaviors in young people was the "turned-on professional" or the "firsthand inquirer" in any area of investigation. This is a person actively contributing to the world's knowledge, a producer as opposed to a consumer. Contrast a medical researcher in the lab, say, and a family doctor, or a composer and a musician who plays the violin following an existing score. (We reiterate: the world needs consumers and producers!)

Learning from the turned-on professional or firsthand inquirer leads a creative child to accumulate "knowledge *how*," which as the words suggest is a level of involvement a cut above the typical classroom experiences of "knowledge of" and "knowledge about" a subject. He begins investigating his real problem, in other words, by picking up specifically useful methods of inquiry.

You might be wondering, "Isn't this all a bit much? Can I really expect my fourth grader to act like a professional investigator? Kids may be bright, but are they truly capable of this kind of activity?"

The answer is yes, they are. Studies have clearly shown that young children can indeed engage in the type of mental processes and critical methods used by an adult scientific researcher or a documentary filmmaker, poet, or puppeteer. The American psychologist and educational theorist Jerome Bruner, after studying the learning behaviors of children, concluded, "Intellectual activity is the same, whether at the frontier of knowledge or in the third-grade classroom. . . . The difference is in degree, not in kind."

"All well and good," you might say, "but if my child wants to make a film, how can I help him with that? I know nothing about cameras or directing or anything remotely related to films."

It is unsettling for adults — parents and educators alike — to realize we don't know something. Teaching in a middle school early in our careers, we were told at one point to "do something" for our students in science. "Where's the curriculum?" we asked. "There is none," said the superintendent. That was scary. The textbook curriculum is a process over which you have control, including a teacher's guide that tells you what to say and when and how to say it. Without a curriculum, you're standing naked before the world.

So we simply started by following the kids' leads, offering them an opportunity to choose what they'd like to study, and following up on what seemed to engage them. This was a beginning, but soon we wondered, "What do these youngsters need to professionalize what they are doing? Who can show them how to reach more demanding and intriguing levels of investigation?" Thus we began our reliance on firsthand inquirers — mentors-in-print and mentors-in-person.

Over the years, in classes in science, mathematics, and English, we attempted to set up resource centers where kids, at least some of the time, could pursue self-directed, project-based learning with a little advice from professionals. In one resource room, a group of students were interested in writing. We found for them a how-to book on how to write and publish a book. Another group wanted to build robots. Still another group designed psychology experiments. We were able to locate people in the community who were willing to come in and talk about constructing machines and about studying human behavior.

Mentors-in-print and mentors-in-person remain a staple in our work with gifted young people today and a core element in programs based on our models. For example, a teacher who supervised an enrichment program on filmmaking for a small group of students helped them organize a documentary they wanted to make about the battles of Lexington and Concord and Paul Revere's ride. As their plans developed, these kids ran into a number of tough issues.

- "How does a film crew set up a shoot so there are no telephone poles in the background?"
- "Can we make a shoot look like it's night even though we're filming during the day?"
- "Where can we find out which British regiments fought here and what their uniforms looked like?"
- "How can you make a church in one location look like it's next to a river that's somewhere else?"

The students didn't know the answers; neither did the teacher. But after a little digging, he was able to recommend a couple of excellent books that addressed just such filmmaking subjects. He also suggested the state historical society as a fine place to start to learn more about the old British regiments and their uniforms. A little more digging, a couple of phone calls, and he located a graduate student in the film department of a local university who said he could spend an afternoon with the kids to impart a few useful techniques.

A good teacher or a good parent can't possibly possess all the expertise necessary to help a child emulate professional methods in a specialized area — unless, of course, the teacher or the parent happens to be a specialist in that particular area. To be a guide-on-the-side to your child in the ways we'll explain in chapters 6 and 7, you do not need to know history or filmmaking. You *can,* however, steer him toward information about what a historian does and what a filmmaker does. There are countless splendid resources to uncover: mentors-in-print and mentors-online. And finding a way to give your child an opportunity to interact with an enthusiastic professional or firsthand inquirer, a mentor-in-person, can be invaluable.

Many parents take their kids to art exhibits, dance performances, film retrospectives, and Civil War battlefields or reenactments. Of course, these are wonderful kinds of exposure for any child who's keen on art or dance or film or the Civil War, and even one who isn't particularly drawn to these topics is bound to gain something from the experience. Such outings are fine ways for parent and child to explore an area together. But in order to immerse himself in real problem solving, a youngster should be offered opportunities that go beyond simple "museum experiences," by which we mean passive visits, such as sitting in the audience for a ballet or a film, or taking a guided tour of an art gallery or a restored historical site. More than "looking at" outings, your child needs opportunities for "looking into" and becoming involved with that which is on display, being presented, or being produced.

So some questions may be, depending on his identified interest, "Can he spend some time observing an artist or graphic designer, a museum curator, a choreographer, or a filmmaker at work, and perhaps actually take part in some of that professional's activities, if only in a small way? Or can he spend some time with a firsthand practitioner, not necessarily a creative producer, in the field he has singled out?" That may be less difficult to arrange than you might imagine.

One mother remembered bringing her nine-year-old to her office on Take Our Daughters to Work Day several years ago. "I'm a magazine editor," this mom said, "an occupation that Jessie has no interest in. She knows I work hard, and she appreciates what I do, but that day she sat in my little office pretty much twiddling her thumbs. It was so *not* interesting to her to watch me read copy, make some phone calls, type on the computer, or to do a little filing.

"Going home I thought, 'This kid loves anything and everything to do with pets, and she should have a going-to-work day with a mom who's a veterinarian.' Which she doesn't have, but that gave me the idea to call the veterinary hospital in our neighborhood, where we'd adopted our two cats. The associate vet was actually gung ho about having Jessie come by for an hour after school. We arranged this, and Jessie became so excited. It turned out that the day of her visit they were treating a dog with a leg fracture, and she was allowed to help prepare the material for the cast and then get the dog settled in a recovery cage."

Jessie's involvement with the local vet continued for several years. Though her activities at the hospital did not involve creative-productive investigations of the sort we've been describing, she got behind-the-scenes, hands-on experience not only in the treatment of animals but also in the running of a busy practice and business. She's currently in college studying veterinary medicine and science.

In a mentor-in-person, a gung ho attitude is highly desirable. People who are "turned on" by their chosen field will naturally convey the excitement of working in it. Also, a mentor who can appreciate a youngster's curiosity and enthusiasm and wants to nurture those splendid qualities is ideal.

ABOUT THE PRODUCT: INVESTIGATIVE ACTIVITIES BEARING FRUIT

The word *product* might suggest a concrete something that can be looked at and felt and passed around. Or maybe it brings to mind something that can be sold. These are legitimate examples of what a product might be, but our inventory encompasses a broader range of possibilities, and in chapter 6 we've listed quite an amazing number of products.

In our discussion, the product, or the end result of a child's involvement in an investigative activity, is meant to entertain, inform, or influence the way people think or behave.

Why does the product matter?

Consider the similarity between independent problem solving and school-based extracurricular activities. The kid who joins the band or the softball team or the newspaper is there because she wants to be. She is interested in playing the trumpet or throwing a softball or writing an article. It is a self-selected activity and her choice. She does not usually receive a grade for her performance. Her success is measured in other terms.

In addition — and most interesting to us — this young person's extracurricular involvement has one important characteristic: there's a product at the end of the line, and the product has an audience. The band performs for a graduation ceremony or a holiday assembly for parents; the team takes the field and plays a real game with a rival; the newspaper gets printed, and someone reads it. Without people to attend the concert, cheer for the team, or read the paper, isn't there likely to be less motivation to rehearse or train or perfect the prose? Some intriguing research indicates that adult successes and accomplishments cannot be traced to or predicted by outstanding academic talent (the straight As or high test scores). But strong correlations *have* been found between nonacademic accomplishments during the school years, such as enthusiastic participation in extracurricular activities, and subsequent adult achievements. Similarly, kids who become involved in independent investigations do their best work when they know it's going somewhere.

Some youngsters conceive legitimate products for their efforts on their own. Jonathan, a boy who attended a program that we designed, invented lawnmower shoes. His father had hurt his back and was advised to limit his movements — specifically, no bending over or mowing the lawn. Jonathan was told this regular chore would now be his, and he confronted his real problem, which was that he hated doing yard work and wanted to find a way to make it as easy as possible. Hence, lawnmower shoes: footwear that had a switch and small blades and motors on the bottom. He created two prototypes of a workable gadget that he imagined would be valued by anyone with a relatively small lawn to mow and a desire to amble along comfortably while doing so.

But not every young person will recognize how a personal investigative activity can lead to a creative and desirable product. Parents can help. As you observe your child getting involved in a self-selected real problem, you might have a better idea about products and possible audiences than she does. In fact, thinking about an audience first will often suggest or streamline the idea of a product. The useful questions for a kid to answer, with parental input if necessary, are:

1. "How can I communicate what I've been doing?"
2. "Who would be interested in what I have created or discovered?"

Many youngsters in our enrichment programs have taken a love for a particular craft or hobby into this larger realm of product and audience. One small group of amateur cooks conducted taste tests and made up illustrated cookbooks for special occasions. Some turned their products into small businesses, such as selling key chains and decoupage boxes. Along the way, they had a taste of what can be involved in purchasing, advertising, marketing, record keeping, and other aspects of the commercial world.

An eight-year-old named Samantha fell in love with quilting. Her mother was an excellent seamstress who made the family's clothes and home decorations, and she had plenty of fabric for Samantha to use. This parent was impressed by her daughter's sewing skill. "She uses needle and thread, not the machine, and her stitches are amazingly precise and ordered, with simple but very pretty overlay stitching. And she already has a great eye for design and color patterns. These are only small, doll-sized quilts, but they're lovely."

Samantha used her quilts for her dolls and gave one to her cousin.

This was a fine beginning, of course, but perhaps she and her mother might have explored how Samantha's craft interest could be professionalized — again, raising the level of challenge. Her budding quilt-making skills might have, for example, led to researching aspects of colonial handiwork, and the evolution of the quilt from humble utilitarian household item to modern-day pricey art collectible, with an illustrated display in a local school for students of fashion and design.

Stretching of this sort — that is, taking an interest and a talent a bit further and sharing it with an audience — is hugely effective in the promotion of self-efficacy, that conviction a child internalizes that she can do bigger, more important things than she realized. The product gives realness, purpose, satisfaction, and enjoyment to a kid's efforts. But more than that, and even better than that, it is a vehicle through which a wide variety of enduring and transferable skills are developed — the kinds of learning experiences that enhance both the present and the future.

ABOUT THE AUDIENCE: REACHING A BROADER MARKET

A real audience has several characteristics that, again, make higher-end learning qualitatively different from schoolhouse learning. The primary difference is that a real audience is not a captive one.

The father of a youngster who became fascinated by Egyptian hieroglyphics said his daughter was excited about giving a demonstration in the assembly her school held once a month, a showcase for special talents or hobbies. She had invented a sort of faux hieroglyphic writing, cleverly incorporating modern online characters with ancient symbols, and showed how it could be used to create one-of-a-kind greeting cards and notepaper. The girl came home looking unhappy. "She said the whole elementary school has to go to this assembly," her father said, "and a couple kids were listening to her, but most of them weren't paying any attention." That experience was a bitter disappointment for this girl who had a neat idea she wanted to share, but since the students were not particularly required to "pay attention," it's not too surprising that the majority of her audience did not, and that was their right.

Contrast this example with the way children's work is showcased in other schools. In a school that uses our enrichment approach, Lunch Bag Seminars are planned during the busy cafeteria lunchtime block. A few children who want to share their products or work advertise on the school PA system that they will be hosting a seminar on a particular topic, like dinosaurs or the history of computers. Students with a sincere interest in that area bring their lunch to a quiet classroom and listen to the seminar being presented by the "practicing young professional," as a teacher or parent-volunteer sits in the back of the classroom.

A real audience is composed of people who come together because of a shared interest or a desire to benefit from the product they're hearing about, reading about, or watching. In the box below, we provide a few examples of the creative work of students who pursued independent activities and the different types of outlets and venues they found for them. A quick look at the list will reveal that these are not avenues that children will typically think of or access on their own. They need a little support from the involved adults in their lives.

Parents can also add perspective to the matter of the audience. Your child might be unlikely to hit the jackpot and have his illustrated children's book accepted by a major publisher (though that has happened). Competition and rejection are always possible when trying to bring original work to a wider audience, and a youngster should be prepared for them. But it's worth giving thought to what realistically might constitute a receptive outlet.

One woman told this story: "In the laundry room in the basement

A Few Examples of Products and Audiences

Kids we've come to know have found audiences for their products through:

- A written presentation at a city historical society
- A contribution of audio and video tapes to a state historical society
- A review of children's books in a local newspaper
- Oral presentations at civic clubs, business organizations, and church groups
- Displays of artwork and scientific reports in banks, shopping centers, and schools
- On-air presentations on local radio and TV
- Letters to the editor of literary and scientific magazines and local and state newspapers
- A performance of folk songs and an explanation of their history at a retirement home
- A page of math puzzles and quizzes in a national children's magazine

of my apartment building, someone taped up a kid's drawing on the wall. It's a large drawing of trees in a park. Under it is a little sign, written by the child, that says, 'This painting was originally conceived and entirely painted by . . .' — the kid's name, age five. Some of the words are misspelled. So at first I thought, Aw, that's cute. Seeing it up there over the following weeks, I thought, You know what? It's kind of presumptuous to think everybody wants to look at your child's drawing. Stick it up on your refrigerator with a magnet or put it in a little frame and give it to Grandma."

We're after an audience that goes beyond the (probably) willingly captive one of Grandma and the relatives, but one that is still within the realm of possibility in the real world.

SOCIALLY CONSTRUCTIVE CREATIVITY: CHANGING THE WORLD (A LITTLE)

Melanie was a shy, quiet girl known for her kindness. In fifth grade, she watched out the bus window each morning as the driver stopped to pick up a small, upset-looking boy. His mother had to verbally encourage him to get on, and when that failed, she gave him a gentle push. Over a couple of weeks, Melanie became increasingly interested in this little fellow who wore thick glasses and usually had tears rolling down his face. After making a few inquiries, she learned that he was in second grade, his name was Tony, and he was visually impaired. She began to discuss him with her mother, who encouraged Melanie to sit in the front of the bus and to talk to the boy. The next day, she did. She asked why he was crying.

"I hate school," Tony said softly. "Well, lots of us don't absolutely love school," Melanie said, "but nobody else is crying about getting on the bus." Tony explained that kids made fun of him because of his glasses; sometimes they tripped him going into the school building; he was given special large-print books for his subjects, but he couldn't find anything in the library he wanted to read for fun. "When everybody goes to the library, I have to pretend to read because I can't get books with big enough letters." Melanie asked him a few more questions and found out he loved adventure and mystery stories and books about sports.

Melanie gave this some thought and approached her enrichment teacher with the idea of making Tony her "project." The teacher helped her outline a plan. First, Melanie got a couple of slightly older and well-respected boys to be Tony's escorts, so to speak, walking him to and from the school bus and sitting with him in the lunchroom. The harassment died down, and Tony became regarded as a cool kid, having his own bodyguards and all. Then, she recruited a number of fourth, fifth, and sixth graders who were known to be good at writing and drawing to create large-print books that dealt with Tony's interests in sports and adventure stories. She was the editor and production manager for the Tony Series.

This transpired over many months, and a lovely change took place in Tony. He no longer hated school. He was proud of "his" books, especially because other kids also signed things out from his special section of the library. Tony became kind of a local celebrity. When Melanie was asked about her work, she said, "Well, it didn't change the world, but it changed the world of one little boy."

Melanie loved her project. In fact, she grew up to become a social worker. What was it about this fifth grader that led her to devote her time and talents to alleviate another child's unhappiness? Why do some young people use their gifts and talents in responsible projects that "change the world," making it a little better for others?

In our current research with gifted and talented children, we are attempting to answer those very questions, looking at qualities such as altruism, moral conviction, hope, and vision. We are examining the relationship between the characteristics of gifted people and their motivation to address the collective needs and problems of individuals and communities at large. Unquestionably, however, encouraging socially constructive giftedness is critical for our life and times.

Some years ago, the social psychologist Urie Bronfenbrenner expressed the need for developing — and the failure to develop — empathetic tendencies in children: "No society can sustain itself unless its members have learned the sensitivities, motivations, and skills involved in assisting and caring for other human beings. Yet the school, which is carrying the primary responsibility for preparing young people for effective participation in adult life, does not . . . give high priority to providing opportunities in which such learning could take place."

That much is true, sadly, right through all the years of official schooling. In delivering a commencement address at Harvard, the college from which he famously dropped out just before graduating (having been disciplined for running a business writing software out of his dorm room), Microsoft cofounder and pioneer Bill Gates told graduates: "I do have one big regret. I left Harvard with no real awareness of the awful inequities in the world — the appalling disparities of health and wealth and opportunity that condemn millions to lives of despair."

Direct teaching about empathy and similarly complex capacities doesn't work very well. School-based efforts to promote involvement in the greater world and the greater good tend to have little lasting impact on most kids. Many take community service these days, a requirement, but compelling young people to participate in socially valuable projects often results in minimal and even reluctant compliance. Said one preteen: "You had to sign up for something, and we had a choice of about eight things you could do. I picked cleaning up this empty lot and helping turn it into a garden kind of place. It was pretty dumb. Most of us just did community service until the teacher adviser signed off on this sheet that said you put in the number of hours you had to."

But the simple idea we talked about at the beginning of this chapter — how to help a child discover a real problem based on his interests and then the means to see it through to a successful and useful conclusion — provides an alternative, a possible entry to socially constructive gifted behaviors. Like Melanie and her work on Tony's behalf, and the boy who was instrumental in reducing drunk driving in his town, many children we have come to know focus on issues that improve the circumstances around them.

Jacob, the young son of a woman who, as it happens, attended one of our graduate programs, started Computers for Communities. After learning that his sister's school was throwing out about forty computers and replacing them with new ones, Jacob decided something better could be done with the rejects. With two savvy friends, he repaired and upgraded the old models, then worked with social services in his town to identify families that could use them. He and his friends made the deliveries and also gave the recipients a short tutorial in computer setup and use. (This effort never would have happened had his parents not supported the idea, by renting a truck to pick up the tossed computers, giving up their garage space for the summer so the boys could do their work, and logging many miles driving the kids on their rounds.)

A group of athletically minded high school students who believed their city needed less room for cars and more room for walking, jogging, and biking visited and photographed recreation centers and facilities in their community and others nearby. They examined books and articles and sent away for brochures and catalogs distributed by manufacturers of recreation equipment. They discussed various ways in which their city's outdoor life could be improved and subsequently developed a sophisticated proposal for a system of bicycle paths. After a great deal of advocacy through a public information campaign, an analysis of costs and potential benefits, and political action aimed at the recreation department and city council, their plan was approved and funds were allocated to build bicycle paths in high-traffic sections of the city.

After hearing a powerful presentation by the young leader of Free the Children, an advocacy group that addresses child-labor issues around the world, a middle school student in Connecticut embarked on a multiyear commitment to work on this problem. Dianna helped form several school chapters of the organization, raised money for the emancipation of children sold into servitude because of parental debt, and traveled to South Asia to lobby officials about the use of child labor in the rug-making industry. Subsequently, she became a Peace Corps volunteer in Africa and had an international internship in The Hague.

A group of kids analyzed water samples as part of an area study on the extent and effects of acid rain, and their findings were requested for use by the state Environmental Protection Agency.

David, a ten-year-old, wrote a guidebook that was adopted by the mayor's office as the official historical walking tour of his city.

Some real problems — and some amazing original products, which came about through hard and imaginative work that included obtaining useful materials, analyzing data, writing letters, planning time lines, organizing notes, and all kinds of other real-world techniques and resources. Not only did these young people do something good by involving themselves responsibly in the well-being of others: our research shows that kids who participate in authentic service projects based on personal strengths and interests become more confident, engaged, and determined to succeed — in the present moment and in the future.

Evaluations of these enrichment opportunities over the years have pointed to one overriding and universal finding: the greatest source of satisfaction almost always results from children's freedom to pursue topics of their own choosing in a manner with which they feel most comfortable.

In Part Two, we offer dozens of practical suggestions that will answer the following questions:

- What topic or topics would your child choose to pursue?
- How can she do that most comfortably?
- How can you support and encourage her efforts?

Practical Paths to Developing Your Child's Gifts and Talents

✳

CHAPTER 4

Passions of the Mind and Heart

Getting at Interests

Pamela Rasmussen, a highly respected ornithologist whose massive two-volume work, *Birds of South Asia,* was the product of two decades of meticulous research, developed a sudden interest in birds as an eight-year-old girl in Oregon. The "push" that at least to some degree set her on the path toward her outstanding accomplishments as an adult might be considered harsh, even potentially counterproductive. In an interview, Rasmussen described a day her father came into the room where Pamela and her younger sister were playing with their dolls, and said, apparently in a tone of some disapproval, "Why don't you girls get interested in something useful?"

Perhaps his words struck a receptive chord in a bright girl with gifted potential. Perhaps she found that playing with dolls *was* a little boring. Whatever the concurrence of thoughts, emotions, and timing, it seemed she was ready to rise to the challenge of her dad's higher expectations for her.

A bit later, Pamela's mother gave her a gift, the junior edition of an illustrated book called *Birds of the World.* Though never having paid much attention to birds before, Pamela was hooked. "I just thought the way the birds looked was so wonderful," she remembered, and the eight-year-old pored over the pages again and again. Soon, she took her deepening fascination to a swampy area near her home, spotted a bird, and was able to identify it as a long-billed marsh wren. Knowing its name, she said, "was thrilling."

College, a master's degree in biology, and a PhD involving a dissertation on cormorants in Patagonia followed, as did her "dream job" as assistant to S. Dillon Ripley, the bird expert and one-time Secretary of the Smithsonian Institution. Over the years, Rasmussen's explorations took her to museums throughout the world to study specimen collections and on field expeditions to India, the Andaman Islands, Burma, the Himalayas, and other distant locations. *Birds of South Asia,* her magnum opus, presents her precise descriptions of 1,441 species, some newly identified, in a form that has been much praised for its unique combination of scientific precision and accessibility to the average amateur bird watcher.

We can imagine the level of focus and task commitment Rasmussen amusingly described as her "attention-surplus disorder." But first, she fell in love with the study of birds.

The ornithologist's mini-history suggests several intriguing questions:

- Why does a youngster develop a particular interest in a particular subject or area of activity?
- Is the "Aha! falling-in-love" moment necessary in terms of uncovering an interest and sustaining it over time?
- How does parental influence enter the picture? Is "get interested in something useful" likely to have a positive effect?
- What amounts to "something useful" anyway, and who decides?

In this chapter, we consider some answers.

INTEREST AND ACHIEVEMENT: THE CONNECTION

Why a youngster becomes caught up in a fascination with birds or American history or quilting is often something of a mystery. The inherent "interestingness" of a task or object itself sometimes can be the catalyst that prompts a child to long to know more about it ("I thought the way the birds looked was so wonderful"). An individual's personality and physical makeup may also contribute to the *why*.

What role fascination plays in performance as well as attitude, on the other hand, is not a mystery. This much is just common sense: The more you like a thing, the more eagerly you tend to pursue it, the more time you're willing to devote to the pursuit, the more able you are to push beyond setbacks and difficulties and get something done — and the greater enjoyment you experience.

But much research has examined the interrelationship of cognitive ability and feelings, and how they in turn influence learning and accomplishment. The developmental psychologist Jean Piaget called *affectivity* — liking, pleasure, eagerness, curiosity — the energy source or the fuel for behavior, including task commitment. You don't get to solve a problem or discover something new, he said, without "intrinsic or extrinsic interest" in doing so. Intellectual functioning works better, it appears, because of the energizing role that is played by feelings. Even an interest that is essentially passive — such as being a rabid Los Angeles Lakers fan — sharpens certain mental processes. The rabid fan will easily pull from memory the first year the team won the NBA championship, the names of coaches, and Shaquille O'Neal's average points per game. Someone who's not especially keen on basketball might have trouble remembering if it's the Los Angeles, Boston, or New York Lakers.

As part of our ongoing work of introducing enrichment learning in schools, we have wanted to gauge some of the long-range effects on students who take part in the programs. As described earlier, our models start from the conviction that young people are most likely to become *engaged* in a thing — a topic, an area of study, issue, idea, or event — when they are given the opportunity to *select* what genuinely interests them. Engagement has a strong payoff in sense of direction and overall achievement, as well as in feelings of self-esteem and self-efficacy. Research studies on our enrichment model bear this out.

For example, the single best indicator of college majors and expressions of career choice on the part of young people has been intensive involvement in self-chosen projects based on early interests. Another research finding: High-achieving students who participated in enrichment experiences for five years or longer and displayed higher levels of creative productivity than their equally able classmates were remarkably similar to their peers, with one notable exception: The more creatively productive group had early, consistent, and more intense interests.

Interests matter. In fact, so often when a child is given the chance and encouragement to pursue his interest in a focused and self-determined way, to stretch and challenge himself to do his best work, he pulls himself up to a higher standard all around.

In the first three chapters, you read about a number of young people and their singular passions, including Ross, the boy who loved anything and everything about trains, and Bruce, the history enthusiast. But, unlike Ross and Bruce, not all children *know* what interests them, partly because, being children, they have limited awareness of what is "out there" that might catch their fancy. Some enjoy a variety of subjects, pointed enthusiasms that may wax and wane. In one of our pilot programs in an elementary school, we identified the top twenty interests of the students: dinosaurs; calculators and computers; cartoons; art projects; volcanoes and earthquakes; monsters and mysteries; math games and puzzles; life in the ocean; animals and their homes; magic; holidays; languages; drawing; rocks and minerals; making new toys; stars and planets; outer space, astronauts, and rockets; reptiles;

chemistry and experiments; and castles and knights — a rundown that probably sounds familiar to any parent of a lively youngster of preschool through middle school age. There is nothing wrong with short-lived and fluctuating enthusiasms, though they tend to preclude the kind of in-depth involvement that leads to independent investigative activities and creative productivity. And indeed, history tells us that the gifted contributions of accomplished individuals have always emerged from concentrated efforts in specialized areas.

Can a parent help a child discover what might be or become her own "specialty"? Absolutely.

ACTION INFORMATION: CLUES TO ENGAGEMENT

Finding what interests a child is a central element of our school-based enrichment programs. To get at this aspect, we often look to *action information,* which is to some degree the polar opposite of status information, or everything that can be systematically measured and recorded about a youngster — her grades, her test scores, and the other letters and numbers that tell how "smart" she is. Action information grows out of what intrigues a child, what grabs her attention. That spark may occur when she is influenced by a person, an idea, a piece of knowledge, or an area of activity or occupation, as was Ross with the world of railroads. If the influence is strong enough and positive enough to promote further involvement, we say a *dynamic interaction* has taken place.

Jordan, like most eight-year-olds, loved pizza. He and his father enjoyed a regular Friday evening practice of bringing home a pie from the local pizza place. Jordan was delighted by the way the baker twirled the dough in the air around his raised fist, thinning and shaping it into the flat round that would then hold the cheese and tomato sauce. Why didn't the spinning dough break apart? What made it so gummy or gluey? He wanted to know.

Jordan looked into the subject on the Internet one Saturday morning and printed out a recipe for pizza dough. With his father's help, he mixed a batch, which did not result in an edible pizza, though he found it was fun to watch the dough puff up and then punch it down. Jordan became interested in the whole matter of yeast and why it did what it did. Researching further, he learned that it had a number of uses and curious properties, and that he could make starter yeast himself. For several months, he involved his dad in baking breads, all based on one simple recipe that Jordan then tried to spice up with his own additions. A chocolate chip variety turned out well enough, he decided, to be given to their next-door neighbors as a gift.

This was a dynamic interaction of a culinary sort. In getting there, Jordan learned to follow a step-by-step process from start to finish — systematic investigation leading to a final (and delicious) product.

The suggestions we offer here are designed to help you help your child settle on an activity that sounds intriguing and that might become a trigger for her subsequent involvement and a dynamic interaction or two. Sometimes initial explorations of interests — surveying the territory — will produce one grand "Aha!" moment, but not always. Falling in love, instant fascination, and the drive to keep delving, learning, and mastering are all wonderful. Interests don't always arrive as a bolt from the blue, however — nor do they need to. Growing involvement so often brings with it the sweet reward of growing enthusiasm and commitment, along with satisfaction and fun.

ZEROING IN ON INTEREST: A GENERAL ASSESSMENT PROCESS

"Get interested in something useful," coming from Mom or Dad, probably won't be an effective motivator with most kids, any more than, "Go outside and get some air" will have the power to wean a child away from afternoons in front of the TV or computer. But many parents do wish their child would develop a passionate interest, or a deep

A (Very) Quick Look at "The Big Picture"

Gifted behaviors flow naturally from a child's interest, or interests, and indeed, there's usually more than one. Creativity feeds task commitment (and vice versa), and in combination these traits lead to the development of abilities at higher levels. To put some shape and form to the vast world of possibilities that exists, we have organized the big picture among ten general areas of interest:

- Performing arts
- Creative writing and journalism
- Mathematics
- Business/management
- Athletics and outdoor-related activities
- History
- Social/consumer action and environment-related activities
- Fine arts and crafts
- Sciences and technology
- Legal, political, and judicial

engagement in a positive pursuit. Some worry that a son or daughter appears uninterested in anything other than playing video games. Some aren't sure what area of investigation holds the most promise for leading a smart but unfocused youngster into "something useful."

One parent remembered her daughter Carla, now a young teen, as a bright, curious toddler who asked "why" a hundred times a day. "I wanted to give her a taste of a whole lot of activities as she grew older, and see what would stick, what she would choose to pursue," she said. So she consistently enrolled Carla in after-school or weekend activities, until age eleven or twelve when, according to her mom, she "could say 'No, I don't really want to do that.' So over the years, I sent her to ballet classes, music appreciation, karate lessons, ice skating lessons,

Saturday art instruction at the museum, Chinese kite making in the park, a theater group for preteens, and probably more I've now forgotten. I think, for the most part, she enjoyed these experiences, some more than others. I also think she's been a lucky kid to be able to try out a lot of stuff, though she hasn't followed up in any intensive way on any of those things."

Most caring and involved parents do have the instinct and make the effort to expose their children to a variety of subjects, issues, places, and pursuits. And these *are* lucky kids, children who are given wonderful opportunities to develop skills and to sample what the world has to offer. At the same time, if a child's involvements are based on someone else's agenda, and all his available nonschool time is channeled into structured and adult-organized programs with, often, pre-set goals, he might skip right past a thing that has the potential to engage his thoughts and feelings fully and promote creative interactions.

It's fine to make available a smorgasbord of activities and see what — if anything — "sticks," as Carla's mother said. There's also a simpler, cheaper, and possibly better way to help your bright child uncover a "specialty." Talk to him.

Ask your child what interests him.

Explore possibilities within that expressed enthusiasm.

Kick around some ideas on how a neat, exciting, enjoyable self-selected and self-directed project might evolve.

Something we call the Interest-a-Lyzer might give you useful hints on conducting such a zeroing-in process. An element in many of our enrichment programs, this tool aims to identify possible enrichment activities for a particular child or small group. It asks a number of questions: What do you like to do? Do you have any pets? Any collections? Do you belong to a club or team? What sort of music do you listen to? And then it poses a series of "imagine that . . ." or "what if . . ." statements designed to dig a little below the surface and find that spark.

Classroom teachers usually have no trouble recognizing each youngster's general preferences or bent: This boy enjoys math, that one enjoys reading, this girl is good in science, that one is athletic. The teacher is typically less aware of how a child likes to occupy himself outside of school or what fires his imagination — action information. Our school-based Interest-a-Lyzers are designed to fill in those gaps.

Parents usually know a lot more, of course. A son wants to be a punk rock guitarist. A daughter spends hours lying on her bedroom floor drawing. He adores anything to do with animals; she collects rocks and minerals. Maybe your kindergartener is a "ham," a kid who likes to perform or put on shows. Maybe your sixth grader is a "thinker" who from early childhood concerned himself with issues of what's right and what's wrong. In the home, then, between one parent and one child, an interest assessment takes on a more informal and conversational tone.

But for a little help in this process, you will find Interest-a-Lyzer selections from our work in enrichment programs in the boxes in this chapter. These, clearly, are meant not as scripts to follow or exact words to use, but as suggestions that can be adapted to fit your circumstances. And the selections in any one box are not limited to children in that age category. The exploration between parent and child takes its own unique shape. Ideally, the questions underscore the point of the process, which is to encourage your child to spend a little time thinking about what he likes — or how he might pursue what he *already* likes in a more involved, logical, and eventually productive manner.

Start a conversation. See where it leads. You may be surprised at patterns or major interest areas that bubble to the surface.

The key is that your child shows the way. There's no timetable. He might want to muse for a while about some ideas he has, or write out his thoughts in a notebook. Kids are sometimes asked in one situation or another to list what they like to do, what hobbies they enjoy, and so on. The Interest-a-Lyzer has a bigger purpose, which is to assist a child in conducting an in-depth self-analysis of his areas of interest or potential interest. When we first began introducing the form, we heard quite a few comments like this one from a middle school student: "I'm sorry that I didn't have any answers to these questions today, but you really made me think about a lot of things. When you come back next week I'll probably have some answers." Bingo! There's a fine goal, getting your child to "think about a lot of things."

Steering a youngster, possibly against his desires, toward a topic that sounds good, useful, important, or intriguing to Mom or Dad is more of what the kid gets in the course of a typical school day and essentially defeats the purpose of a personal interest exploration. One mother said she found it difficult to avoid "leading questions. Thomas and I had watched a nature show about how elephants swim underwater, and he was fascinated. So I heard myself saying, 'Remember how you loved those elephants we saw? I bet you'd really like to learn more about elephants.' He said, 'No.'"

A corollary to this bit of advice is to avoid the tendency to pounce on any hint of a child's selected interest. Pouncing, with all the best intentions, usually backfires. Another concerned parent was thrilled when her seven-year-old, Abby, "got involved in making small puppet-like figures out of odds and ends — sticks, colored pipe cleaners, bits of cloth. Some were people, some were animals. They were imaginative and full of expression, truly clever and witty. So I jumped in with all four feet. I took Abby to fabric stores, craft shops, loaded her up with a whole bunch of stuff. I got her a book about building miniatures. A lavish book about Queen Mary's dollhouse. I said she ought to construct dioramas or stages, have the characters displayed in scenes, and I'd help her with that. Abby let the whole thing drop. Whether I butted in too much and sort of derailed her enthusiasm, or whether this was just a passing fancy, I don't know."

Sometimes it's not easy to know. Young people do have passing fancies. Or they think a topic or activity sounds "kind of neat," but not much more than that. Or an expression of interest may in fact reflect a superficial notion of what in-depth involvement with the subject is all about. And of course, parents often *do* necessarily assume an active role in coming up with supplies, marshalling resources of one sort or another, suggesting a possible audience, and providing other support services that a child cannot access on his own.

Following the gist suggested by our Interest-a-Lyzers is a good way to stay on the track of a general assessment process — a reconnaissance mission — and resist an inclination to pounce or take the lead. One major parental role is that of reality-check provider. The kid who expresses a powerful interest in riding the shuttle with astronauts isn't going to get there. But maybe there's another angle to space travel and astronauts that he can look into.

At the same time, a reality check can go too far if its effect is to kill off entirely a burgeoning romance with a subject. One father told of his daughter's sudden infatuation with the idea of creating beautiful buildings, which followed the family's visit to Frank Lloyd Wright's Fallingwater house in Pennsylvania. The majestic house situated on several levels, the rushing mountain stream, the surrounding trees, all this seemed to have had a sensuous and aesthetic impact on the girl, who borrowed books about Wright from the library and talked about becoming an architect. "That's great," her father said, "but you don't start out building places that look like that," and went on to describe what he suspected were probably the tedious aspects of architectural training — the need to learn about cement, the apprentice years spent designing things like plumbing and wiring, and so on. That youngster's balloon was deflated in a hurry, which was never the intention of her father in his efforts to "be realistic."

It's usually counterproductive to temper initial romanticism with an immediate, heavy dose of realism if you're getting into any discussions about occupations with a child. Romanticism is precisely what so often lures him into deeper exploration. A fuller, truer picture can emerge as his interest develops and deepens. Who knows? The girl who fell in love with Fallingwater house and building beautiful buildings might have relished spending some time watching an architect — one of those willing and gung ho professionals with a talent for conveying enthusiasm — make drawings or design working models.

GETTING SPECIFIC: THE PROCESS OF INTEREST FOCUSING

Often, a child's interest is vague or so broad that she will benefit from help in getting a handle on it. One girl liked creative writing and language arts, a vast arena of activity and learning with many potential roads to head down. As she considered several kinds of writing, she decided it would be fun to concentrate on poetry, and that in turn sparked a fascination with haiku in particular. Interest focusing involves some further zeroing in and weighing of options with the aim of arriving at a specific and manageable goal or objective, and, ideally, a creative product, a "something" that is the result of a child's concentrated involvement over a stretch of time and that can be shared with an audience.

Focusing has a lot to do with the *how* factor, or in what way a youngster might want to follow up on a topic, which in turn can suggest the goal or objective.

Here's an example. Ten-year-old Rachel went with her mom to their local YMCA to hear a talk about yoga. What interested Rachel that afternoon was not so much the yoga, but a sign language interpreter standing to one side of the stage who translated the talk as it went on. Rachel was transfixed by the movement of the interpreter's hands and the speed with which she "spoke." A day or two later Rachel's mother rented the movie *Children of a Lesser God,* which takes place in a school for the deaf. In one scene that particularly fascinated Rachel, the speech teacher immerses himself in the school's swimming pool in an attempt to gain a sense of how it feels not to hear. A

For Kindergarten through Third Grade:
Some Interest-a-Lyzer Questions

- What is your favorite book? Why do you like it so much?
- Imagine that you can travel to any time in history. Where would you go? Why would you choose that time?
- You're a famous author about to write your next book. What will it be about? Can you think of a title?
- If you could have any pet you wanted, what would it be?
- Have you ever thought of inventing a new game? What kind of a game?
- Pretend you and your class are going on a trip and you're in charge of picking the place to go. Which would be your top three places?

___ museum	___ science center
___ sports game	___ show like Ice Capades
___ music concert	___ mayor's office
___ newspaper office	___ firehouse
___ TV studio	___ planetarium
___ courtroom	___ police station
___ zoo	___ amusement park
___ play	

- Pretend we're going to move to the moon. What will you take with you?
- What are some things you like to write about?
- Which of the following do you think you would like to try?

___ go to the opera or the ballet	___ make things with clay
___ make a secret code	___ play chess
___ help animals	___ build with blocks
___ speak another language	___ take things apart to see how they work
___ make cartoons	___ count things, like leaves on a tree
___ do science experiments	___ cook or bake
___ plant a garden	___ do jigsaw puzzles
___ play a musical instrument	___ play math games

running and somewhat explosive debate throughout the movie concerns the relative merits of using sign language or lip reading, and that also got Rachel's attention.

She decided she absolutely had to learn sign language. To her, it looked graceful, dramatic, and exotic. Her parents supported this enthusiasm by bringing home a training video and a book on the subject, and Rachel spent her free time over the next month or two practicing. Signing turned out to be much tougher than she had anticipated. She didn't get very good at it at all, and began to refer to herself as "a klutz." Her interest lessened, then died; the book and video were abandoned.

This youngster was willing and able to commit herself to a selected problem, but she might have fanned the flames of her initial enthusiasm if she'd considered a somewhat *different* problem. Maybe Rachel's perception of herself as a klutz stemmed from a lack of manual dexterity that made the practice of signing especially difficult for her. In any case, other follow-up options existed. She might have interviewed a sign language interpreter about the demands and satisfactions of the work, and what led her to it in the first place; studied the history surrounding arguments for and against lip reading; or tried to understand the social realities of deaf young people and their feelings about living in a hearing world, among other possibilities. She might have tried to formulate an idea for a product or service, maybe an article that would help others gain greater insight into this disability — or whether deaf people consider it a disability at all.

The point is, there is almost always more than one way to dig in.

Michael, a second-grade student in an enrichment program, generated an unusual and original project with a little adult guidance, and his activities illustrate the path from focused involvement to creative productivity. Michael had indicated a strong interest in Tchaikovsky. His teacher asked him a few questions about that: how and why he'd become interested, whether he'd read any books about the composer, whether he liked looking in different books to learn more. Michael explained that he took piano lessons, that he'd been listening to a passage from *The Nutcracker Suite,* and that he began wondering how Tchaikovsky wrote music.

Asked what made him think of this, Michael said he noticed that the music in *The Nutcracker* included both sad and happy parts. After some further teacher/student brainstorming, Michael decided that what he really wanted to know was if Tchaikovsky wrote sad music when he felt sad and happy music when he felt happy. Or maybe when he was sad, he wrote the happy parts to cheer himself up. In order to find out, he'd have to learn something about Tchaikovsky's life: When did he live? Did he have a nice childhood? Did he always love music? Did he always have a piano to play? Did he have sad periods in his life when he was composing music? If so, what did he write during those periods? He searched for information to answer his questions — or to solve the real problem he'd set for himself: did the composer write sad music when he felt sad and happy music when he felt happy?

Michael thought he'd like to try writing a "talking children's book" on the music and life of Tchaikovsky. Encouraged to find out whether his school or town library already had such a book, he learned that one did not exist. So he had a splendid incentive to do his best work at completing his product; and doing so required a lot of in-depth investigation of a historical nature, all centering around the happy/sad question that intrigued him. Six months later, this young boy gave his book to his school library, thirty printed pages and an audio version that played selections of Tchaikovsky's music composed during periods of happiness and tragedy — a reflection of his love for his topic and of his own effort.

Michael was fortunate to connect with a teacher who asked the right questions and thus helped him explore his enthusiasm and focus on a creative and manageable product.

Unfortunately, the opposite can happen and dead-end suggestions too often land on a motivated child in school. One youngster, for example, expressed an interest in sharks. Her teacher reacted in what he thought was an appropriate fashion: "That's terrific. I'm glad to hear you have such a great interest in sharks. Why don't you do a report about them?" Those awful words, "do a report about . . . ," led to a predictable result: a presentation of facts and drawings based entirely on information copied off the Internet and from books. While the girl prepared a neat, accurate report, her investigative activity was limited to looking up and summarizing already-existing facts. She did not provide fresh information, insights, or conclusions to what the world already understood about sharks.

Now, clearly, an elementary school student is unlikely — and not expected — to unearth discoveries about shark behavior that will have the professional community of shark scientists all abuzz. In addition, some practice in basic research and reporting is a necessary part of a good education for any young person: you can't pursue new knowledge without first reviewing old knowledge. And our shark-loving youngster might have enjoyed putting together her neat, accurate, illustrated presentation.

But "a report" is a pretty bland end result of a child's exploration of a subject that has begun to engage her; it tends to fall in that category we have called schoolhouse learning. Almost always, a self-selected interest can lead a youngster toward more exciting investigations and a more genuinely creative mode of involvement and final product. In answering questions regarding the product dimension of our enrichment model, we have a favorite expression: We do not necessarily expect small children to do great things, but we can expect them to do small things in a great way.

SPECTATOR OBSESSIONS: POINTS OF ENTRY TO A WIDER WORLD

Bobby, a third grader, was a baseball fanatic. He never missed a Yankees game on TV, collected baseball cards, and talked about baseball constantly and exclusively. It was the one subject he chose to write about in school when required to produce something in writing. Bobby's two best friends were similarly infatuated with the game.

Was it healthy, his parents wondered, for an eight-year-old to be so absorbed by one topic? Wasn't it a kind of superficial topic? Was Bobby shutting out peers who did not share his singular interest? Besides, they had to admit, listening to their son talk nonstop baseball was a little tiresome.

Like Bobby, some kids have their magnificent obsessions; there is no need to tease out a potential area of interest by the routes we've been describing — it's right there. Often, the child is mostly an amasser of data, a spectator, a fan. Nevertheless, such a passion can be the starting point from which parents might steer a youngster toward higher-end learning explorations.

Rather than urging Bobby off his baseball kick, for example — which probably wouldn't have worked — his parents bought him a biography of Jackie Robinson, the first black player in the major leagues. They talked to Bobby about Robinson's teammate Pee Wee Reese, the Southerner who famously put his arm around Jackie in a public display of acceptance. His parents got Bobby to read the sports pages of the morning newspaper over breakfast; played guessing games and estimates about players' averages; took out books on baseball that were a bit above his reading level, and so on. Gently, he was encouraged to read, learn, and think about civil rights, social history, and mathematics in addition to baseball. And his reading skills improved, to boot. He became interested in the history of the Negro Leagues, and actually managed to interview one of the last living players. A report about the leagues that he gave before his class became a discussion point about racial discrimination. All of this increased Bobby's feelings of pride in himself and what he was able to accomplish, and that motivated him further.

A boy named Harry was a rather indifferent student in fifth grade, one of those youngsters about whom teachers tend to say "needs to

For Elementary School: Some Interest-a-Lyzer Questions

- Imagine that your class has decided to create its own video production company. Which job would you like? Which would be your second and third choices?

  ___ actor   ___ advertising agent

  ___ director   ___ scriptwriter

  ___ musician   ___ costume designer

  ___ business manager   ___ scenery designer

  ___ computer effects spe-   ___ lights and sound person
      cialist   ___ camera operator

  ___ prop person

- Imagine that a machine allows famous people from the past to travel through time. If you could invite some of these people to visit, whom would you invite first? Who would be your second and third choices?

- If you had the time and the money to collect anything you wanted, what would you choose to collect?

- Imagine that you can spend a week "shadowing" any person in our community to investigate a career you might like to have in the future. What would be the occupation of the first person you'd select? The second choice? The third?

- Imagine you have been given a job as a feature writer on a newspaper. Which of the following columns would you like to write?

  ___ movie reviews   ___ video game reviews

  ___ book reviews   ___ Web site reviews

work harder." Harry's parents thought their son wasn't working harder because he wasn't happy in school. "He's a smart kid," Harry's mother said, "and he did fine earlier, but we moved to another city and this school he goes to now just doesn't seem to be a good fit for him. The boys are all into sports, which he's not. He's had trouble making friends. He told me the other kids think he's a nerd."

___ political cartoons   ___ camping and hiking
___ local history   ___ music critic
___ stock market analysis   ___ business trends
___ personal advice   ___ humor
___ editorials   ___ math puzzles
___ celebrities   ___ chess advice
___ cars and bikes   ___ sports analyst
___ travel   ___ pet care
___ social action news   ___ computers and technology
___ fashion column   ___ consumer advice
___ science
___ crossword puzzles

- If your school had the following clubs or programs, which ones do you think you might like to try?

___ newspaper   ___ collections club
___ yearbook   ___ ecology club
___ 4-H club   ___ drama club
___ cooking club   ___ invention convention
___ math club   ___ science club
___ chess club   ___ literary magazine
___ baby-sitting club   ___ computer club
___ language club

Midway through that year a science segment suddenly sparked Harry's interest in meteorology, and he started reading everything he could find on the subject. His immersion continued, and he became known, his mother said, "as a kind of walking encyclopedia of all sorts of facts relating to weather." Some of the kids began to call him Hurricane Harry. The boy became less of an indifferent student overall, his grades were better in all subjects, and he started talking about becoming a meteorologist.

His mother was pleased about this positive turn of events, but had a nagging concern. "I think one of the reasons he developed this intense involvement was because it distracted him from the social problems he was having. This was something he could do, a way to make himself feel special."

That may have been the case. Still, Harry's parents (or teacher) could encourage him to consider how to take his great love of weather and the exploration of meteorology a few steps further. Could it be arranged, say, for Harry to spend an afternoon at a local TV news station observing how forecasters interpret radar readings on the weather? Or to spend time with the person who monitors rainfall measurements in the city park? Just having a real-life encounter or two with professionals who gather and analyze information might deepen this youngster's involvement.

The examples of Bobby, the baseball fanatic, and Harry, who loved reading about weather patterns, make an important point about this matter of a child's chosen interest and how it can be encouraged. Although in our work with gifted and enrichment programs we emphasize creative productivity — chasing a real problem and a real product — as the highest good, so to speak, not every individual learning path will or must result in an original product or service intended to have an impact on an audience. A child who is "turned on" to a particular interest can indulge that in several ways:

- He may wish simply to accumulate and store information for future use or consideration.
- He may explore his passion out of sheer enjoyment and personal satisfaction. It's fun. He'll have a great time, while discovering that learning can be a joyful experience.
- He can use his discoveries to fuel an active fantasy life, dream-

ing about becoming a great actor or shortstop or hurricane spotter, let's say.

Each is an important and useful manifestation of a child's selected interests, though they are more latent and receptive than active. Not every child — or adult — is built for investigation and inquiry. And we emphasize again that exploring and understanding the existing knowledge in an area of learning, even becoming a "walking" encyclopedia, is fine.

A child has a right to interests that are not productivity-oriented. Some kids may have no motivation whatsoever to become creative producers or firsthand inquirers in their selected areas, but every child has a right to pursue his interests.

INTIMATIONS OF THE FUTURE: "WHAT DOES SHE WANT TO BE WHEN SHE GROWS UP?"

Do you see in your child's budding interest the seeds of a career someday? Does that possibility gladden your heart or does it start you stewing over whether she'll ever find a good job, make a decent living, or "get somewhere" in life?

Here's our take on the matter: Raise your child to use her talents, build on her strengths and interests, and eventually pursue work that she loves, and you have done well.

Another story close to home: When our daughter Liza was three years old and taking ballet, it quickly became apparent that she loved the stage more than she loved the dance. In a snapshot from that time, she stands there, one of the snowflakes from *The Nutcracker,* arms spread wide, relishing the whole experience of being in front of an applauding crowd. The dance teacher finally went out and led her off the stage.

For Middle and High School: Some Interest-a-Lyzer Questions

- If the principal at your school asked you to design the perfect elective course for kids with your same interests, what would the course be called? What would be taught?
- If your school gave money to each individual student for a field trip of her choice, what three places would you choose to visit? Why?
- Imagine that your science teachers are planning a speakers' bureau based on a variety of topics. What are the first, second, and third presentations you'd be interested in attending?

___ toxic waste	___ nuclear energy
___ health issues for teen-agers	___ greenhouse effect
	___ environmental issues
___ genetic engineering	___ scientific research and
___ endangered species	methods
___ weather mapping	___ meteorology
___ forensic medicine	___ rain forests
___ robotics	___ astronomy

- If a conservative and a liberal attorney were invited to your school for a debate, what three debate topics would you choose? Why?
- Imagine that you and your friends have been asked to prepare individual time capsules for future generations, and you were allowed to include ten personal possessions that were representative of you. What would go in your capsule?
- You have had a dream in which you have been transported back in time and have become an active participant in a historical period. Which period was that? Whom did you meet there?

At age five, after seeing *Show Boat,* she left the play in tears. We asked why she was crying and she said, "Because it's over! I don't want it to be over!" In first grade she became involved in a series of en-

- If you could conduct an interview with a man or woman you admire, past or present, who would it be? What three questions would you ask that person?
- If you could be an exchange student in any country for half a school year, what country would you want to visit? Why?
- If you had the opportunity to learn foreign languages from native speakers, which three languages would you want to learn? Why?
- An after-school group has been formed to meet and discuss important issues facing young people. Which would be the first, second, and third choices of seminars you'd be interested in attending?

___ contemporary moral issues	___ gender issues
	___ peer relationships
___ national security	___ world peace
___ career opportunities and choices	___ family structure
	___ issues in ethnicity

- If you could design a computer program, what would it do?
- If someone asked you to participate in producing the film of your choice, what type of film would that be?

___ documentary	___ science fiction
___ musical	___ horror
___ biography	___ mystery
___ travelogue	___ comedy
___ fantasy	___ adventure

- Imagine that you've been asked to be a member of a social action committee in your town, and you will work with elected officials on important issues. What three issues do you think need to be discussed? Why?

richment clusters on puppetry and started writing and creating her own miniature shows. Amassing a collection of finger and hand puppets, she organized her friends and cousins to put on plays. She was the director, the boss — that kid would be given the assignment to make tickets, that one would sell them, this one would see that everyone got seated.

When she was in fourth grade, *Titanic* came out and Liza and a couple of her friends wrote a play based on the movie. Organizing a crew of classmates, she had some kids taking care of set design, some doing costumes. The group performed their original *Titanic* as part of an end-of-year program, with Liza producing, directing, and starring.

Over the next several years, she appeared in every school musical, and we, her parents, looked for opportunities for her to pursue her passion during the summers — Camp Broadway in New York City, a theater acting program at a college in New England. All through high school, Liza and the other "drama kids" were in their element. Hosting cast parties now and then, we marveled at how these young people were so in touch with and supportive of each other because of the commonality of interests.

In eleventh and twelfth grades, Liza chose to direct and act in a play as her senior project. Over those two years, she read every play that had won a Pulitzer Prize for the past half century, settling on *Proof* as the one she thought would be most amenable to a high school production. Producing the play involved securing the rights and roping in all the other drama kids. Working on her projects over the years, she would sometimes put in twelve or eighteen hours a day, to the point of euphoric exhaustion. As testament to her hard work and commitment, Liza was accepted at — and enrolled in — a college known for its outstanding drama department.

This girl loves the theater. There is no doubt in her mind that she will someday, somehow, be involved in the professional theater world — a notoriously tough one, with jobs hard to come by and erratic paydays. But to us, her belief in herself and her passionate goal are the prizes — a young person living a happy, creative life, ultimately finding work that is both meaningful and enjoyable. The educator John Dewey said, "To be interested is to be absorbed in, wrapped up in, carried away by, some object. . . . We say of an interested person both that he has lost himself in some affair and that he has found himself in it."

In this chapter, we've considered the routes by which your child might identify an area of investigative activity that appeals to her. In the following chapter, we look at how she can proceed according to styles of learning and expression that feel most natural, and that honor and capitalize on her uniqueness.

✳

CHAPTER 5

The "How" Factor

Tuning in to Your Child's Preferences

in Learning Style and Expression

In a small seaside community in New York State, several ninth graders were encouraged to develop an independent learning project that
might eventually be of interest to the town in general. The young
people decided to investigate an issue that had been receiving local
media attention in recent months: how to retard beach erosion and
whether or not a beach replenishment proposal by the U.S. Army
Corps of Engineers should be approved.

One girl in the group, Margot, assumed a leadership role from the
start. Margot kept the discussions moving, planned timelines, and set
up regular meetings to assess progress. Ellie elected to undertake a
little scientific research. She uncovered and studied the literature on
relevant topics — what was known about erosion patterns, whether
littoral drift naturally replaced sand on the shoreline, and whether
artificial replenishment of the beach would affect marine life such as
algae and mollusks and thus the fish and birds that feed on them.

Three other youngsters — Kevin, Erin, and Billy — filmed the actions of waves at various hours in order to demonstrate tidal movements and how they affected the sand. Learning that a particularly

high tide would be hitting the area on one day, they hoped to video-tape the effectiveness of the sea grass dunes.

Ethan and Georgina, aware of all the heated feelings regarding the corps' project, gravitated toward what they called "the human interest angle." On several weekend afternoons, the two interviewed a few surfers waiting on the beach for the big waves, homeowners who lived along the shore, a couple who lived farther inland in a less affluent section, and the head of the city council who gave them an hour of his time to discuss the upcoming vote. Some believed the sand replenish-ment project was absolutely essential; others thought it would be the worst thing that could happen to their town.

At the end of their investigation, the ninth graders put together a polished presentation that combined reports, film, and oral testimo-nies. It was intended, said Margot, "to give the pro and the con with-out us saying what we thought." They presented at school and again at the local library for an audience of over a hundred people. The beach erosion team members were fairly popping with pride.

We asked the teens why they each chose particular areas to pur-sue. Ellie was a studious girl with a scientific bent who loved "looking things up," she said, and liked to work mostly on her own. Kevin, Erin, and Billy were motivated partly by the fact that Kevin, a bud-ding filmmaker, had a camcorder and could produce good results with it. All three also called themselves "beach rats" who enjoyed be-ing outdoors and "doing physical stuff." Ethan and Georgina said, "We liked talking to people, maybe getting a debate going, mix it up." Margot, the master of ceremonies, enjoyed designing the final prod-uct and thought she was good at "organizing and publicity." Each kid, it seemed, had settled on a path of activity that suited him and that felt like a good fit.

This concept of stylistic fit — and why it matters — is easily dem-onstrated by their example. The self-described beach rats might have been bored silly printing out information from computers. The scholarly minded girl might have found the prospect of tramping around the beach, filming waves and getting wet, highly unappealing. Individual style preferences often manifest in groups working on projects such as this one, and the willingness to accommodate differences is what largely accounts for successful outcomes. Had all the children been shoehorned into one manner of solving their self-selected problem, the whole process might have lost steam early on. At least, it almost certainly would not have been as involving and enjoyable to the kids as it clearly was.

In this chapter, we offer some ideas that should help you appreciate your child's style, the better to help him move forward in exploring the interest he's identified for himself. He knows *what* sounds intriguing and worth digging into; now he will think over or experiment with the *how* — and the *who, when,* and *where* are in there, too. Style, or the kind of approach that comes naturally, is revealed by several indicators:

- preferred mode of instruction
- preferred surroundings
- preferred way of thinking
- preferred forms of expression

We say that these preferences represent the characteristic ways a particular youngster adapts and organizes the assets — the "internal stuff" — that he brings to a learning situation. They come from a mix of personality or temperament, physical makeup, age, and any number of other factors. But it's not always easy for parents to "get" a child's stylistic fit, as some parental comments show. Often, we adults tend to apply our sense of what's proper or right, what works and what can't possibly be working: "He's having so much fun and getting so jazzed up, I don't see how any real learning can be going on." "She acts out, she always has to dramatize things." "It's eleven at night, he's got to be too tired to think straight!"

So this might be a useful point at which to reiterate some of our favorite themes: Gifted behaviors blossom according to your child's unique self — what interests him and how he opts to spend his time and direct his efforts. In the dynamic learning environments you create and encourage, he can enjoy a degree of stylistic wiggle room that in all likelihood is unavailable to him in the classroom. An opportunity most conducive to creative productivity includes freedom for your child to do what he wants to do in a style that honors his uniqueness and capitalizes on his strengths.

GETTING THROUGH: PREFERENCES IN INSTRUCTION STYLE

Educators are well aware that different kids like to be taught in different ways. Children have not only varying interests and abilities, but varying modes of desired instruction too.

Some kids, primarily auditory learners, like to listen to the teacher deliver a lesson, take in what's being said, and engage in discussions. The more visual learners pay attention to what is written on the board, read assignments diligently, and enjoy studying pictures, graphs, and diagrams. Some youngsters are more tactile. They like to touch objects, draw, build, piece things together — hands-on kids, literally. Others learn best when they can involve their whole bodies through role playing, going on field trips, any kind of physical expression of thoughts and ideas. Some like to work on their own, some don't.

Experienced teachers spot the differences in their classrooms. One child comes to life during an animated debate, jumping out of her seat, waving her hand, asking provocative questions. Another child always wants to partner with a classmate who is maybe a bit more knowledgeable about a topic. Another becomes most "tuned in" at a worktable or what is sometimes called an *interest center,* where concrete collections related to a subject invite manipulation.

The important point is that a child is likely to be happier, less antsy, and more awake if at least some of what she's compelled to learn is beamed at her in a style with which she's comfortable. In addition, she is better able to concentrate, absorb, and retain new information. She's more interested in the subject. She says she wishes everything was taught in the same way! This positive result may come about because she can focus most of her energy on the content being presented, rather than having to adapt to a style of instruction that doesn't quite suit her.

Ideally, students are provided opportunities to enjoy their preferences through what is called *individualized instruction.* In most classrooms, however, individualized instruction tends to reflect only imperfectly each child's uniqueness. Typically, kids may simply be offered the chance to move through the curriculum at their own speed, according to the level of achievement each has reached. So the skilled reader is allowed to work on material that is more advanced than the material being used in class and perhaps given a few extra assignments to complete.

Varying pace is a good thing, of course, but goes only so far. In an attempt to identify how kids prefer to be taught, we use an Instructional Styles Inventory form, asking children to tell us what appeals to them and what doesn't: "You're learning something new. Given your choice, how would you like to go about it? What works best for you?" From their responses, greater efforts can be made to match teaching strategies to individual preferences.

Whether achieving a match is possible during the school day or not, an instruction style that best fits your child is important for any kind of independent work. Whatever interest your child chooses to explore, she will inevitably need to go about gathering information, learning about existing knowledge in the field, and about the processes required to get something done. One or two routes to information gathering will probably be more acceptable than others, and actually might mean the difference between a project that delves into deeper levels of engagement or one that dies on the vine.

A thirteen-year-old named Eve was described by her mother as a reserved and quiet child, ever since her toddler days. "She's a person who always likes to observe from the sidelines. I've heard people say to her, 'Hey, Eve, smile, why so serious?' She might look like she wants to be somewhere else or she's not interested, but actually she's taking it all in. Very alert. And she won't say anything until she's absolutely sure she's got it right, she has to get all her ducks in a row."

With characteristic intensity, Eve at one point became interested in issues surrounding freedom of speech after hearing about certain books that were banned in libraries and schools, an action she thought was very wrong and deeply disturbing. Over a couple of weeks, she researched the subject — which books had been outlawed in different countries and when, the political and other reasons behind those actions, and more. Her mother happened to see an announcement for a daylong Saturday meeting of seminars sponsored by a freedom-of-speech advocacy group, including teenagers, and suggested Eve go to it. She'd probably learn a lot there.

"This turned out to be not such a hot idea," her mother said. "Apparently there was a kind of round-robin talk. Eve was expected to get up and give her thoughts. There was a lot of arguing, lots of viewpoints. Then people were pressing her to sign up for one committee or another." Rather than having an energizing effect, attending the meetings seemed to deflate Eve. It was a matter of not necessarily too much information, but of information arriving from too many directions, coupled with an urge for action that Eve wasn't ready for.

This young girl probably preferred a more singular and a quieter form of information gathering, getting all her ducks in a row, before figuring out what, if anything, she wanted to do with her interest and growing awareness. As her mother put it: "She just likes to spend time with her books and computer, informing herself. That's her style."

Style matters.

In the box below, we've adapted the Instructional Styles Inventory in the form of a few questions you might want to ask your child. Or, review the inventory to add your own insights, to confirm or refresh a picture you already hold about what she prefers, given what you know of her nature and what you have gleaned from school reports. Appre-

---

An Instruction Style Survey:
How Do You Like to Gather Information?

Suppose you set out to learn something new. How would you choose to go about it? What do you like best?

Do you like to learn things mainly by using the computer? This means you like mostly working on your own, hunting up information. Or maybe you like computer programs that are set up like a workbook, with statements that end with a question or a blank to be filled in. This gives you feedback right away and shows how well you're doing.

Do you like to learn from other kids? You're most comfortable when another child who is more knowledgeable about a certain topic helps you learn new material or reviews it with you.

Do you like to listen to lectures? You find it appealing to have an expert in a subject talk about the ideas and concepts you need to pick up. It's good to have someone organize and present the material to you and tell you the important points.

Do you like learning by discussion? You enjoy sharing ideas, listening to various opinions, and talking over a topic with others. This is the best way for you to weigh different facts and get the whole picture.

ciating this aspect of your child's learning style can give you some good ideas about the kinds of information resources you might steer her toward.

WHO, WHERE, WHEN: PREFERENCES IN SURROUNDINGS

The father of nine-year-old Jake said, "I come home from work and there's Jake lying on the den floor. Actually, more than lying on the floor, he's stretched out half under the table, on his stomach, with his legs sticking out and propped against the chair. The TV is on, tuned

Do you like playing games or role-playing? Role-playing of real-world situations helps you understand. Board games, contests, and spelling and geography bees are fun ways to learn something new. Maybe you enjoy acting out a historical event, or playing the part of some professional person.

Do you like to work with an older, experienced person who can give you a lot of guidance? You learn best when there's a teacher or another expert who knows a lot about your interest and can give one-on-one expertise and encouragement.

Do you enjoy working with collections? You are most enthusiastic and involved when you can study things organized around a topic or a concept, and maybe experiment with them.

Do you like to research and explore something new all on your own? It works best for you if you don't have too much supervision, if you can develop your own approach to gathering information.

Do you like to work on a project? You like producing something concrete as you go about learning. Maybe you'll work on your own or with one or more other kids who are interested in the same thing.

to a rerun of *The Munsters.* The air conditioner is going full blast. Jake is also apparently listening to music, those little ear things plugged in his ears. On the floor next to him is a magazine, not a plate, on which are the remains of little mini pizzas he's nuked in the microwave. Oh, and there's a book open and some papers under the table. I ask him what he is doing. 'I'm studying,' he says.

"I recognize that the generations may differ in how each one approaches a job. I contrast Jake's position with my own, which is that I need to be sitting up straight, at a desk, feet flat on the floor, six sharpened pencils right there, no background noise, temperature just right. But I do wonder whether it is actually possible, mentally, to study successfully in the midst of the kind of distractions that engulf my son."

One man's distractions are his child's learning environment preferences.

The child who's sprawled on the floor, munching on snacks, with noises pounding while he's "studying," dad viewing the scene in dismay, is perhaps the stereotypical and comical image of the great generational divide. But there is a world of variation in the kinds of surroundings young people prefer. And there is no question, according to research and simple observation, that social and physical aspects of the environment influence a child's performance — but not necessarily in the way the adult looking on might think.

Some children are true night owls, up until four o'clock in the morning working away with no apparent ill effects — until they feel a need to nap in the afternoon. Others are morning larks; if these youngsters can't get at a thing early in the day, it doesn't work for them. Some children concentrate better with snacks on hand; others don't need them.

Many young people demonstrate a preference for independent work that calls to mind a remark once made by Albert Einstein. He said: "I am a horse for single harness, not cut out for tandem or teamwork." This is the self-oriented youngster who likes to work in a solitary setting. Other people are not necessary for the purpose of communal energy or comfort; having anyone around might, in fact, be annoying. For this child, learning takes place most comfortably within a personal, not social, environment.

Peer-oriented youngsters, on the other hand, greatly enjoy being in the company of other kids. Within the group — whether it's one or two others or more — this child does his best work and gets his brightest ideas. Some children prefer an adult to be nearby. And some demonstrate no strong preferences for being alone or in groups or with adults. These youngsters are probably just highly flexible in outlook and personality, children who can float from one learning environment to another without difficulty.

These are some of the correlations between personal preference and environment that impact learning and productivity. When a child is compelled to work in an environment that doesn't quite suit him, creativity and output can be squelched.

The inescapable fact is that your child is probably required to toe the line during the course of the school day. There may be some attention given to organizational arrangements at the teacher's discretion, such as how seats are set up, whether kids work cooperatively or individually, and so on. But if your child is one habitually in creative high gear late at night, he's nevertheless expected to be most alert at nine in the morning. And teachers do not look kindly on snacking in the classroom.

The statements or questions in the box below concern your child's preference for closeness and interaction with others, his inter/intrapersonal social style. They also touch on a number of physical factors that actually do affect learning. Ask him for his thoughts on these matters. Maybe it never occurred to him before that he's happiest and most productive in particular surroundings. That's good to know. And good for you to understand as well, as you appreciate his unique stylistic fit.

A Surroundings Style Survey:
How Do You Like Your Environment to Look, Sound, and Feel?

Company

You learn best . . .

___ on your own.

___ with another kid or in a group.

___ with an adult.

___ Depending on what you're studying, you might like a combination.

Sound

You learn best . . .

___ when it is absolutely quiet.

___ with some background music.

___ when it's very noisy.

___ You don't care one way or the other.

Light

You learn best . . .

___ in very bright light.

___ in some light.

___ in dim light.

___ The amount of light doesn't make a big difference.

Temperature

You learn best . . .

___ when it's hot.

___ when it's warm.

___ when it's cool.

___ when it's cold.

___ Temperature doesn't make a big difference.

Setting

You learn best . . .

___ when the room is very orderly.

___ when you sit at your desk.

___ when you casually lie, lean, stand, or sit on a bed, couch, or carpet.

___ You don't care about the setting.

Time

You learn best . . .

___ in the morning.

___ in the afternoon.

___ in the evening and late at night.

___ You don't care about the time.

Food and Drink

You learn best . . .

___ with a lot of food and drink around.

___ with an occasional snack break.

___ when you chew gum.

___ when you bite or chew on a pen.

___ You don't need any food or drink or anything in your mouth.

Mobility

___ You like to sit down and stick to your work until it is finished.

___ You like to stand and move around a little while working.

___ You don't care one way or another.

LEGISLATOR, EXECUTOR, JUDGE: PREFERENCES IN THINKING STYLE

Two ten-year-old boys, Leo and Aidan, friends since second grade, were putting out a newsletter to send to kids they'd met in camp that summer. Leo was inspired by an old-style printing press — a huge assortment of metal slugs of individual letters that are placed along tracks line by line to make words and sentences, then inserted in a wooden frame, brushed with ink, and pressed onto paper. This antique set had belonged to Leo's father when he was a boy, a favorite hobby now captivating his son.

Working at their project, Leo decided what they were going to write and how the newsletter should look. Aidan went about organizing the letters on the tracks and suggested ways to make the printed page smoother.

Aidan's mother was happy that the two were keeping nicely occupied and apparently having a good time, but something bothered her. "This is how things always develop with those two. Leo is the spark plug. He comes up with the ideas, he gets very revved up about some new project. Aidan will get excited about it too, but he's always kind of playing the support role. It seems to me he's following orders. I wonder sometimes if Aidan is dominated by his friend. Maybe I'd like it if he were more assertive." She added that her son didn't *seem* to feel dominated; this was her own concern.

This parent might have gained insight — and been relieved — by shifting her attention from the emotional or social elements of her son's friendship and his lack of "assertiveness" to how his brain worked. When it comes to the manner in which a child applies himself to an intense creative endeavor, it's useful to understand how he characteristically thinks.

Thinking is an artful, internal activity reflected in particular styles, though most research over the years has focused on the different matter of thinking *skills*. According to one popular concept based on the ideas of Benjamin Bloom — and much admired by many educators — thinking skills move along a continuum from simple to complex, or from the lowest to the highest levels of sophisticated thought processes. In this hierarchy, the first, lowest, rung is knowledge, the second rung, comprehension — in other words, remembering facts and being able to exhibit a basic grasp of them.

But some children in school (often those with the highest aptitude) can be expected to demonstrate the three highest levels of competence, which are identified as analysis, synthesis, and evaluation. In class discussions, reports, and answers to questions, these youngsters are able to draw broad conclusions from retained facts, make comparisons among a number of areas of study, engage in "what would have happened if?" speculations, and present well-reasoned arguments.

In a challenge to this mind-set, we have insisted that *all* children ought to be developing *all* strengths, including the higher-order skills. Why should not (or could not) the "average" kids learn to analyze and evaluate, express the difference between right and wrong, good and bad, the aesthetically pleasing and the unpleasant, what is acceptable and not acceptable? All children should be encouraged to develop the competencies needed for reasoning and making value judgments, even if only at their own levels of understanding.

In any case, some theorists have addressed the issue of thinking *style,* which is how an individual typically sees the problem at hand and goes about tackling it. Psychologist Robert J. Sternberg explains thinking style as the manner in which "one directs one's intelligence," and identifies three distinct styles. Using the metaphor of our government, Sternberg names the legislative, the executive, and the judicial thinker. We might call these children the inventors, the facilitators, and the evaluators.

The Legislative Inventor

She says: "I like to create, formulate, do things my own way."

The youngster with a legislative thinking style — and this sounds like Leo — is a planner and creator. She's the kid who says, "Here's what we're going to do." She prefers to make up her own rules and games, put together her own Halloween costume, draw her own greeting cards, write stories and poems, devise scientific experiments, originate service projects, and create sculptures.

Words that describe the legislative thinker: plan, choreograph, compose, invent, animate, write.

The Executive Facilitator

She says: "I like to figure out what to do, or direct how to do what needs to be done."

The child with an executive thinking style likes to fill in the content or build on someone else's design, as Aidan seems to enjoy. She's the producer, in a sense — the one who has what it takes to bring things in line. This youngster will explain or teach someone else's theories and ideas, and clarify and articulate existing bodies of information.

Words that describe the executive thinker: facilitate, help, simplify, interpret, support, sustain, assist.

The Judicial Evaluator

She says: "I enjoy analyzing, grading, evaluating, and comparing."

The judicial thinker reflects on how things are going. She prefers to judge designs, structures, or content; consider evidence; and weigh significances. A literary person with a strong judicial bent is probably a book reviewer rather than a book writer — one who can play critic, analyze, and compare.

Words that describe the judicial thinker: appraise, value, assess, judge, determine, review.

As you observe your youngster, you'll probably realize that one, or perhaps two, of these preferred thinking styles typically emerges in learning situations. No one style is superior, and indeed young people should practice thinking in all styles, since real-world learning situations require a variety of approaches.

EYE ON THE PRODUCT: PREFERENCES IN STYLE OF EXPRESSION

As we've noted, schoolhouse instruction usually requires that your child prove that he's been paying attention by writing a report or taking a test. Seldom is he asked, "Okay, instead of a report or a test, how would you prefer to demonstrate what you have learned?" It's a shame no one asks him that, because when a child is given an opportunity to express himself in a naturally preferred style, he is apt not only to take more pleasure in his work but to delve more deeply into the material.

Elizabeth, an enthusiastic reader from a very young age, had read and reread all nine volumes in the *Little House* series by Laura Ingalls Wilder during the summer after second grade. Entering third grade, she and her classmates were given the assignment to read a nonfiction book of their choice and write a book report on it. Elizabeth surprised her parents and teacher by reading not one but four popular biographies about Laura Ingalls Wilder.

She had an idea. She loved playing board games almost as much as she loved reading and asked her teacher if she could forgo the required book report and instead create a game that would follow Laura's life across decades and different periods. Maybe the game would inspire other kids to read more about this fascinating woman and about early American history. Her enlightened and courageous teacher thought the idea was excellent and gave the go-ahead.

Getting down to work, Elizabeth realized that the authors of the biographies included different information and also had slightly varied impressions of their subject. Her mom explained that biographies

An Expression Style Survey: How Do You Like to Demonstrate What You've Learned?

Suppose you have been working on a project and have made a lot of interesting discoveries. How do you think you would like to share your findings with an audience? Do you find any of the following possibilities not at all appealing, or a little appealing, or very appealing?

___ *Do you like to talk in front of people?* You give oral presentations or lead discussions about information you have gained.

___ *Do you like being the one who organizes things?* You might circulate a petition for an animal shelter or start a cleanup campaign.

___ *Do you like helping people, being of service?* You volunteer at a day care center, collect clothes or food for a shelter, or raise funds for social causes.

___ *Do you like all kinds of activities involving calculations and numbers?* You invent mathematical games or puzzles or brain teasers.

___ *Do you like to express yourself in writing?* You write essays, short stories, plays, newspaper articles, or letters to the editor.

___ *Do you like to work with design, color, fabrics and other materials, or artistic products that have eye appeal?* You make costumes, paint play sets, create jewelry or sculpture, paint pictures or a mural, illustrate a book, or draw a comic strip.

only interpret lives, but to understand what a person actually thought and believed and how she lived, it might be necessary to read primary sources. This was a pretty big leap for a third grader, and it was one that led her to further reading, including the letters that Laura had written to her husband, Almanzo Wilder, while she traveled. Elizabeth was almost in tears, her mother said, as she recognized the differences between a woman whose books had made her famous and her husband who never wanted to leave the farm.

This young girl worked diligently on her game — Laura's World —

___ *Do you like expressing yourself creatively through music or movement?* You compose music or choreograph dances, sing before an audience, or put together a performance playing an instrument you have mastered.

___ *Do you like working with tools or other kinds of equipment?* You build scenery, a working model, or original inventions. You refinish furniture, take photographs, or conduct scientific experiments.

___ *Do you like dramatization?* You like to act in plays or skits, or perform a mime or a clown act.

___ *Do you like doing things that take you outdoors?* You conduct environmental impact studies in your area.

___ *Do you like working on the computer?* You design interactive computer projects or games, multimedia shows, or computer animations.

___ *Do you like audiovisual products?* You film or edit movies or videos, record and edit radio programs, or select slides and music for slide shows.

___ *Do you like business activities, commercial products, and making money?* You might start your own company or manage investments or market an idea.

conceiving the rules and directions and drawing up questions for the cards that allow players to proceed around the board. A field test with four of her friends lasted only five minutes, however, as the players zipped through the game. Elizabeth realized she'd need a lot more than the forty-five cards she had made. So it was back to her books and source materials for more information about Ingalls Wilder — her growing-up years on the Midwest frontier; the family's moves to Wisconsin, Kansas, Iowa, South Dakota, and Missouri; how they made a living; hardship winters; and so on. When the final version was completed, Elizabeth had prepared over 300 question cards that gave players a sense of the unique woman and her life and times.

Inventing a board game was fun for this girl, and also led her through an in-depth learning experience. There probably would have been less in-depth learning, and a lot less fun, if she had not been given the opportunity to select her problem and then express herself — create a product — in a form that she liked.

Expression styles deal with *how* youngsters prefer to identify and explore a topic, and with *how* they will most comfortably communicate what they have learned with others, if they choose to do so. Style takes off from your child's interest or interests and relates closely to them. Some interests obviously lend themselves to specific products. But often, there might be a variety of ways for your child to proceed, and one or two will suit him more naturally than others. If you and your child talked over the Interest-a-Lyzers in the previous chapter, some expression style clues probably popped up there. From those "Imagine that . . ." and "If you could . . ." and "Which of the following . . ." discussions, maybe you learned that in a video production company, he'd absolutely want to be the actor — or not the actor but the scriptwriter or the person who designed the costumes. Or maybe he thought he'd like to make cartoons, or plant a garden, or count things.

A love of history might be expressed by planning a walking tour of local historical sites (as one boy did for an enrichment learning project), or by producing a dramatic reenactment of the Constitutional Convention of 1787, or by mounting a photography exhibit. Eve, the girl who was concerned about the banning of books, might eventually want to interview librarians, write an article based on their opinions, and try to get it published somewhere. Or, she might set up a table outside the local library and collect 200 signatures opposing book banning, to be sent to her congressional representatives.

To further refine and focus an interest, consider with your child the Expression Style Inventory we've adapted here for some thoughts about products and formats that might be a good fit.

A final word on stylistic fit: All style preferences may change — almost surely *will* change and evolve — over time, with age, greater exposure, heightened confidence, developing abilities, and all the other factors that go along with growing up.

✳

CHAPTER 6

Putting It All Together

Moving from Interests and Styles to Creative Projects

Your child has expressed a genuine interest in something. Or maybe you observe that she's all ears and keenly attentive whenever a particular topic — planning for a NASA space launch or saving the whales — is in the news. But many kids with real enthusiasms will lack the expertise, or even the motivation, to follow up on an interest over a period of time. Very young children may have no idea what to do next or how to identify a "real problem" for further investigation. Parents should help. Encourage your youngster to explore so that she might uncover some hints about what could become a bona fide project to pursue.

In some schools, creative and energetic teachers set up Interest Development Centers in their classrooms. This is a table or bookshelf or otherwise specially designated area that is stacked with a variety of materials — photos and pictures, posters, newspaper stories, books, catalogs, collections — all intended, as the name suggests, to develop interests held by students in the class. Attempts are made to create an enticing, eye-appealing assortment, with the goal of sparking children's "what to do next" ideas.

In this chapter and the one that follows, we offer a number of suggestions for at-home interest development with children. Brainstorm ideas together. Clip a magazine article that relates to your child's interest. If your youngster "always has her nose in a book," help her think about a project that incorporates choices in reading, such as storytelling. If she's a hands-on child, help her surf the Web to find ideas geared toward her preferences — "Building a Robot," for example, or "Home Sweet Home: Design a House." Encourage her to take a "virtual field trip" online, which can be a wonderful opportunity to get a taste of the dynamic possibilities in a particular area of learning. (More later on using the computer wisely and well.)

Through such general exploratory activities, you can tweak your child's curiosity about a subject, expand her perspective, and, ideally, invite her to actively participate in the topic of her choosing.

Many young people with gifted potential become sufficiently motivated to take their curiosity or concern to a higher level, as has been demonstrated by our stories of kids who carry out remarkable explorations with impressive results. In these chapters, we tell a few additional stories for the purpose of highlighting the "how they did it" steps that characterize creative learning. In the broadest sense, these steps might be categorized as an *input* stage (gathering information and materials), a *processing* stage (arranging, rearranging, analyzing, or in other ways manipulating the input), and an *output* stage (creating a product).

In reality, children's projects rarely advance in such a cut-and-dried fashion. The answer to "what next?" can take any number of turns. Various tools — pulling-it-together techniques — facilitate creative work, but accomplishments tend to be cyclical rather than linear. There is often a great deal of back and forth; a child decides at one point that she must retrace some former steps. The concept of a final product may change or an anticipated audience may be expanded, reduced, or modified.

Along the way, parents enter the scene as needed, to offer encouragement, suggestions, and practical support — that is, to assume the role of managerial assistant. We focus here, first, largely on the "start-up" stages of developing a project around a personal interest. Next, we concern ourselves with the "well under way and finishing up" stages and with some general observations about the creative life. What our suggestions will *not* do — and cannot do — is provide a step-by-step set of instructions suitable for any and all explorations. Specific projects call for specific tools. The thing to recognize is when and how to insert yourself in your child's efforts in an appropriate way. Play it right, and you've helped steer her through a real, as opposed to contrived, learning activity.

Piaget believed that some of the best classrooms did not include a teacher. We say that creative investigations involve natural or non-school-based learning. They occur, naturally, in a *laboratory environment,* which is not necessarily the physical place the words suggest, but an atmosphere and a series of tasks carried out when your child, by herself or with like-minded individuals, works creatively toward learning something new and doing something with that knowledge. In the laboratory environment, all the elements we've been talking about over the previous chapters come together — your child's chosen interests and problem solving based on her preferred styles.

While there is no one-size-fits-all manual, a handful of principles or steps underlie and remain constant for all independently pursued work, from the simple to the complex.

SIMPLY ABCS

"Awesome ABCs," a project described on our online learning site, is for young children who have mastered the alphabet. Here is how Mary, age five, worked through the project, from idea to product.

Mary learned that an alphabet book typically has a picture of something that begins with each letter. She decided to make her own version, complete with illustrations of her choosing. To gather ideas and see how others had produced such a book, she checked out several existing titles on the Internet and in her neighborhood library. After looking through them, she believed she could make a niftier alphabet book herself.

In the next step, Mary did some brainstorming about ways to proceed. She thought about things she particularly liked — animals, flowers, dinosaurs, and birds were personal favorites. Testing out these several categories, she wrote down lists of items she could use for each letter. On dinosaurs, she was pretty quickly stumped to come up with twenty-six examples. But with animals, she had no trouble coming up with anteater, bear, crocodile, deer, and quite a few more. So animals seemed like a good theme.

Mary began work on a rough draft, writing down each letter and the animal to go with it. But she was unable to think of one for every letter, so with her parent's help, she located books about animals to find additional names and pictures she might copy. Another snag: what to do about "X"? She got tips from her parent, such as picking an animal that *ended* with the letter — "fox" could work for "X," with the "X" capitalized so readers would understand her approach.

Mary considered the materials she would need — attractive paper, colored pencils or crayons, scissors, paste, ribbon to bind the finished book, and a hole punch. At our Renzulli Learning Site, she was advised to mark out lines with a ruler where she planned to write and also to work in pencil. Another decision: should she draw each illustration or perhaps use a combination of her own drawings and pictures cut out from magazines? Mary experimented with the combination plan and decided she preferred the look of variety.

Further design ideas evolved: Maybe it would be fun to create some pages with just the letter and the picture — "G" with a large picture of a gorilla she found, rather than writing "G is for gorilla."

Her mother threw out another suggestion: What about writing a sentence on some pages, using words beginning with the letter? "The fearless, frisky frog frolicked around the forest." Mary decided that was too much trouble. In the last production step, she and her mom located a Web site that outlined simple ways to bind books using ribbon or string.

Finally, she was encouraged to consider how she could share her book with others — give it to the school library or read it and show the pictures to the younger kids in preschool.

Mary's "Awesome ABCs" project illustrates our point. Even a simple "problem" — such as producing an alphabet book of one's own design and wanting to make it the best — can lead a child through the activities involved in the most sophisticated kinds of investigations: testing ideas, locating information, figuring out a plan of action, assembling materials, experimenting with possibilities, and tapping in to personal preferences. There was also her parent, a wise managerial assistant in the background, extending a helping hand from time to time.

BRAINSTORMING ON THE ROAD TO A SELF-SELECTED PROBLEM

Before problem *solving* must come problem *finding*. A selected problem answers the question, "What do you want to know about this interest of yours?"

It's useful, and encouraging, to recognize that any basic, one-word interest can be the nut from which a variety of workable, researchable projects may emerge. Brainstorming is how a child — with some input from his parent and some searching on the Internet or in books — identifies a smaller idea or two within the larger one.

A colleague reports the experience of a teacher who said his students were interested in, and seemingly only interested in, listening to rock music. A youngster who loves rock music might want to become a guitarist or drummer in a punk rock band, or a weekend DJ on a local radio station, or the producer of a concert. But if none of those options were possible or appealing, where else could these kids go with their rock music obsession in order to turn it into something of a more creative nature? Together, teacher and kids came up with a number of questions, or problems, to consider:

- Do children, parents, music store owners, and online music providers feel that CDs and MP3s should include content ratings or warnings?
- How many elementary-age kids watch MTV and how often?
- How did rock music evolve?
- Does listening to music while doing homework reduce the quality of work?
- Do students who like rock music do worse in school?
- Does playing rock music affect plant growth?
- Are there developmental stages in learning to play an instrument?
- Is there a relationship between the kinds of music kids like and the kinds of music their parents like?

In exploring any one of these topics, all under the broad umbrella of an interest in "rock music," some of those kids would inevitably use skills similar to those employed by professional researchers. And they might also answer the question in the form of information that is of interest to others. Whether any of that teacher's students chose to do so is beside the point here — the point is that a general interest can always be refined, usually along many avenues. We use the analogy of the floodlight and the spotlight: The floodlight casts its beams broadly, illuminating the territory without having clear-cut boundaries. The spotlight is concentrated and intense. In considering interest areas, we first want to explore widely, then select and pinpoint a specific and intriguing path.

Two examples:

Tessa, a six-year-old, and her mother had a lively chat following the Interest-a-Lyzer discussion points we outlined earlier. Tessa expressed a fascination with rainbows. Part of their conversation went like this:

MOM: Why do you love rainbows so much?

TESSA: Well, they're beautiful and they have all those colors in them.

MOM: Were you thinking about making some paintings of rainbows?

Tessa wasn't much into drawing and painting.

TESSA: Anyway, everybody makes drawings of rainbows. All the girls, anyway. Rainbows and clouds and hearts and things like that.

MOM: I wonder why it's such a popular subject.

TESSA: Probably because it's a happy thing. It makes you happy to look at rainbows. Also hearts, because that means love.

MOM: The boys don't paint rainbows?

TESSA: I'm not sure, but not so much, I think.

MOM: So, I wonder what would be an interesting thing about rainbows to look into.

With her mother, Tessa entered "rainbows" in an Internet search engine on the family computer and the two of them discovered that the world of rainbows was a vast one. There were sites explaining the science, how the combination of raindrops, angle of sunlight, and other factors produced the prism-like effect. There were many examples of rainbows in art. There were rainbow fish and rainbow boas.

Rainbows were to be found in fiction, in the titles of books and in folklore, such as the story of the pot of gold to be discovered at the end of one. There were sites suggesting related crafts and experiments for individual kids and for the whole family to enjoy. "Rainbow" was also the title of albums by a number of pop groups.

Clearly, a girl who wanted to "do something" about rainbows might head off in a number of directions.

Tessa decided after thinking about it further that she was curious about the fact that rainbows made people happy. Why was it that everyone loved seeing a rainbow? Was it because the colors were so pleasing, or because rainbows came after a rainstorm, or because there was something "magical" about them, "like it meant some amazing thing could happen in your life," as she put it. These were tough questions. Neither she nor her mother could think of a logical next step toward answering them, so Tessa decided she'd read some stories for kids that included rainbows and see if she came up with ideas that way.

Peter, an eight-year-old, liked animals. From his toddler years on, he had loved zoos; whenever the family visited other cities, he always asked his parents if that place had a zoo and if they could go to it. Brainstorming and focusing his interest came about as his parents regularly took him to the local zoo and talked to him about what they were seeing and learning.

Two particular issues caught his attention. His mom showed him an article about a polar bear that swam back and forth endlessly in its artificial lagoon. The conclusion by its trainers was that the bear suffered from boredom that might be alleviated by enclosing food in blocks of ice so that the bear had a bit of a challenge and maybe a bit more fun in its day. Peter's father mentioned that when he had been Peter's age, their local zoo looked very different than it currently did, with large apes and cats penned in small and bare cages, within which they had limited room to turn around. Peter asked questions about the zoo displays. Were the animals ever allowed somewhere to run around? What was in the cages with them? How close could a visitor get to the cages?

The boy was deeply disturbed about all this, the unfairness of the fact as he saw it that people sometimes put animals in such confined spaces. But he was also relieved that life for that polar bear and the previously caged big apes and cats had improved. He and one or another of his parents spent time looking at computer images of zoos around the world and Peter absorbed a beginning lesson in when, where, and how zoos began to be redesigned to accommodate the needs and natures of the animals. Learning the feeding schedules for the sea lions at his local zoo, he got his dad to take him one day and asked the feeder questions about his job. After a number of weeks of this on-and-off digging into the matter of zoos, Peter's enthusiasm for the subject was stronger than ever and he began to appreciate the dynamic nature of his interest.

Both these children were gathering information and their thoughts, possibly on the way to coming up with an independent project to explore.

There hardly exists a topic about which the Internet cannot pour out an astonishing wealth of information, and a simple Google search is a good way to begin focusing a problem of personal appeal. Do help your child develop a critical eye toward resources available over the Internet. Many parents have become ferocious monitors of what their kids are "up to" on the computer, motivated by fears of a child landing in an unsavory chat room or accessing inappropriate pictures, and that is a necessary parental role to assume. But spending some time reviewing sites related to your child's interest and talking a little about their helpful or less helpful features can greatly facilitate moving forward on an independent project; in the box below we have some ideas on how you might go about that.

Casting a Critical Eye on the Internet: Evaluating and Reviewing Web Sites

Type in a word or two, hit "search," and your child will see ten, or two hundred, or half a million Web sites pop up. Where to start? It's important for young kids to learn how to evaluate Web-based resources. For one reason, much time can be spent in wandering among various sites that are fun or pretty or interesting, but not especially relevant to what he's after.

Discuss with your child the features of a site and how to determine from an opening thumbnail sketch whether it's one he wants to explore or how it connects to the project he's working on. Some useful questions to ask and discuss:

- From the description on the first page, can you tell what type of site this is? Is it a game site, or one with lots of information, or one that leads you through a creative process?
- Can you read and understand what's on the site?
- Do you have questions about whether the information is accurate?
- Can you find other sites to check the reliability of the information on this site?
- Do the pictures, illustrations, and writing grab your attention and make you want to stick with it and explore some more?
- Does this site have the kind of information you thought it would or the kind you're looking for?
- Do you think it will give you new ideas or help you learn more about your topic?
- Does it teach you something new or help you improve on or practice something you already know?
- By using this site, can you create something to share with others?

A young child can get practice in manipulating the Internet by starting small — selecting two or three sites that will add to his existing information, and then doing something small with that.

From Internet search information, or from sitting down and thinking over the subject with a parent's help, a youngster can uncover subtopics within a general interest, as Tessa and Peter essentially did. *Webbing* is a simple technique by which one maps on a piece of paper a number of possibilities. Radiating out from a central topic, say "American deserts," a child might draw lines to "history of people who lived there"; "topography"; and "what grows in the desert." From that last topic, secondary lines would lead to "plants," "animals," and "weather and climate," with tertiary lines to "rainfall and irrigation methods," and so on. The subject "circuses" can branch off into "European circuses"; "American circuses"; "how to join a circus"; "performers," with additional branches to "animal trainers" and "trapeze artists"; "where circus people live in the winter"; "designing costumes"; and a handful of other circus themes.

A library book about American deserts or about circuses can be another rich source of ideas; looking through the index or the table of contents, a child will often come across any number of subtopics that would not have occurred to him on his own.

This kind of browsing through the accumulated knowledge about a thing might go on over a period of time for a youngster who's deciding what it is he wants to know about his interest — finding a problem. There's more than one benefit from this time spent. In browsing, he not only becomes more familiar with the subject; he acquires experience in sorting through a mass of information and in making better-informed guesses as to what kind of problem is a fruitful area of investigation and what would probably lead nowhere.

Focusing an interest through brainstorming and initial searches might not at once suggest a reasonable-sounding project. Curiosity may percolate for a while. But it's the beginning of thinking creatively.

In our enrichment programs, we emphasize the point that there's no need for a child to create a major, involved, independent project right off the bat (or ever, for that matter). For example, you might suggest to your youngster that he locate a site that will enhance a subject he's currently enjoying in school. Is the class learning about mammals? Is he enjoying the study of mammals? Perhaps he can uncover five mammal facts that he believes will be new information for his teacher or the other kids, write them down on a piece of paper or print them out, and take them to school to share at the end of class.

MORE DEFINING AND REFINING

Sometimes a young person has a broader interest, less specific than rock music, rainbows, or zoos. It might be in a particular field of study, an interest of an essentially scholarly nature. In an earlier chapter, we described the activities of a boy who loved history and carried out an original idea. We return here to the example of a history buff to demonstrate how a youngster might refine her enthusiasm on the way to becoming an active, small-scale, firsthand investigator.

Suppose your child likes reading stories about history and watching shows on the History Channel. She doesn't have a favorite topic (unlike the boy who was fascinated by the lives of the American presidents). And suppose also that you do not possess extensive knowledge of, or interest in, different categories of history. However, you are now a confirmed believer in the value of independent higher-end learning and creative productivity and you'd like to get your child doing more than reading "about" and watching.

Here's the approach:

Before she can consider what historians do and how they do it, your child needs to answer another question: How does a historian go about choosing and focusing a topic? Brainstorming of the sort we've described previously might be less than fruitful. Starting with "history" as the core of a webbing exercise, for example, might lead to the American Revolution, the state of Ohio, World War I, Egyptian pharaohs, Mayan civilization, and Renaissance art . . . quite obviously, a tempting but virtually infinite number of possibilities that gives little help in refining.

Knowing a historian who's willing to talk about his field and can do so in a way that conveys the excitement of it is a benefit. In the absence of a living informant, however, the mentors-in-print we've described can be invaluable. In this area, an excellent choice is Louis Gottschalk's book, *Understanding History: A Primer of Historical Method,* which gives the following suggestions about problem focusing:

The beginner, with or without aid, can easily discover a subject that interests him and that will be worthy of investigation — at least at an introductory level. He needs only to ask himself four sets of questions:

1) The first set of questions is geographical. They center around the interrogative: "Where?" What area of the world do I wish to investigate? The Far East? Brazil? My country? My city? My neighborhood?

2) The second set of questions is biographical. They center around the interrogative: "Who?" What persons am I interested in? The Chinese? The Greeks? My ancestors? My neighbors? A famous individual?

3) The third set of questions is chronological. They center around the interrogative: "When?" What period of the past do I wish to study? From the beginning till now? The fifth century BC? The Middle Ages? The 1780s? Last year?

4) The fourth set of questions is functional or occupational. They center around the interrogative: "What?" What spheres of human interest concern me most? What kinds of human activity? Economics? Literature? Athletics? Sex? Politics?

The young history enthusiast is shown how to approach a vast area in an authentic fashion and settle on a topic that is both personally attractive and manageable in scope and size. *Where, who, when,* and *what* questions are a pretty good tactic by which to narrow down many subjects.

Such aid in finding a road "into" an interest may come in all forms and from all directions. The mother of a highly motivated and talented fourteen-year-old girl recognized that her daughter consistently demonstrated strong interests in science and in environmental concerns. Science units in school had always been Rose's preferred classes; at home, she often watched TV specials or read articles about energy conservation and the design of "green" homes. Rose's mother said she "made it a point to keep my eye out for information in these areas."

This parent had graduated from a women's college and in one issue of her alumnae magazine she read a feature about a small group of current upper-class students who had organized a program called EcoReps. One imaginative program they originated was to present each of the several hundred incoming first-year students with a compact fluorescent lightbulb and a fact sheet explaining that it consumes 75 percent less energy and lasts ten times longer than a standard bulb. Through these gifts, the EcoReps hoped to engage the newcomers in green campus efforts such as conserving energy and reducing waste.

Rose's mom showed her daughter the article. The girl thought the business with the bulbs was terrific and wanted to learn more. "These college girls sounded wonderful," said her mother, "all activists, doers, some studying for science careers. Great role models. I think this whole thing of the older students bringing along the younger students is what sparked Rose to get creative herself. She started talking about designing some kind of conservation learning plan for little kids, kindergarten kids." Rose's mother said she'd make some phone calls and ask if one or two of the EcoReps would be willing to meet with her daughter and tell her more about their plans. Rose said she couldn't wait to talk to them.

"Keeping an eye out" for ideas and people with the potential to spark a strong, but perhaps still unfocused, interest in an area is a fine parental role. And if one or another of the instruction style preferences we reviewed in chapter 5 seems clearly the right fit for your child, that might be a clue as to where to cast your eye. Is your child one who learns best through hearing a lecture by an expert? Or in back-and-forth discussion with slightly older peers? Or by pouring over a set of instructions on her own in a book or online?

THE PARENT AS READINESS ASSESSOR

Here's part of a conversation with a thirteen-year-old boy; his impressions are a cautionary tale about what can happen when parents are perhaps too zealously determined to support a child's enthusiasm: "I'm interested in a bunch of things, actually. But every time I get really into some hobby or something I'm doing, my parents are all over me about it. For a while, I was really interested in these rocketeer groups, some people who use solid-fuel rocket engines to power these big balsa wood and aluminum planes that they build, radio-controlled wings, really cool stuff. My parents thought this was just great and they started loading me up with kits, stuff about organizations I should join, exhibitions we would all go to together. I appreciate this, I really do. But then I get grilled about whether I followed up on something or other, did I send away for those plans, how come I haven't started with that kit. They're on my case all the time.

"It's like I get on a little bandwagon about something and my parents hop right on there too, and I might get off at some point but they keep right on going. With the rocket groups, I didn't actually want to *do* that myself right then, I was just interested in seeing what these guys were doing."

This bright and serious young person added that he occasionally wished his parents would "just leave me alone a little more" and sometimes he felt he was "disappointing them."

So this might be a good point at which to pause and mention a few issues parents can consider in order to ascertain the depth or the nature of a child's interest — and whether they and he are on the same bandwagon — remembering that sometimes a child's initial enthusiasm fizzles. Or, in the natural course of things, his skills in one or another area strengthen — suddenly he can read a lot better or write a lot better than previously — and that points him in other directions. Sometimes he'll decide that the "what next" idea he had in mind will take too much work and probably won't be fun. And sometimes he'll discover an area he'd enjoy studying and learning a little about and then stops there when his curiosity is satisfied.

Gifted behaviors emerge when a child's ability, task commitment, and creativity are jointly activated in response to a particular stimulus, the thing with which he has become smitten — or at least pretty interested in. The questions in the box on the next page touch on these matters of interest, ability, creativity, and task commitment. Is your child ready, willing, and able to dig into creative-productive work?

MULTIPLE MODES OF EXPRESSION: DECIDING ON A PRODUCT

If your youngster has caught the bug for something and is making her first moves to explore it with enthusiasm, it's an excellent time to help her consider the endgame: Where does she want to take this? What product could emerge and who would be interested in it? Thinking ahead about a product and an audience has the effect of further focusing an independent learning activity, shaping the steps it might involve.

One delightful project called "Centuries of Silliness," completed in an enrichment program, had its earliest roots in a three-year-old's fascination with clowns. That was when Betsy went to the circus, the first of many over the years to come. Midway through middle school, she began researching the history of clowning — a multifaceted topic,

A Readiness Assessment Checklist

It's never wise to urge a youngster on further than he might wish to go. Without a real problem born from his individual passion not much creative work is likely to emerge. Ask yourself:

___ *How long has my child had an interest in this topic?* The longer, the better.

___ *What is his general attitude about the project he's talking about?* If he's eager and excited, that's a sign of his commitment. A cautious and tentative attitude suggests a more tepid or latent interest.

___ *Is his interest faddish and thus likely to be short-lived?*

___ *Has he done any preliminary reading or listening? Does he have a decent store of knowledge about the topic already?* Very little preliminary "finding out about" might mean he's not ready to move forward.

___ *How original is the project my child has in mind?* Creativity is demonstrated by a unique idea rather than a plan to replicate existing work.

as she learned — and with her mom's help decided to concentrate on clowning and jesters in European life, specifically seventeenth-century English and French clowns. This was such rich, vivid material: the costumes that have continued down through centuries, such as oversized shoes, waistcoats, and giant ruffs around the neck; the painted-on whiteface; the characters Harlequin and Pierrot and the lovesick, sad clown with the tear on his cheek. Betsy decided it all had to be presented in a grand show to inform and amuse, just like the clowns.

She worked with her best friend, and the two girls wrote and perfected a forty-five-minute script, set up a small stage, and built large puppets in the style of the clowns of different ages and countries. After a trial run, the girls realized the production would sound a lot more professional — and amusing — with more voices. So they recruited their parents and several teachers to perform. "Centuries of

___ Is he thinking about making some kind of change, improvement, or new contribution to the topic he hopes to pursue?

___ How elaborate is the idea or plan he has for this project? A detailed plan is more promising than a sketchy one in terms of how deeply his involvement will take hold.

___ How action-oriented is this project he's considering?

___ Is he generally good about or resistant to the possibility that the work he does might need revising, rewriting, or polishing?

___ How does he feel about the time and energy all this will entail? Is he capable of concentrating on it for what might prove to be a long stretch?

___ How many other demands does he have on his time and energy? If he's involved in ten other activities, he might be spread too thin to be able to accomplish much creative work.

Silliness" was a big hit at a school assembly and the two girls also hoped to "take it on the road" to scout meetings and other groups.

Here was the likely coming-together of an interest and the product that grew from it. Betsy was a kid who loved the idea of performing, entertaining, and creating the lively visual impact of bright figures on a stage.

In our earlier section on expression styles, a quick checklist explored questions related to how your child might naturally prefer to demonstrate what she's learned or what she's been doing. If she loves getting up in front of people and talking, she might relish putting on a show or giving an oral presentation. If she's more technologically oriented or dislikes any kind of public speaking, she'll more comfortably gravitate to another form.

Young children do benefit from suggestions about the kinds of

Product Suggestions

Children often are unaware of or do not understand the range of products into which they may translate their interests. Very young children have such limited experiences that when asked what they might produce, they invariably think only of "a report." The suggestions here can open up your child's mind as she recognizes the many more possible options.

Artistic Products

- mural • cartoons • collage • set design • home decoration
- book cover • movie • pottery • sculpture • fabric design • video
- weaving • filmstrip • maps • aquarium • calligraphy • mobile
- advertisement • painting • greeting card • drawing • fashion design
- Web site • terrarium • graphic design • jewelry • poster • puppets
- wrapping paper • art photography • horticultural design • sewing
- engraving • mosaic

Performance Products

- skit • puppet show • reader's theater • chorale • role playing
- concert • dramatic monologue • poetry reading
- comedy performance • parade • simulations • improvisation
- musical performance • historical reenactment • dance
- demonstrations • mime • video • science experiment

Spoken Products

- debate • comedy routine • forum • speech • panel discussion
- book review • radio play narration • master of ceremony • newscast

products they might consider. In the box above, we have scanned the wide world of possible products that fall within different modes of preferred expression — each one of these was created by one or more kids in real life — and listed a few of the possibilities for you and your child to think about.

- poetry reading • dedication ceremony • infomercial • storytelling
- weather report • rap song • sales promotion • oral history

Visual Products

- digital photo show • computer program • travel brochure • chart
- computer printout • timeline • athletic demonstration • sculpture
- graphic design • calendar • graph • painting • diagram • silk screen
- advertising slogan • ice sculpture • caricatures • photography

Construction Products

- drama set • toys • robot • relief map • game • rocket • habitat model
- solar collector • multimedia presentation • fitness trail
- hydroponic farm • greenhouse • bulletin board • masks • garden
- puppet theater • catalog • diorama • scale model • maze • ant farm
- furniture

Service/Leadership Products

- speech • debate • organizing a business • Internet discussion group
- election • organizing a group • volunteer activity • school patrol
- editorials • fund-raising • club or class webmaster

Written Products

- pamphlet • advertisement • Web site • newspaper article
- brochure • journal • autobiography • folktale • book • poetry
- family tree • limerick • captions • marketing plan
- position statement • recipes • riddles • banner • legends • slogans
- crossword puzzle • bibliography • song lyrics • consumer report

INPUT AND PROCESSING: ON THE INFORMATION-GATHERING TRACK

When a youngster conceives of a project, having decided what, exactly, he wants to know about or do with his interest, his immediate concerns are:

- What do I need to accomplish this?
- How can I get what I need?

The answers involve pulling together materials and *raw data,* which can be thought of as relatively unorganized bits and pieces of information that clearly will be useful in achieving his aims. Even the poet, we might say, uses new combinations of words, ideas, and feelings as raw data in creating an original poem.

In their guidebook, *Looking for Data in All the Right Places* — very good for parents, too — our colleagues Alane J. Starko and Gina D. Schack identify three broad approaches to research and data gathering that are serviceable for young children: the *descriptive* approach, which attempts to find out how things are now through making direct observations, conducting surveys, taking photographs, and so on; the *historical* approach, which finds out how things used to be through hunting up primary sources, such as diaries and journals and old newspapers, that shed light on the past; and the *experimental* approach, which seeks to answer "what would happen if?" through manipulating or changing the variables of a subject and observing cause and effect.

Depending on your child's investigation, gathering data may lead him to such resources as videos, magazines, slides, films, technical papers, artifacts, blueprints, speakers, biographies, record books, letters, catalogs, polls, TV and radio programs, personal interviews, atlases and maps, or the contents of a box of old photographs and letters. It may lead him to the encyclopedia and similar reference books to conduct some real-problem research. This is, as we have been emphasizing, research for the purpose of reviewing existing knowledge — acquiring a well-prepared mind — in order to create something, and not for the purpose of "writing a report." Raw data may be the responses to a questionnaire about how often kids exercise outdoors, measurements of the relative growth of petunia plants in different kinds of light, or the findings from a comparison of published alphabet books.

The tools or techniques he needs to gather this information may be as basic as a pencil and a notebook, a camera, a tape recorder, or a ruler. Or they may be a great deal more sophisticated. In enrichment projects, we have observed all of the following — and more — put to productive use: conductivity meter, dissecting kit, solar cell, telescope, litmus paper, sound meter, oscilloscope, barometer, blood pressure monitor, sextant, editing equipment, and stethoscope.

Even the youngest kids have successfully utilized some extremely professional data-collecting methods and tools. In a science enrichment project, three second-grade girls became interested in learning about acid rain after hearing a speaker talk about its devastating effects on just about everything — plants, wood, sidewalks, roads. The girls began collecting samples of rain, sleet, and snow; tested them for levels of acid; maintained records for months in a carefully prepared log; and ended up helping to prove that the rain falling in their part of Connecticut was much higher in acidity than had been thought. They had help, of course, from their parents and their teacher, but the work was theirs alone. (They also became committed to social action: they wrote a short letter to the editor of the local newspaper and held petition drives in several local supermarkets to send to their congressman.)

The key questions — What methods do professionals use to carry out their work? What resources and materials do they need? — will guide you in your role of managerial assistant as you help your child go about acquiring necessary data and skills. If *you* do not know the answers, someone does.

For example, most professions have professional societies and associations and there's a Web site for virtually every possible field of study. Starting from the official Web site of a particular association, your child might learn about the kinds of jobs held by people in the field, state and national conferences, available newsletters, publications, and much more. He can find information on the tools or instruments professionals use and how they carry out a methodological investigation.

A teacher supervising a group of kids working on an enrichment activity about local history helped them prepare for interviews with war veterans by what he described as "three clicks of the mouse." From the search engine Google, he clicked on "Social Sciences," which produced many topics related to that general field and a dialogue box that allowed him to type in and search for "Oral History." This second click yielded fifty-two links, including one entitled "Oral History Questions," his third click. To his delight and surprise, he was presented with and able to print out four pages of questions appropriate for his students to use in their interviews.

At relatively tender ages, many children do quickly become remarkably adept at computer-based data gathering all on their own. This is the generation, after all, for whom the computer holds no fear; it's been there — in the library, the schoolroom, on the kitchen counter — from their earliest days.

One girl wanted to explore her family's past and found online most of what she needed to get going. (A family genealogy is a hugely popular project with many youngsters and one that can accommodate a number of expression preferences — a graphic representation of a family tree, a pictorial display board, a computer database, a fictionalized account of how families merged, a brief nonfiction family history book, a dramatization of key events in a family's history, even a family tree greeting card.)

Eleven-year-old Kathryn was transfixed by the stories told by her grandmother about *her* mother and father, Kathryn's great-grandparents, who emigrated from Sicily. Taking cues from their daughter's interest, Kathryn's parents invited her to learn more by arranging visits to Ellis Island and the Tenement Museum in lower Manhattan, the area in which her great-grandparents had lived and raised a family.

The girl was deeply moved by these experiences, especially the look and feel of the tiny, cramped apartments. She wanted to delve more deeply and worked through a variety of online sites that told her how to gather information about family names, ship arrival records, immigration lists, records maintained in city agencies, listings of genealogical archives, and a lot more. She also learned the meaning of legal terms encountered while researching records and she quickly became experienced in recognizing whether a resource was trying to tell her something or sell her something. From the Association of Professional Genealogists site, she discovered a couple of books she thought would help her learn added skills, such as preparing worksheets and interviewing living relatives.

After almost a year of investigating, Kathryn had created descendancy and ancestry charts on both her mother's and father's sides of the family, and many more historical bits and pieces — old photos, maps of Italy and of Ireland, where her father's family was from. She went on to design a handsome booklet and had it reproduced through an online service. She then asked her mother to hunt up the addresses of all known relatives and mailed each one a copy. (All this had one lovely outcome when several far-flung family members got in touch with Kathryn with more stories to share. Buoyed by her success, she began checking historical societies and museums with the thought of possibly involving herself in an ongoing oral history project of some sort.)

Another powerful source for methodological assistance and data-gathering suggestions: the mentor-in-print. Find a how-to book for your junior investigator. Returning to the example we mentioned above, *Understanding History* offers the reader much more than help in problem focusing. It goes on to give a wealth of practical advice on note taking, determining authenticity, using songs, poetry, and folklore as sources of historical data, even techniques for writing an article or manuscript about your findings, down to the nuts and bolts aspects of using proper punctuation, preparing drafts, and revising.

It is one of literally hundreds of books (we have listed a number of our favorites in Appendix I) about investigative methodology in different subjects. Most of them were written for young readers — but they're excellent support services for the parent/managerial assistant. Does your youngster want to collect fossils, write a screenplay, forecast the weather, give a speech, or write poetry? There's a how-to book for him. You will find *The Kid's Guide to Social Action, Let's Put on a Show!, Make Your Own Puppets & Puppet Theaters, Philosophy for Kids,* and *Kid Cash.*

Even in the age of the Internet, mentors-in-print can be most inviting to young explorers. In addition to identifying basic principles, most demonstrate how to carry out research; give ideas for specific studies; and suggest special equipment, materials, sources of data, and places where research results might be published or presented. In other words, they explain how to put together those bits and pieces, or process data in the truest, most accurate, most polished way. In fact, some are essentially laboratory manuals that guide a child through all stages of an authentic investigation in the field.

It really is impossible to overstate how genuinely excited kids become when engaged in raw data gathering! There can be a kind of magic to it.

MAKING A PLAN

Three twelve-year-olds were intrigued by the story of Amelia Earhart, the dashing aviator who at age forty abruptly disappeared over the

South Pacific, along with her plane and copilot. The girls wrote: "We think Amelia Earhart was a hero to many people. We want to learn about her as a person and a pilot and share this information with other kids." They proposed to find Earhart's planned flight route, learn how she prepared for it, and — the big question — discover what went wrong. No one knew for sure, but they thought they might be able to find some clues that would bring this legendary aviation puzzle a little closer to a solution. They wanted to explore, also, Earhart's effects on American society and how her life and accomplishments might be commemorated.

Thinking ahead to a product, the girls envisioned a mural-timeline of Earhart's final flight and a photojournal of her life to display in their school art exhibit. Most intriguingly, they hoped to create a *WebQuest*. In this online activity, participants are linked to Web sites that supply various pieces of information about the subject, a trail of clues to put together. The girls were excited at the thought that students around the world might help figure out the mystery: what happened to Amelia Earhart? To accomplish all this, they'd need to gather many photographs and known facts about her life and her last flight and find out what skills were needed to produce photojournals and build a WebQuest. These actions, they wrote, would take them into interest areas of computers, journalism, and photography in addition to history.

It sounded like a plan.

A management plan helps a youngster map out an overview of her work and the steps she'll need to take. One added beauty of a management plan: two or more children working jointly on a project can underscore the particular talents and strengths required, and thus each child's preferences. The kid who's really good with computers will contribute one aspect; the child who loves photography and working with visual effects will add her own expertise.

If your child is beginning an independent investigation, encourage

The Project Management Plan

Project Description
Write a brief description of the problem or topic that you plan to investigate. What do you hope to find out or learn?

Study Areas
Which of the following general areas will you study as you carry out your investigation? (Think of all the ones that apply.)
• architecture • arts (drawing and painting) • athletics/sports
• building things • business/management • computers/technology/gaming
• creative writing • drama/performing • foreign languages
• geography • graphic design/animation • helping/service • history
• journalism • mathematics • music • photography/video
• reading/literature • science • social action

Format
What form or forms will the final product take?
• artistic • audio/video/DVD • constructed model • drama/performance
• musical presentation • oral/discussion (speech, teaching, presentation)
• photographic presentation • service/leadership • technology/computer
• visual display • written piece

her to write down in a notebook or on a computer a plan of action following the questions we list in the box above. Assure her that the purpose of writing it all out is to provide a helpful tool for proceeding; it's not a tricky device to prod her along or to make you happy. A management plan must retain an element of realness, of personal investment and importance. Although practicing professionals may not actually write it all out, they do in fact explore in their own minds each of the items we have listed.

The section we've called "Project Description" might alternately be labeled "The Problem I Intend to Solve" or "Here's What I Want

Getting Started

What are the first steps you should take to begin your work? What kinds of information will you need to find and what questions will you need answered in order to get started? What help do you think you'll need from your parents?

Skills, Resources, and Materials Needed

Make a list of the resources you'll need to do your work: how-to books, videos, exhibits, Web sites, special equipment (camera, tape recorder, questionnaire), and experts who might provide assistance. Write down contact names, addresses, phone numbers, and other details. If you need new data to solve your problem, how can it be gathered and classified? If the data you need already exists, where can it be found?

Intended Audience or Audiences

Who would be most interested in your project? Consider organized groups (clubs, organizations, societies, teams) at the local, state, regional, and national levels. Consider contests, places where your work might be displayed or published, and Web sites that include similar kinds of work. Write down contact names, phone numbers, e-mail addresses, and so on.

to Find Out and/or Do." The higher the degree of clarity with which the problem is described — and that might be in the form of a statement, a few questions, or lists of objectives — the more naturally and logically will flow all the subsequent activities involved in its solution or accomplishment. Again, the statement should closely approximate the ways in which a professional states a hypothesis or lists specific research questions. Creative-productive people in the real world always pursue a problem with more functional goals in mind than merely finding out a lot of facts about a person, place, or thing. If you and your child have had a successful focusing-in and narrowing-down brainstorming session around her area of interest, the project description part of her plan should be as clear as a bell.

"Project Description" goes hand in hand with "Intended Audience or Audiences." Right from the start, your child can be thinking about the final form her investigation will take and about who potentially will be interested in it.

"Getting Started" and "Skills, Resources, and Materials Needed" provide a running account of the procedures that will be used from beginning to completion. The information they include may be sketchy at first and mushroom later on, with modifications to come as some steps or activities are followed through and as your child becomes more familiar with the topic and aware of a greater variety of resources. It's a good idea to try to ensure that successes will be achieved in the beginning steps, to keep motivation going.

As you help your child with a Project Management Plan, it is worth remembering that some children seem to be born with outstanding organizational abilities; others only develop them over time, and some never quite as well. And most kids beginning to learn independent study skills benefit from having a timeline. In addition, to help your child develop task commitment and understand effort, she might need encouragement to devote a regular period each day or every other day or once a week to her project. Remember, too, that some kids can be organized to begin work in a few minutes, work hard for half an hour or an hour and get a lot done. Others may need half an hour simply to locate their supplies, find the right pencil, and prepare their work space.

Young people who think seriously about their plans come up with wonderfully detailed outlines for themselves, early snapshots of what they hope to accomplish.

Here's some of what two boys wrote about their project:

Project Description: "We think roller coasters are really cool and we want to learn how they work. How do they keep people from falling out of roller coasters? How are roller coasters built? How do they get roller coasters to be so fast without a motor? We will make a model of a roller coaster and test it with a marble."

Getting Started: "Set up a notebook for each of us to use as a scientific log. Watch a *Newton's Apple* video about roller coasters. Take notes in log books. Practice designing a roller coaster on the Internet using a virtual roller coaster Web site. Take notes about which designs work and why. Talk to crafts teacher and shop teacher about materials for building a model. Get all of the materials on the list in the *Newton's Apple* hypercoaster project. Build the model using the directions. Try some test runs with a marble. Take notes on what works and what doesn't in log books.

"Once we have a design that gets the marble to the end of the track, we can measure the speed of the marble. We can do this by dividing the length of the track by the time it takes the marble to get to the end. Measure the speed on several runs and get an average. We'll try changing the track to make the marble move faster. We can use the information in our log books to help us design a fast roller coaster. When we have the fastest track we can make that still gets the marble to the end, we'll write down the length of track, hill heights, and the length of the spaces between hills so we can re-create our coaster. We can double the height of our hills to make a hypercoaster!"

They plotted out all this after preliminary Internet searches, before they actually began building. But writing out a plan helped them lay down a logical series of steps. (These boys thought that if their hypercoaster was a success, they might enter a competition they read about online, the Discovery Education 3M Young Scientist Challenge.)

In other project descriptions and identification of self-selected "problems," kids have revealed their delightful, far-ranging curiosities about the way the world works:

"What ever happened to the Neanderthals?"
"I would like to learn where butterflies live."

"I want to know if regular people can make machines that work or only professional scientists."

"I plan to know more about the greatest moments in sports history."

"Why are Alexander Calder's mobiles special? Why do so many people like them?"

If a Project Management Plan might sound entirely too official or perhaps even too "homework-like" to your child, don't call it that.

The uncle of one fourteen-year-old boy described several conversations he had had with his nephew. They illustrate the idea that helping a youngster to start thinking of a plan to organize and professionalize his work can take an informal tone and still achieve results.

"Eddie and I have bonded for a long time," the uncle said. "He loves cartoons, especially Gary Larson's *The Far Side.* I gave him a *Far Side* cartoon-a-day calendar and he started making his own cartoons, very imitative of this Larson style. They all revolved around things going on in our lives, like when I put new tires on my car and when Eddie had his bedroom painted at home. I was getting these in the mail from him like once a week. They were good, the drawings more so than the captions. They had that same kind of off-beat, weird sense of humor, pretty clever for a fourteen-year-old.

"So I thought, I could just let this kid keep sending me his cartoons and keep telling him I got a big kick out of them, but he should get some validation from other people than me. The next time we got together, I asked him if he was thinking about being a cartoonist when he grew up. Eddie said it was really tough to be a professional cartoonist, get a regular strip. That's undoubtedly true, I told him, but you're jumping the gun here. Let's imagine you wanted to show your stuff to some newspaper guy who might hire you to do a strip. Or somebody who publishes comic books. What would you need?"

He should have about two dozen sample cartoons, Eddie thought. But then: Should these be a random assortment, à la *The Far Side,* or should there be one main character, like Dagwood or Beetle Bailey? How does a cartoonist create a character or a plot? How could Eddie develop a distinctive style, something that didn't look like he was imitating other people? How can you tell if a cartoon about changing tires on the car is going to make sense or be funny to somebody who maybe doesn't have a car? Should you start with a caption and draw a picture to fit it, or the other way around?

"The upshot of all this talk," said Eddie's uncle, "was that the boy really wanted to do something with his cartoons, and we mapped out a number of steps he could take. Get some books about drawing. Try to research the careers of cartoonists, how they got started, find the answers to some of these questions about developing a style and writing captions. Maybe he could actually talk to Gary Larson, who knows? Get some better-quality supplies. Try to get some of his stuff published in a kids' magazine."

It was a plan.

GOING THE EXTRA MILE

Allison, a science-loving seventh grader, became interested in learning more about the colors of the stars after watching an episode of *Nova*. She loved photography, too, and got the idea that she might combine her enthusiasms by taking pictures of stars. Her parents, having no knowledge of stars or how to photograph them, called the director of an astronomy club they read about and asked for suggestions. That contact began a series of activities and events that ended up, a year later, with Allison winning first place in her division at the state science fair for her project researching and photographing the spectra of stars.

Along the way, her parents aided and abetted her efforts: They arranged for their daughter to meet with a local astronomer who volunteered to be her mentor and with a group of kids her age who were studying at the small planetarium in the city science center. Following a suggestion from her mentor, Allison's parents called the manufacturer Bausch & Lomb and were able to arrange for the loan of a special camera and telescope. The ideal time to conduct astronomy photography in their area, they learned, was in the winter. Her parents drove Allison and her borrowed instruments to nearby mountains on many a freezing evening so she could gather her data. They described Allison's investigations to the head of the astronomy department at the local university who agreed to allow the girl use of the high-powered university telescope, under the watchful eyes of two doctoral students, in order to complete the final stages of her project.

All in all, it was a splendid experience, they said, though it was too bad that star photography couldn't be carried out just as successfully on balmy summer nights.

Going the extra mile as managerial assistant to a creatively engaged child might mean, literally, going a few *hundred* miles in the car, such as all over mountains in the Northeast in the cold. Or, it might mean offering support of an entirely different nature — some possibilities follow in the next chapter. If you are uncertain as to what's needed, ask your child:

- What can I do to help you?
- Are you running into any snags?
- Would you like to bounce a few ideas off me?

Your child should be the leader and emerging expert; you are the assistant, or the guide-on-the-side.

Pursuing original research and data gathering, we've noted, can be magical for a child, unlike anything he's done before. You may look on in pleasure, perhaps astonishment, as your child stretches in learning and his accomplishments go way beyond what might generally be expected as his "level." He may be reading highly advanced books and other resource materials. His vocabulary may expand. (A small group of kids who worked together on a horticultural project learned the Latin names for plants, along with the names of parts of the plants, the concept of germination, and many other terms used by professional growers and landscapers. Because of their keen interest in the topic, they were able to handle the Latin vocabulary with aplomb. During one observation, a child was heard to ask another if she would bring over the *Ilex opaca* so that it could be planted before its roots dried out, tossing off *Ilex opaca* with ease and a complete lack of self-consciousness.)

Interestingly, efforts have been made over the years to determine how *creative* children are by giving them "creativity tests." These might involve, for one example, presenting the youngster with a page of blank circles and asking him to turn them into drawings. The idea is that the more possibilities he imagines, the more unusual they are, and the greater detail they incorporate, the more creative the child is. But conclusions have been reached over the years that such tests actually reveal very little. Certainly, it cannot be predicted that the kid who produces a sheet full of the most elaborate pictures from some circles is the one who will soar to great accomplishment.

On the other hand, something pretty wonderful takes place while a child pursues an independent learning project and a personal objective. A subject he loves has the power to "bring out" advanced thinking and feeling processes and the "powers of the mind" — interpretation, analysis, comparison, hypothesizing, appreciation, classification, value clarification, awareness, and creativity. These are the very abilities, research demonstrates, that are most widely applicable or transferable to any and all learning situations and that hold the key to a child's future achievement.

※

Guide-on-the-Side

How to Be Your Child's Enrichment Ally

As one of the principles behind the *guide-on-the-side* parental role, we recall an observation made by the philosopher and educational theorist Mortimer Adler in a speech at the University of Connecticut: "For the gifted person, the person who really wants to learn something, too much instruction is insulting." For the parent supporting a youngster's interests and creative productivity, the trick lies in refraining from volunteering "too much" — in the matter of instructing, correcting, or in other ways running the show — while recognizing the appropriate moment to step in. What might be needed is a well-timed word of encouragement, an added perspective, kindly but realistic feedback, or some opening of doors and greasing of wheels when a youngster's efforts are ready for a wider audience.

In our involvements with young people, we have seen over and over how excited kids can become about the *process* of learning. Yes, the topic may be attractive, but an even more powerful pull and enticement lie in the finding out — and the joy that comes with it. If your child is exploring a real problem of her choosing, one growing out of her evolving interest in a subject or area of study and fueled by her creativity and motivation, she is engaged in this truly thrilling process. And she might indeed be insulted, or at least annoyed or distracted, by too much imposed direction from on high, i.e., from Mom and Dad.

So, being a guide-on-the-side means chiming in but not taking over, being available but not intrusive, expressive but not judgmental. Just how that involvement plays out between parent and child depends, of course, on the particulars of the people and the project. But from talking with hundreds of talented and creative kids over many years, we've learned the general areas in which children benefit from the right kind of adult guidance — the subject of this chapter.

STOKING THE FIRE: HELPING KIDS STAY ON TRACK

One of our favorite projects, carried out by a ten-year-old participating in an enrichment program, resulted in *The Louisa May Alcott Cookbook*. Gretchen loved the literature of Louisa May Alcott and cooking equally — each an interest she had picked up on her own. Fascinated by the foods mentioned in Alcott's novels, she began experimenting with how authentic nineteenth-century dishes could be reproduced, making substitutions for ingredients no longer easily available. The project she conceived would marry her two interests — a cookbook that combined up-to-date versions of vintage recipes with vignettes from *Little Women* and *Little Men*. So, for example, a brief passage from a scene in the March household (the children bringing their Christmas breakfast to a poor family) ends with her comment, "Anyone would be pleased to be served this lovely breakfast, even if it weren't Christmas," and a recipe for buckwheat cakes.

This effort occupied her for a year and a half and eventually her enthusiasm for reading the books and researching the foods wasn't enough to sustain her through the writing of each scene and the great attention to detail necessary for testing recipes. Following helpful suggestions from her teacher, Gretchen refreshed her stamina by introducing more variety into her self-imposed assignments — one day writing out a scene, another day getting supplies, another day experimenting with a recipe — rather than trying to accomplish all at once.

(*The Louisa May Alcott Cookbook,* by the way, was eventually published by Little, Brown.)

Youngsters occasionally will become discouraged or ready to call it quits entirely. Even when things are proceeding fairly well, there inevitably are peak times and down times, as happens in most kinds of original work. Kids can easily become overwhelmed when a project starts feeling just too tough or complex, with no end in sight. That's when motivation can begin to waver. And that's when an adult perspective can help things get back on track.

If you sense that your child is hitting a wall of commitment fatigue, that might be the time to suggest he switch from one aspect of his project to take up another for a while. Or, he might choose one piece of the whole that he can complete in its entirety and look on with a feeling of accomplishment.

PUTTING TOGETHER A PROGRESS PORTFOLIO

Another strategy to keep your child on track and motivated is to devise a simple system to record achievements, tangible proof that something is happening and progress is actually being made.

In many school programs following our designs, teachers are encouraged to use a tool we call the *Total Talent Portfolio.* This is, simply, a large folder containing the best information that can be learned about a child's strengths and abilities. In the Renzulli Learning Systems, an electronic version of this portfolio is an ideal place for computer storage of a child's cumulative work. In particular, we watch for indications of a serious and persistent interest in one area or another: this youngster always takes out library books on the same topic, regardless of reading difficulty level; that child draws detailed designs in the margins of her notes and notebooks. Comments might be included on which style of instruction a child seems to respond to most enthusiastically — class debates or independent study or working with peers — and about preferred modes of expression. In addition to the teacher, the school librarian, sports coach, and other school professionals might contribute their observations. The goal is to tailor learning, as much as possible, by capitalizing on the gathered information.

But here is the outstanding feature of the Total Talent Portfolio: unlike many typical folders that are amassed largely from the input, assessments, and choices of the adults, our model emphasizes the role of the student. The youngster herself selects most of the pieces to include, and she is the one who formulates and refines the criteria. In other words, she has the opportunity to put a value on varied accomplishments according to how greatly they matter to her. Kids come up with wonderfully rich descriptions of why a particular item is in the portfolio. Some sample assessments: "This essay is here because it's about a special memory." "I really tried my hardest on this report and revised it three times." "This clay-bead bracelet is not finished yet, but I know it will be my best, and I put it in because it has a really neat pattern." "These are colored graphs I created on the computer and even my little brother could understand them!" "I like my new idea for animal pens because now the pigs can't get out." "This watercolor demonstrates how I can use different brushes."

You can appreciate that the Total Talent Portfolio is a living, breathing collection that takes shape gradually and testifies to growing skills, competencies, and commitment. Our research shows that kids who take an active role in keeping up their portfolios benefit in significant ways. They tend to pay closer attention to what they're doing. They think about and judge their efforts according to personally meaningful goals and develop a clear understanding of what constitutes their best work. They use advanced thinking skills, such as analysis and evaluation, to determine how well they are proceeding and to track their progress. One of our daughters literally "mined" her portfolio for ideas to use in her college applications.

An at-home adaptation — we'll call it the Progress Portfolio — might be an invaluable next step beyond the Project Management Plan described in the previous chapter.

Like many parents, you probably have in a closet somewhere a box full of your youngster's earliest drawings: the first big joyful splotches of color; the later stick figure picture of Mom, Dad, and the family dog; the earliest paper constructions and clay creations from preschool or summer day camp; and so on. The Progress Portfolio is the same idea, but with a focus on the creative learning project on which your child has embarked. It might be a large accordion-type folder, or a cardboard carton, or any other receptacle that can hold work-in-progress materials and information. These materials might include:

- photographs
- early drafts of a piece of writing
- sketches
- journal entries
- first attempts at building something
- taped conversations or interviews
- research notes
- feedback or comments from a friend or friendly critic
- an evolving list of possible titles for a painting or photographic essay

Your child should date each selection. Provide her with a packet of sticky notes to attach to pieces, as reminders of ideas or directions for refining her work. She might choose to make a weekly habit of adding to and updating her Progress Portfolio.

Pursuing a complicated investigation, a child can lose sight of the forest for the trees. Or of how the trees are indeed going to eventually become a forest. Here's an example of how a Progress Portfolio encouraged one girl to carry on her project when she became discouraged:

A curious seven-year-old, Jennie got into several animated discussions with her mother on the topic of breakfast. This meal, her mother insisted, was an extremely important one, the right way to get ready for the day ahead. Jennie's mother rued out loud the fact that Jennie's father had never picked up the breakfast habit, despite her efforts to get him to do so. "My mom said you can't teach an old dog new tricks," Jennie said. But her dad was a healthy person, wasn't he, the girl wanted to know. Her mother agreed that yes, he was a healthy person, but it was still better to start the day with a good breakfast.

These thoughts prompted Jennie to conduct some online research into why breakfast mattered and what type of breakfast was a good one. She learned about the desirable impact of protein and fiber on the brain and body, and the less desirable impact of sugary things, which pep one up initially but cause one to feel tired a short time later. Jennie read that children who eat breakfast do better in school and she decided she'd see if this intriguing bit of news could be proven based on kids she knew. She also entertained the bigger idea that she might be able to find out if adults did better at work or experienced greater energy throughout the day if they ate breakfast. A goal was to marshal persuasive evidence for her father, "so he'll have breakfast and get more healthy."

"Everybody knows who gets the best grades on tests and stuff in my class," she said, so figuring out who was doing better in school, at least in her limited population, wasn't a problem. She wrote up a simple questionnaire that she proposed to hand out to her classmates, a "yes" or "no" as to whether they had breakfast each morning. Deciding that that would not tell her much, Jennie then came up with a more elaborate version that asked the participants to note *what* they ate, whether they ate the same thing every day or only occasionally, and if they felt energetic at the beginning of class and tired later on. That had some holes in it: "There's lots of reasons you can feel tired, not just because of breakfast."

Jennie then considered that maybe she should offer a list of four or five items, such as cereal, doughnuts, toast, orange juice, and eggs, and ask kids to check off which they ate. That didn't do the trick, "because lots of kids don't like eggs. Also, most kids like to eat leftover pizza, like I do, and my mom says that's okay for breakfast." With the adults, a few relatives and a couple of family friends, she decided the best approach would be to ask questions about their energy levels while at work and circle back around to the breakfast issue. But a trial run was only confusing when her aunt said that sometimes she ate breakfast, sometimes not, and it didn't seem to make much difference — but she absolutely could not function without strong black coffee in the morning.

Though she didn't realize it, all this was getting Jennie into some pretty sophisticated territory involving defining an hypothesis, eliminating biased or "loaded" inquiries, constructing appropriate data-gathering instruments such as surveys and interviews, and making sense of the results. She was working "without a net" — she hadn't developed a Project Management Plan, which would have helped her prepare herself with some useful tools and approaches. By proceeding with her investigation only according to what seemed to work or not work, Jennie devised fifteen versions of her written questionnaires and interview questions after two months. Fortunately, encouraged by her mom, she had kept them all in a Progress Portfolio with the dates noted on each. When she became discouraged and was at the point of chucking her whole idea, she studied her collected work-to-date and was amazed at how far she'd actually come.

"When I started this," Jennie said, "I didn't know what I was doing!" Her earliest versions struck her as "babyish." She could appreciate that, just by her own brain power and determination and thinking through the necessary factors, she had made significant and appropriate refinements to her plan. And that gave her the needed charge to carry on. With her mom's help, she found an excellent how-to book on writing questionnaires and carrying out surveys.

A Progress Portfolio can be a most useful way for your child not only to keep the stages of an exploration organized and in sequence, but to monitor results, see encouraging evidence that she's really getting somewhere, and help her stay on track at a point when she's feeling discouraged. It's a tangible reminder that creative-productive people always spend much time working their way through the details of their products, and that success is achieved in increments. Thomas Edison once said, "I have not failed. I just found 10,000 ways that won't work."

UPPING THE ANTE: ESCALATING THE KNOWLEDGE FIELD

Higher-end learning investigations can sometimes turn into fun-filled, enjoyable activities, and not much more than that. Enjoying what he's doing is obviously all to the good, but for your child to develop gifted behaviors he may need encouragement to "up" the level of involvement using advanced content, methods, or processes. An illustration:

Kids in one elementary school enrichment program were organized into the Environmentally Friendly Construction Company (many programs eschew the familiar *club* label in favor of guild, society, company, institute, league, or group as a way of underscoring the more "professional" or serious nature of what they do). Their selected activity: building environmentally kind birdhouses and feeders. This might seem to involve the fairly straightforward business of finding plan specifications; locating appropriate, perhaps recycled wood or other materials; and cutting, sanding, nailing, and gluing the houses together.

Those activities did represent some of the steps the youngsters followed, but far from all of them. Guided by their enrichment facilitator, the children obtained not only how-to books on the construction of birdhouses and feeders, but also information on marketing, advertising, and bird biology. They learned about the birds native to their area and their migratory patterns and mating habits. They discovered what different birds like to eat and their preferred nesting locations. When they had completed the finished products, some kids prepared posters with colorful drawings and photographs of the birdhouses for sale. A couple of others who were interested in computer activities and desktop publishing created printed materials to go along with each birdhouse or feeder. They also offered workshops for other children interested in trying their hand at building environmentally friendly birdhouses.

A lot of learning took place while the youngsters pursued their goal of producing birdhouses; again, information, materials, and problem solving skills became relevant — and memorable — because they were acquired on a need-to-know basis. The young birdhouse creators were dipping into areas of ornithology, geography, geometry and measurements, architectural construction, purchasing, record keeping, advertising and salesmanship, computer graphics, teaching, and photography — not to mention teamwork.

Whatever your child is up to, can you point him to the next step, or one next step, broadening the knowledge field? Carrie, an eighteen-year-old, said that as a very young child she'd always liked reptiles and her parents allowed her to keep tanks that at various times held different small snakes and lizards. She learned about their care, diligently fed them appropriately, and cleaned the tanks. "These were my pets, I gave them names," Carrie said, "and when one died, we'd have an 'official' burial out in the backyard. I'd put it in a small box, put a little marker over the spot."

On a summer day before one such burial, her father took her aside. "My dad, who's a physicist, said, 'Let's try to understand more about this lizard, what an amazing little creature it is.' So he laid it on a clean cloth, got his X-Acto knife, and we dissected it. He pointed out the lungs, the heart, we studied the skeleton. It was fascinating. I was maybe only about seven, then, but I got a new way of looking at these reptiles. Not just as my pets, but as amazing little creatures, like my dad said." On entering college, Carrie planned to begin a premed course.

Another, simple example: The parent of a five-year-old said that practically every evening her daughter arranged an elaborate display across her bed and desk of many small items — some toys, plastic jewelry, a couple of old books, a couple of old boxes of crayons, shells, pretty rocks — that were "for sale." Each of these items had little notes attached indicating the cost — five cents here, eight cents there. Mom and Dad were invited to shop and there was much negotiating as to price, layaway plans, and so on.

This was pretend play or fantasy play, the mother said. Which it was, but it was also a young child's expression of interest in setting up a shop, running a business, and dealing with the public as a store owner. At our suggestion, her parents bought the book *Better Than a Lemonade Stand,* about how to start a small business, and mother and child read it together. The girl was fascinated, her eyes opened to the wider world of buying and selling.

SAFE RISKS: LEARNING TO RELISH A CHALLENGE

Some youngsters love facing a challenge. A setback or two does not daunt them, a new area to explore is perceived as a welcome opportunity. And others — equally bright, equally capable of gifted behaviors — shy away from the new and untried. These are children with unique strengths who find it easier, or more comfortable, to not stretch themselves to do something with their strengths. They are also children with an enormous capacity to grow when they receive parental encouragement to take chances.

One parent told this story: "From the time she was little, Lila was a kid who said 'no' right off the bat to anything different, any change. It's in her DNA. So I was always pushing her to stick her toe in the water, try things out, join this group, go to that performance, whatever it was. We'd talk about this. 'What's the worst that can happen?' I'd say. Well, she wouldn't know anybody there, she wouldn't be able to do it, she wouldn't this, she couldn't that. 'That's the worst?' I'd say. 'Doesn't sound so terrible to me.' My point with her was always, 'Try it, it's a safe risk.'

"I knew she would be fine and I knew she'd be pleased with herself after the fact, and nine times out of ten I was right. The summer she was twelve there was a two-week-long kind of mock-UN program, very minor scale, being held for kids her age on a college campus in a nearby city. She was interested in the program, but no way, she wouldn't go. 'Here's the deal,' I said. 'You go, if in four days you can't stand it, call, we'll come get you and bring you home.' She went, looking like we were shipping her off to Siberia. Two days later I get a phone call — would I please immediately send her other pair of sneakers, her camera, ten other things she had to have.

"As time went on, my daughter got bolder and braver. First year of college, barely eighteen, she surprised us all by signing up for a study abroad semester in Europe. She's now in grad school, going great guns, doing complicated work in political science, traveling all over the place doing research. I don't think she remembers my little confidence boosting talks. That's okay. She's proud of herself, that's what matters."

Venturing to take safe risks — tackling the new, the untried, possibly failing or not coming out on top — is critical for talented young people who choose to or have been conditioned to "play it safe" by sticking with what they know they are good at, who reach for a sure-fire success over an opportunity to learn something important and understand the benefits of expending "effort." After all, genuine creative productivity — solving real problems — always involves some degree of stepping forth into the unknown, with no guarantees. The great artist Pablo Picasso said, "I am always doing that which I cannot do, in order that I may learn how to do it." Perhaps the reluctance to take chances does have something to do with DNA, as Lila's mother said; however, it is also the case that children can be taught to embrace challenges.

From her research studies involving students in elementary through middle schools, psychologist Carol Dweck has noted the difference between kids who hold a "fixed" view of intelligence and abilities and those who believe in an "expandable" or "growth" view. The fixed view youngster is mainly concerned with how smart she is and with proving that to teachers, to the world, and to herself by maintaining top grades. Consequently, she prefers tasks she can already do well, avoiding those on which she may make mistakes. Making a mistake, in her self-perception, means not that she has to try harder, but that she is, in fact, incompetent or inadequate. Not smart.

Those with an expandable view of intelligence, who believe that most people are capable of learning new things, are what Dweck calls "mastery-oriented." Focused more intently on learning rather than on feeling or looking smart, they like a brisk challenge. They pour effort into what they're doing; they persist in the face of difficulties. Being mastery-oriented, she says, is about having the right mind-set. And having the right mind-set leads over time to heightened abilities, accomplishment, and feelings of self-efficacy — to getting bolder and braver.

Independent learning experiences — the creative-productive adventures we've been describing — can be the ideal arena for kids to absorb messages about the importance of taking safe risks and facing — even enjoying! — challenges. In your child's other learning arena, the classroom, she's more likely to be noticed and rewarded for measurable evidence of her "intelligence": a 95 percent on an arithmetic test, excellent. The fact that the arithmetic problems were, for her, a snap, no challenge at all, is a sadly overlooked part of the picture. It is not suggested that just doing what she can already do well is in some way a waste of her time.

Encouraging her to take safe risks — what's the worst that can happen? — is one powerful way to promote a mastery-oriented mindset in your child. Offering praise — appropriate praise — is another.

PRAISE AND THE "A FOR EFFORT" ISSUE

"In the parenting books and articles, you always read that there's a good way to praise a child and a not-good way," said the mother of seven-year-old twins. "So if your kid shows you a drawing, you don't say, 'Wow, Timmy, you're so clever, you're so smart, you're our brilliant little artist!' Praise the drawing, not the kid, is the idea. 'I like how you painted that boat, Timmy, the colors are really bright.'" This advice struck her as somewhat phony. "Suppose the boat is a mess? It doesn't look like a boat at all. Suppose you think he should be able to paint a better looking boat if he took more time with what he was doing?"

Another parent, after attending a performance of her preschooler's ballet class, remarked, "The way all the mommies and daddies were reacting, it was like we were watching Margot Fonteyn. Wild applause and 'woo-hoos!'"

These are interesting issues, especially as they relate to the parental role in guiding a child's gifted behaviors. Studies in early child development (roughly the first three years of life) show that parents do tend to go to extremes in praising a child's accomplishments, momentous or not, and that this is, in fact, desirable. A young child needs to feel that someone is intensely involved with him, or in essence, rooting for him. Of course, as kids get older they become capable of testing reality and measuring themselves according to more than the reactions of their parents.

If we want young people to engage in higher-end learning, uncover their interests, realize their strengths, and deal with real problems according to the ways of the real world, we must help them appreciate realities that are painfully apparent to anyone who has ever tried his hand in the real world of creative productivity. For instance, there is always a competitive element involved, even if only with oneself in meeting deadlines and achieving personal standards of satisfaction. Quality matters. Sloppy work is rejected. If the first version of the boat doesn't look anything like a boat, you are expected to try again.

Never discourage a young person from becoming a true investigator and creator because he has not acquired advanced level methods, theories, or conclusions. Any child should be applauded for serious efforts made, the imaginative application of workable strategies, and the willingness to accept a challenge. At the same time, part of a parent's role is to make sure a child does not spend months producing something that has been done before and is readily available. For example, one boy wanted to write a book for kids on great moments in the history of baseball. His father suggested a trip to the library, and together they found a book for children on just that topic. Along the same lines, youngsters should not be deluded into believing that they are on the forefront of knowledge or achievement in a field or area of endeavor (unless, of course, you truly think they are). Parents do need to help a child become aware of the basic differences between beginners, journeymen, and grand masters.

That brings up the questions: Can your child's product be improved? And how can you encourage improvement?

THE MATTER OF QUALITY: HOW GOOD IS GOOD ENOUGH?

Creative people know that proceeding from inspired idea to polished end result takes not only work, but clear-eyed evaluations and revisions. Even highly talented individuals seldom achieve perfection on the first go-round. At times, it may be necessary to scrap one's efforts partway through and start over. The *Peanuts* dog Snoopy opened each of his novels with the clichéd line, "It was a dark and stormy night," but he never sold any. Maybe if he had reassessed and tried a second version, he would have had better luck.

In school-based programs quite often all the products produced by all the participating youngsters are treated as of equal quality. For example, in a program in the area of creative writing, one sample of each child's work was photocopied, the whole bound together in an attractive cover, and sent home to parents at the end of the school year. Someone got to read the pieces, which was better than no one reading them, but the audience was basically a contrived one. In addition, since the attractive booklet represented a collection of the required work of all students — rather than the submitted work of aspiring and committed young poets, short story writers, and essayists — some of it was undoubtedly of higher quality than the rest.

However, in many kinds of original problem solving, how does a child know if her results are good or bad? Top drawer or could-be-better and getting-to-best? The psychologists Jacob Getzels and Mihaly Csikszentmihalyi, in their writings on creativity, have pointed out, "when the solution is obtained — *if* it is obtained — [the problem solver] may have no immediate criterion for its ultimate correctness. . . . He cannot compare it against a predetermined standard. . . . He can accept or reject the solution only on the basis of a critical, relativistic analysis — as is the case with works of art." In other words, in the absence of right/wrong measuring sticks, the individual must take the major responsibility for evaluating what she's done.

In school-based programs, of course, the teacher or facilitator usually must come up with, if not a grade, some form of final judgment concerning the outcome and how successfully a youngster achieved the goals of enrichment learning. In programs based on our models, the facilitator will consider several questions designed to assess the child's efforts:

- Did the child clearly state the purpose of her work, defining the topic or problem early, with an end product in sight?
- Did she focus or refine the topic, making it a specific problem within a large area of study?
- Did she use a variety of appropriate and relatively advanced resources?
- Did she organize her work in a logical way, following a series of sequential steps?
- Was her goal to go beyond merely reporting on or summarizing existing information, and produce something new?
- Has she found an appropriate audience?

All these are worthwhile criteria in evaluating investigative processes. If you have been a managerial assistant and guide-on-the-side in the ways we have outlined so far — helping your child zero in on a problem; offering suggestions about checking out Web sites and how-to books and resources; logging the miles in the car, driving her here and there as needed; reviewing the Project Management Plan; and so on — you know how well things have been going. Probably quite well. When it comes to judging the quality of the final product, however, or knowing how good is good enough, it might be enormously useful to encourage your child to seek out, with your help perhaps, someone who can offer "a critical, relativistic analysis" (in the words of Getzels and Csikszentmihalyi).

Kids who energetically commit themselves to independent projects tend to view what they're doing honestly and hold high expectations for themselves. But to develop a sense of professionally polished work, there's probably no better time spent than for your child to get feedback from a person or persons who know how to make judgments about quality — one of the mentors-in-person we've mentioned, or just someone who knows something about the subject at hand. That should be an individual with the sensitivity to appreciate the difference between a ten-year-old's study and the work of a PhD candidate, but with the willingness to point out the difference between quality and carelessness or misguidedness at any level — and, also, with the ability to be both forthright and kind.

FEEDBACK: WHAT KINDLY CRITICS DO

Vera was a girl with a bright imagination who enjoyed mystery stories. She traced this enthusiasm back to when she was around five and her father began reading to her every evening after she got into bed. "He didn't read kid stories, like Beatrix Potter and that stuff," Vera said. "He read me all the Nancy Drew books and then all of Sherlock Holmes and some stories by Saki. I didn't understand everything, but I just loved reading time and I loved the stories. They were weird and exciting."

At thirteen, she decided that she wanted to try writing her own stories, and envisioned a series of books featuring a young woman mystery solver. After reading a few of the Sue Grafton alphabet mysteries, she realized she would need to give her main character a specific job in a specific location or the story wouldn't seem real. This problem was solved when she decided to base her protagonist on her beloved Aunt Lucy, a thirty-five-year-old woman who managed a modern art gallery. This had everything, Vera thought: "It was a fancy place, very fancy people who got dressed up to go to my aunt's exhibitions, all this interesting art and paintings and drawings that were sold for huge tons of money." There could be robberies, forgeries, maybe a murder.

Dreaming larger, Vera started thinking that instead of books, she would try to write a TV show about her character. In a burst of creativity, she wrote two scripts for her proposed series, one that was twenty pages long and the second — she was running out of steam and ideas — four pages.

This was a girl whose preferred instructional style was to learn from "grownups who can tell me useful things." Vera's father suggested she had enough material to talk to an independent TV and film producer with whom he shared office space. Her father said, "This fellow, Sam, knows the business inside and out. He's kind of a tough-talking character, but the sweetest person you'd want to meet, an ear for everyone." The producer agreed to read Vera's work; she accompanied her dad to the office a couple of days later and the two of them sat down for a session with Sam.

Vera's father remembered, "Sam started out, 'Kid, you got terrific ideas here. I'm impressed!' He liked the glamorous setting, he said, and there was some good action, some funny parts. Other parts were too rushed through or would have been handled better in a more visual way. Then he described how a writer gets to the point of having a show on TV, saying, 'I've only learned this stuff myself over years and years of banging my head against the wall!' He talked about the process — how to develop what writers call a treatment, plus characterization, pacing, and planning story arcs over a period of time — a lot of elements that obviously required practice. 'Check out a movie called *Rear Window*,' he told Vera, 'terrific mystery, and that one started out as a short story.' Maybe she could try her hand at writing just one short story featuring her woman sleuth, to establish the character in her own mind.

"He talked about all this in a way that informed my daughter about the realities of a very tough business, but at the same time made it sound like an exciting and dynamic area, and bravo for her that she was interested in it. Also at the same time, he had specific suggestions on how to evaluate or revise what she'd dreamed up so far. He talked to her as a serious adult giving a serious young person the benefit of his expertise."

That's an excellent rundown of the type of feedback an appropriate critic will offer a child and of the manner in which it should be conveyed:

- Note with admiration what she has done well.
- Note what needs improvement.
- Explain how professionals follow through on their creative ideas by editing their work and learning from the efforts of others in their field.
- Point her in a direction or two that might expand her skills and experience.
- Talk like a serious adult to a serious young person.

THE POWER OF AN AUDIENCE

Much of the creative work that young people produce really does have the potential to affect the human condition in a positive way. Much of what kids come up with can, as our examples over these chapters have shown, serve to inform, entertain, or influence the thinking or feelings of others — bring pleasure, add understanding, make the world a little better. One boy's interest in the old buildings in his city led him to develop a descriptive guide that was subsequently adopted by the city council as its official walking tour. Working through social services agencies, a group of kids rescued and repaired outmoded computers to bring computer capacity to homes previously without it.

Finding an outlet or an audience inspires a child to a higher degree of professionalism or to view himself in a more professional role.

A ten-year-old named Julio had a talent for drawing and liked making sketches of his neighborhood. His interest was primarily in buildings and other structures; over time he had amassed a sketchbook full of precise pencil drawings — similar in style to architectural renderings — of a town house, a kiddie park filled with climbing and other play apparatus, a bridge, and more. One drawing depicted the facade of a nearby church, an old and ornate Gothic-style building. Julio's mother thought it was a masterful piece of artwork. One day she stopped in at the church rectory office. She introduced herself to the resident priest, showed him her son's drawing, and asked if the church might have any interest in using it in some way. The father said he'd like to reproduce it at the top of a newsletter the church regularly sent to parishioners.

When his mother told Julio about this development, the boy said: "Oh, my gosh! I got the perspective all messed up on the left side. I have to work on it more." This he did, correcting the perspective and then laboriously inking over the pencil outlines, which he thought would make his drawing more reproducible. These efforts involved going to an art store to buy India ink, a fine-nibbed pen, and an art eraser, with which he carefully rubbed out his pencil marks at the end.

His response demonstrates the kind of motivational power of a child knowing his work is headed for a "real world" outlet. Even without a professional evaluation of his drawing, Julio developed a more keenly critical eye himself to what he was doing, once he realized that many other eyes would be seeing it.

Another story of young artists and the audience they found:

Three girls who loved art had become friends when they all were involved in after-school and weekend art lessons. Their parents came to know each other in the course of driving their youngsters to and from the lessons and buying painting materials, and when the girls came up with the idea that they should be able to exhibit their art somehow, these moms and dads were all for it. So the children spent a few months completing several pieces of their best work and the parents looked around for a location for the show. The most likely candidate, the one gallery in their small city, was not available. Several other possibilities also failed to pan out and the search for a location was proving frustrating. Then one of the parents began to think about his own workplace.

The manager of a bank branch, he broached the idea with his Board of Directors about a local student art show to be set up in the bank lobby. They wholeheartedly supported it and the venture then took off. The art teacher at the girls' school announced the upcoming show and some other youngsters decided to join. When the girls realized they would have a public venue, they worked harder than they had before and went through many revisions to come up with their very best efforts. The founding group kept tabs on what the others were doing and made sure they would have enough finished art for a proper display. Six months after the original brainstorm, the exhibit opened, with an announcement in the local paper and signs posted in the bank. Positive comments about the art were made by many of the customers, and the girls even received several offers for purchase of their work. This was the big time!

Other involved parents, with a little footwork, a little phone calling, a little thoughtful attention to possibilities, have found many such receptive audiences.

So, what and where is a realistic platform for your child's work?

HUNTING FOR OUTLETS

Finding an appropriate and relatively realistic audience might take exercising some creativity of your own. You may serve as referral agent, promoter, and door opener. It's one of the parental managerial functions that can mean a truly qualitative difference between independent creative work and the typical projects done in school.

One mother thought her teenage daughter's handmade jewelry designs were good enough to be sold. Over the space of a year-and-a-half, Marcie had produced about two dozen bracelets and pairs of earrings, each one a unique construction of jewel-toned beads and small charms attached to thin copper and silver wires, which she gave as Christmas gifts to friends. Through a women's professional organization she belonged to, Marcie's mother heard about a woman who had a well-established line of jewelry that was sold in several high-end boutiques. She cold-called the woman, described her child's interest in making jewelry, and asked for any advice about how and where her daughter might show her work.

"I had no idea what kind of reaction I'd get," said this parent. "I mean, you might come across like a pushy, stage mother type — my kid makes these beautiful things, you've got to see them. But she couldn't have been nicer." This brave bit of outreach had a nice payoff when the woman sent Marcie fliers listing the times and locations in their area of upcoming *look-sees,* where budding designers show examples of their pieces to store buyers who might be interested in displaying them on spec. She added "Good luck!" Marcie decided, with some fear and trepidation, to give that a try.

Consider whom you might tap for suggestions regarding the audience aspect of your child's product and how you might approach them. You should probably not buttonhole a professional in a demanding manner. But you might find an agreeable way to gain her cooperation in suggesting ideas for "where to go with this." In general, you want to learn from this creative-productive individual some answers to the following questions:

- What are all the products associated with your talent, skill, or service?
- Who are the most authentic audiences and potential audiences for your products?

- How do you go about identifying and locating these audiences?
- What are the established vehicles — such as journals, competitive events, art shows — for communicating original work in your field?
- Do these vehicles exist at local, regional, state, and national levels? Do you know of contact persons in these areas who might be receptive to viewing the creative work of gifted young people?

A Few Likely Outlets

For Written or Oral Products

- Local newspapers, shopping guides, and city or state magazines often accept articles, editorials, children's book or movie reviews, cartoons, letters, a science column, puzzles, quizzes, and games contributed by young people.
- Many state and national organizations have newsletters that publish the work of young people.
- A number of magazines specifically publish the stories and poetry of young authors — *Stone Soup* (www.stonesoup.com) is one example. *Kid News* (www.kidnews.com) is a free news and writing service for young people around the globe. *The Writer* (www.writermag.com) is another source of information for writing and publishing opportunities.
- Some kids have organized story hours in local or school libraries to showcase their work.
- Others have established an oral history tape section in local or school libraries.

For Visual Displays or Demonstrations

- Public buildings and business offices may be receptive to requests to display young people's work.

- If such outlets do not exist, how can we go about establishing them?
- Would you be available to help us?

Parents often find themselves surprised at the quality of practical advice they are able to uncover by having a friendly chat with someone who knows something about their child's interest.

As a parent guide-on-the-side, you might be door opener and

- Local or state organizations — such as historical societies, civic groups, environmental preservation organizations, and advocacy groups — often provide opportunities for young inventors and entrepreneurs to present their work.

For Theatrical and Film/Video Products
- Senior citizen centers, day care centers, church groups, and professional organizations may be happy to host showings or performances.
- Some young people have arranged to create and present a regular science slot on local children's TV shows.

All fields of organized knowledge have available resources. Simply entering a broad subject area into a search engine will lead your child, with a few clicks on the links that appear, to all kinds of information about how the creative products in the field are communicated to interested audiences. The Web is itself a powerful audience for many young people's products, featuring poetry sites, story archives, and virtual science fairs.

---

adviser, suggesting one or more of these realistic outlets. You might rehearse with your child the appropriate way for a contact to be made, what should be said, what might be asked. But in most cases, the follow-through is her responsibility. Writing query letters; submitting work for possible publication, presentation, or display; and receiving positive or negative replies are all part of the creative process and a major source of motivation for aspiring writers, scientists, artists, and other action-oriented young people.

Another form of outlet: contests and competitions.

LOOKING TO WIN: A DIFFERENT KIND OF CHALLENGE

Almost all the boys in nine-year-old Charlie's class were involved in athletic activities. Most played soccer; several were in swim training, a few of them already taking part in local meets. Charlie's interests were of a literary nature and his parents thought of ways they could be supported. His mother discovered on the Internet an annual event called the Reading Rainbow Young Writers & Illustrators Contest and she and Charlie looked it over. Scanning the titles and cover designs of the submitted entries, the boy got excited. There were first-, second-, and third-place winners, with ribbons awarded. He and his mom talked about some of the realities of taking part. For one thing, with more than 40,000 entries, there were a lot of kids vying for a ribbon. But Charlie thought this was something he wanted to try and he began studiously polishing a story he had written and illustrated.

Contests and competitions are great experiences for many youngsters, maybe especially for those who don't participate in athletics. With early exposure to competition, kids learn how to compete with honesty and integrity, to experience disappointment, and to recognize that it's important to lose with courage and grace — or to win with humility and, at the same time, with pride in one's accomplishments.

Those are some of the lessons that are learned through participation in competitive sports, after all; the swimmer sees he can train hard, lose, and still continue swimming and striving.

Whatever your child's interest area, there's probably a contest or competition that will match it (in Appendix I, we list some of our favorites in a variety of fields). This is a natural audience for his interest-based activities. Most of us have heard about the extensively covered national science fairs, but there are literally thousands of other competitions — in areas such as photography, fashion design, inventions, greeting cards, play writing, technology, Web design, and more. Preparing for and entering a contest or competition can be tremendously exciting for a youngster. He aspires to higher levels of excellence and begins to understand more fully his own creative potential. He experiences in a real-world setting these issues of winning or losing.

Other big life lessons: Electing to participate means he must improve organizational, time management, and self-regulation skills. Deadlines have to be met, instructions must be followed to the letter. Contests can also teach children about personal safety issues, such as how and when to provide information about home addresses and phone numbers and whether or when parental supervision is necessary.

You can be a guide-on-the-side in this arena by determining whether a specific contest is a good match for your child's interests and abilities and what's involved in taking part. He might need your help to understand the rules regarding eligibility requirements, how to submit material, and so on. And a Project Management Plan and Progress Portfolio can be developed and reviewed regularly in order to stay on target to get in the game.

Since we may be sounding at this point a bit Pollyannaish, we add: Losing is not fun. Realizing that the competition is often stiff will not usually dissuade a determined and confident young person from believing that his best work will nevertheless be judged best of the pack.

After disappointment but before he can embrace any idea of losing with courage and grace, he may need a shoulder to cry on (which, of course, is something we all want occasionally). You can offer one — and at the same time remind him of, and applaud him for, his willingness to accept a challenge, his effort and perseverance, and the care and trouble he took to refine his product. Those words do register.

JOINING FORCES: WHEN KIDS WORK TOGETHER

Our examples have mostly concerned young people working on their own, but many terrific projects come about through the collaborative efforts of two or three or even a small horde of kids.

Generally speaking, it's important to make the effort to enable a child to be involved with an appropriate peer group — birds of a feather — where there exists an appreciation and value for the same endeavor. That might be especially important for the child with a passion that is highly unusual for her age — she loves classical music, for example — and who might be lonely, isolated, or feel like a "nerd" in her school class. If your youngster is with others who share her interest in analyzing rocks or acting in plays, it's a safe environment, one within which she can feel comfortable and supported. A boy who works with several friends at an animal rescue and adoption society in his town said: "In our group, nobody's into who's popular or who's not. Nobody cares about that stuff. We're just doing our thing. We all want to help the animals."

And there is another element when birds of a feather work together that distinguishes independent explorations from your child's school life. In school, she typically spends all her time with kids her own age. In the out-of-school world, people almost always group themselves or are grouped according to common interests or common tasks, regardless of small (or even large) separations in age. Pursuing her enthusiasms with like-minded kids, some younger, some older, adds to the "realness" or laboratory environment (as we've called it) of higher-end learning.

But in addition, when youngsters gather around the same interest, they reach *critical mass* — a grand mix of the necessary ingredients that produces the best results. A six-year-old might have a wonderful, creative, rough idea; an eight- or nine-year-old might have the know-how to begin implementing it. In thinking style preferences, one may be the inventor, another the facilitator, another the evaluator. In some enrichment programs following our models, children spanning four grade levels have joined forces with great success.

Of course, the larger the group, the greater the number of variables in terms of personality and other factors that may or may not interfere with progress. Two stories demonstrate this point.

Annie was captivated by her visit, during fourth grade, to a local newspaper to watch the internal workings of a small city pressroom. The visit had been arranged by her parents because of Annie's interest in journalism. This was an exciting scene: reporters at their desks, editors arguing in a conference room, the crackle of the police radio in the background. She came away with the idea of starting a mini-version in her school, a monthly newspaper with regular features, news from each classroom, and interviews with key players such as the principal, nurse, favorite teachers. Discussing the idea with her parents and teacher, a plan was hatched: her parents would provide some start-up funds; the principal gave his permission; Annie would be allowed to substitute her work on the paper for some regular language arts assignments.

The paper got under way, with Annie as the editor and several other kids signing on as assistant editors, cartoonists and artists, book critic, movie critic, and "roving reporters."

Before the first month was over, Annie ran into problems. Some reporters did not meet deadlines. Some classroom contributors failed to contribute entirely. Some of the stories had to be completely rewritten. A temperamental artist objected to preparing a second draft of illustrations. Then there was the principal who seemed to want to read every story. Would this lead to a censorship issue?

But as the deadline for the first issue came closer, the kids began pulling together, and the premier, eight-page edition was put to bed at last. Annie kept up the *Chronicle* each month for the next two school years (before training her successor). The problems didn't disappear — the need for revisions, the recalcitrant contributors, the personality conflicts — but Annie grew and persevered, becoming stronger and more focused.

Fourteen-year-old Joseph created and spearheaded a service project devoted to bringing sandwiches, juice, and an hour or two of company to elderly and largely shut-in residents in his neighborhood. To set up his Saturday morning goodwill program, the boy met with the director for volunteer services at a local senior center; with the director's help, he phoned a number of elderly persons who had indicated that they would be happy to have home visits on a regular basis and came up with the names and addresses of twelve receptive individuals. His parents would finance the purchase of food items, a relatively small outlay for bread, sandwich fixings, and apple juice.

Figuring that two visits were the most one kid could handle in the course of a morning, Joseph set about recruiting five additional volunteers. Posting a notice on information boards in school and his apartment building — "Bring a sandwich, a smile, and some company to one of our elderly neighbors" — he heard from a few kids who said they'd like to join. Joseph explained that he would make up the lunch bags in his kitchen early Saturday and his dad would then drive him to each of the volunteer's homes to drop off the bags.

The first Saturday, things went well; after that, downhill. One volunteer called to say she wanted to switch to another neighbor, because the person she visited didn't talk much and it was kind of boring. Another said he would be busy the following two weekends. Another requested that her visits be reduced from two to one each time. On the third Saturday, Joseph, with his mother in tow, found himself handling five of the visits, which occupied most of his day. He felt let down by his volunteer crew. The service ran for about three months that fall, when Joseph decided to discontinue it "until further notice." If he tried it again, Joseph said, "I'd want to be sure these kids really wanted to take part. I just figured that since they signed up, everybody was as interested in this as me, but I guess not."

The experiences of these two young people point to some important lessons a child may pick up working on a group project — especially if she assumes leadership:

- Even if all involved start out on the same page, levels of commitment or motivation may wax and wane as time goes on.
- Not all participants may be embracing the task as a "real problem" of personal relevance. (One of the boys in Joseph's volunteer group said he joined "because my mom wanted me to do it.")
- Personality differences may enter the picture.
- Needing to critique a peer on the quality of her contribution can be tremendously difficult and call for a degree of tact and sensitivity that takes practice to reach.
- The best way to plan practical aspects, such as scheduling and arranging for roughly equal divisions of labor, may only become apparent after some false starts.

These are hard, but splendid, lessons, involving Howard Gardner's multiple intelligences. Collateral learning, as John Dewey called it, can be gained only in the heat of battle, so to speak, as a creative endeavor involving several kids takes shape over time. Parents, having surely themselves picked up some such skills in the course of navigating their own challenges in the adult world, can add useful perspective. They can share their experiences — not in a "here's what you should have done differently or what you should do next time" tone, but in "I remember facing a similar situation" manner. Parents can relay the truth that experience is often the best teacher, and that sometimes we learn more when things don't go exactly as planned.

THE CREATIVELY PRODUCTIVE FAMILY

A few final thoughts about creativity, parenting, and the overused, somewhat clichéd, but nevertheless critical advice about being a good role model for children.

Our colleague Robert Sternberg, a foremost cognitive psychologist, has described his theory of *Successful Intelligence* (the title of his book, which is subtitled *How Practical and Creative Intelligence Determine Success in Life*). Successful intelligence is marked by an individual's ability to think in ways that will help him develop personal excellence. One key is *creative thinking:* looking beyond the known to consider what is not known and doing things perhaps a little differently from others, and in the process generating new and interesting ideas. "The most powerful way to develop creative intelligence in children," he writes, "is to serve as a creative role model." Think of the teachers who influenced you most, Sternberg suggests: Who were they? What did they do?

Thinking back, one parent remembered: "My first semester at college: I arrived just the coolest kid, I thought. All school to that point had been no sweat for me. That first term, I got my first ever Cs, from the professor who taught a required class in Modern Civilization, a broad survey course. In the papers I turned in, this professor wrote comments in the margins, and they all essentially said a version of 'Oh, really? Why do you say so? How do you back up that observation? What makes you think this?' He carried on his lectures along the same lines, not exactly playing devil's advocate, but pointing out that the first way of viewing something wasn't necessarily the right or the best way. He steered us to all kinds of interesting reading, not just the standard issue textbook we had. And he never made you look ignorant or feel ignorant.

"The scales fell from my eyes. What he led me to understand, and it happened very quickly, was that for the previous twelve years I hadn't been thinking very much at all, but instead rather glibly putting down what seemed to sound right or clever."

That experience, he believes, had a significant influence on his future work life, and, later, his feelings about parenting his own children. "I wanted them to learn not to accept everything on face value. Question assumptions. Try out possibilities. Make mistakes. Both my boys, now preteens, are highly imaginative kids. And they're developing their own approaches to life, to what they want to do. I encourage them to be envisioning next steps, not necessarily mapping out a whole career plan but recognizing their strengths and where that could take them."

He did consider himself a role model, this father said, "because my sons see that I follow these principles in my own life. Kids are very aware of what their parents are all about; they're watching. They've seen me take chances in my work. Try something difficult because it was the right thing or the right time."

A mother of four believes that being a good role model included "demonstrating commitment and passion yourself. You should have your own things that you love to do, your own passions. Not just random hobbies, or only random hobbies, but something you truly love, something you can't wait to get back to every day or whenever. You don't *tell* kids, you *show* them that it's exciting and fun and hugely satisfying to keep stretching and producing."

Her house, she said, "is a pretty loosey-goosey place. We don't have a lot of rules besides the few you need to keep some kind of order to the day. But everybody's got projects going on all the time, the kids, their dad, myself. We let the kids express themselves in their own ways. Whatever they want to do — as long as they're serious about it, they're willing to put in effort and time, and strive to do their best — we're all for it.

"And we get so much out of each other's activities. They take us into areas we wouldn't get on our own. My one son is into organic and hydroponic farming, that's what he wants to do! He's got half the basement set up with strange blue lights. My one daughter is learning about equine therapy. She volunteers in a program that helps autistic kids who ride horses. They're all different, my children, but they support each other and we're in it together — so one weekend we're visiting a horse farm, one weekend we're at a horticultural exhibit. It makes for an interesting life!"

Almost surely, that's an attitude that also bodes well for the future of gifted young people, according to much research into the intriguing question of why and how some people develop their talents within specific domains and some do not. For example, the educational theorist Benjamin Bloom and his colleagues conducted extensive interviews with 120 individuals who had excelled, reaching an international level of accomplishment before the age of thirty-five, in three areas: academic (research mathematicians and neurologists), artistic (concert pianists and sculptors), and athletic (Olympic swimmers and tennis players). Talent blossomed most often, they found, when a positive family environment existed, as parents or other family members provided high levels of support. In fact, most families assumed that the young person's talent would be developed as part of the family's life.

In an interview, Erik Friedlander, a highly admired, avant-garde cellist, recalled childhood summer trips in a pickup truck and a camper: he, his sister, and their parents heading out for a couple of months of driving, taking photographs, and camping. His father, Lee, is a noted photographer whose work has been shown at the Museum of Modern Art in New York, and the trips were both family fun time and creative-productive time for his parents. The son developed along another path, but the lessons he absorbed back then remain. "I had a model of someone who just pursued what they needed to do for their art," he remembered. "So when I wanted to try to do something different with the cello, I didn't feel like, 'Well, maybe this is impossible, I shouldn't try this.' I know exactly what to do about this: You just do it."

As Albert Einstein said, "Setting an example is not the main means of influencing another; it is the only means."

PART THREE

Special Considerations

✳

CHAPTER 8

Twice Exceptional

Children with Gifts and Talents, and Learning Disabilities

A college student vividly recalled her earliest school years. Kindergarten had been for her both terribly boring — "far too easy" — and overly stimulating because of all the noise and activity in the room. She was moved up after a couple of weeks. But: "Skipping kindergarten and going directly to first grade created an unanticipated problem. I wasn't able to read or write even though I seemed to have the readiness skills." At the beginning of third grade, she was placed in remedial reading, math, and writing. "I was devastated to be in those programs, because it was now clear to my whole class that I was one of the slow kids. None of my friends were in *those* classes. Why did I have to be? I was just like them in gym and art. Why was I so different in the regular classroom? These were questions that continued to plague me throughout my educational experience."

This is the painful paradox faced by countless children — perhaps as many as 180,000 in our schools. They are smart, often with superior cognitive ability, but show serious weaknesses in reading, writing, spelling, following directions, or other skills that would enable them to do well and display their intelligence. They are also creative, imaginative children, good thinkers and task oriented producers — just like their "gifted" peers. Some research has found that among students identified by schools as learning disabled, more than one-third also demonstrate gifted behaviors. Many have personal interests they pursue with passion. And yet their academic performance is characterized by failure after failure.

We call them *twice exceptional*. For such young people the combination of talents and disabilities is, at the very least, confusing and frustrating. Most, for too long, simply don't understand what's wrong with them. These children, concluded one researcher, "are the most misjudged, misunderstood, and neglected segment of the student population and the community."

Some youngsters are never accurately diagnosed because their gifted abilities hide their learning difficulties, and their learning difficulties hide their giftedness. Some teachers still find it quite inconceivable that a child who's reading two years below grade level, say, might also be capable of gifted work. School-based services for the learning disabled typically not only ignore a child's strengths, but fail to teach coping techniques — learning-how-to-learn strategies — the child can use to succeed despite limitations. Especially as they get older, social and emotional issues complicate the picture for young people who may feel as if they don't belong anywhere within the school system — or among their peers — and who then may exhibit behavioral or psychological problems.

Of late, there has been greater appreciation within professional and educational circles of these youngsters' uniqueness and consequently of their need for particular classroom accommodations and specialized instruction. Nevertheless, very few data-based studies have addressed twice exceptional elementary and middle school children. Much of what we know about the support they require to deal with the interaction of superior intelligence and learning disabilities has come from young adults who themselves navigated this often torturous road. In retrospect, they have been able to tell us how they felt, and what worked and what didn't. Personally, our understanding has broadened not only from our research, but from our experiences as the parents of a talented child with learning disabilities. The remarks at the beginning of this chapter were written by our daughter, Sara, for inclusion in *The Handbook of Secondary Gifted Education* (edited by Felicia A. Dixon, PhD, and Sidney M. Moon, PhD).

For any parents of an obviously bright and gifted child who's struggling academically — and who perhaps has been or will be identified as learning disabled — the overview we present here should offer insights, ideas, and hope. It's compiled from our interviews with older students, from a number of research studies concerning this special population, and from additional observations by Sara — today a college graduate on her way to a successful career.

What we do know:

- When children who have both gifted abilities and learning disabilities are encouraged to understand that a disability is a personal attribute within their power to control, they can begin to view themselves in a much more positive light. They *are* smart.
- These young people typically have enormous capacities for persistence and hard work and a drive to do well.
- Parents can be powerful advocates by seeing that their children receive adequate attention not only to what's wrong but to what's right, and that they enjoy opportunities, resources, and encouragement to develop their gifts and talents.

REMEDIATION AND REPETITION: EDUCATIONAL APPROACHES THAT FALL SHORT

Our colleague Susan Baum, who has worked extensively for many years with twice exceptional children, told the story of Chris. A charming and friendly youngster, Chris was such an accomplished artist that his work was displayed in a one-man show in elementary school. As a preteen, he was running two successful businesses outside of school. Clearly, he was capable of demonstrating ability, creativity, and task commitment. His academic performance was extremely poor, however, and he was diagnosed by a child study team as learning disabled. Thus began a barrage of remedial efforts, including placing him in a class for students with severe neurological impairments.

A happy turnaround came in sixth grade, when Chris was mainstreamed and benefited from the attention of a responsive special education teacher. There, he was allowed to capitalize on his strong suits through a flexible approach to schoolwork: developing projects and giving oral presentations instead of being compelled to turn in written reports, for example, and using peer monitoring to complete assignments. Chris began doing well.

In junior high, those gains largely evaporated. Chris spent one hour a day in a resource room where he was drilled in organizational and writing skills. Nothing was done to modify assignments in ways that utilized what he was good at and that allowed him to experience greater success. In short time, he lost interest in school. His self-concept deteriorated; he considered himself a failure and began to keep company with other kids who were failing. Chris's parents eventually found a private school for their son where remediation was offered along with enrichment activities.

This abbreviated history of several years in one young boy's school life outlines a familiar story. Often, there is a striking dichotomy in levels of achievement between what the child accomplishes in school and what she does outside of school. Once identified as learning disabled, that diagnosis dictates what happens next, oftentimes something of a disaster as the youngster is grouped with other "disabled" kids who might in fact have vastly disparate disabilities and needs.

In special education, attempts are made to repair her learning deficiencies. Within a highly structured environment, she usually works alone under the teacher's supervision, trying to catch up on work missed in class or toiling away on basic skills in vocabulary development, phonics, memory, math, or writing — all removed from a "real" context of any interest to her. Drills may be designed to move the child at a slow pace through a series of simple tasks, which she finds frustrating. Her probably outstanding thinking abilities remain unchallenged. There's little recognition of, much less attention paid to, personal characteristics and gifted potential that might be tapped to help the child believe she can actually get something right.

Support services may be inconsistent, disorganized, and of varying quality and effectiveness from one year to the next. After repeated profound blows to any feelings of self-esteem, the child is in danger of losing the motivation to succeed. She writes herself off as a lost cause.

But the misjudgments, the misunderstandings, and the neglect might be under way even long before any learning disabled diagnosis is reached.

For many high-ability youngsters, entering school comes as a shock. These are kids, after all, who probably have been admired for their smartness and precocity. They may have been early talkers, learned all their letters, numbers, and colors at a young age, have an impressive vocabulary. Some may have been identified early on as gifted. Then suddenly, they find it hard to sit still, pay attention, express themselves in writing, and fit in with a large group of age-mates. Worst is the self-realization that they simply can't do what all the other kids seem capable of doing.

They may go to great lengths to disguise their shortcomings through various ruses. Many rely on superior verbal skills to "get by" and mask humiliating deficiencies. Being gifted, and perhaps quite insightful and knowledgeable in areas that interest them, they can talk intelligently about what they know. In fact, the gap between verbal and performance scores may be noted by teachers, who are likely to conclude the child "just needs to work harder."

Sara remembered developing "strategies to keep my inabilities a secret. . . . I thought that if I could be invisible and keep my teachers and peers in the dark about what I couldn't do, I could escape the embarrassment." Like many youngsters with difficulty reading, she made use of her excellent memory, memorizing the school books that were read to her at home and then pretending to "read" them herself the next day in the classroom.

For these and other reasons, twice exceptional youngsters are frequently identified much later, often in middle school or high school, than are learning disabled kids who are not gifted. Meanwhile, they suffer.

WHAT TWICE EXCEPTIONAL CHILDREN EXPERIENCE

A number of twice exceptional university students took part in a study we conducted with colleagues to understand how they coped with their problems and how they learned how to learn. All were involved in a university learning disabled program, and all had also been identified as gifted on the basis of IQ, achievement test results, and other indicators. Their difficulties included, variously, reading, spelling, handwriting, and math disabilities; trouble processing information; poor short-term memory; dyslexia; difficulty with verbal and written expression; and attention deficit disorder. All were doing well. All were eager to take part in our study, which included open-ended questionnaires and interviews both alone and with one of their parents.

Of the group, two had been diagnosed as learning disabled in second and third grades. For the others, recognition of a disability did not "officially" come until much later, for some not until they began college. Only one had been identified earlier than college (in seventh grade) as gifted.

They discussed the practices they employed to compensate for their shortcomings, strategies they adopted only late in their educational careers. But first, they talked at length about the negative experiences of elementary and secondary school.

Recalling those classrooms was painful. Some said they tried to forget what happened, "blocking it out." But all told the same stories: being repeatedly punished for not completing work, made to repeat a grade, placed in self-contained special education classes in which the majority of children were developmentally delayed or experiencing severe behavioral problems.

Both peers and teachers treated them poorly:

"I remember one English teacher. To this day, I hate her. She would just have the idea that if I couldn't do it, if I couldn't get an essay exam done in the time, then I just didn't deserve extra time."

"In fourth grade I had another terrible teacher who used to keep me after school when I couldn't get my times table test done, or when I would get a bad grade. . . . The other kids made up rhymes about me because I couldn't memorize my times table. I got detention every time I made a mistake."

"I remember being so angry at the kids who would get the As and stuff, because I actually knew more than they did, but nobody would let me say anything. If they had given me oral tests, I could tell them anything that they wanted to know, but they always gave me the written stuff. I would be on question three or four, and the time would be gone, because it took me so long to figure out what the questions were."

One boy who was placed in a class with other special education students said, "It was awful, it was degrading. I was very resentful of it. I don't remember that part of my life that well." Being compelled to repeat a grade, he thought, was "a disciplinary thing." When asked if he had been a discipline problem, he replied, "I wasn't before I got into the special class."

"I always felt like there were two people. One that I present to people and the other one who is inside me, but can't speak, and knows everything, and I get so absolutely frustrated. . . . So I sit there. . . . I just know all this stuff and I know all the answers. If I could just figure out how to say it, or how to get it out."

"I could know the word, know it well and say it wrong. I felt dumb in elementary school. . . . The kids would say, 'you're so dumb.' I believed them."

"I learned real early that the quieter you were, the less trouble you would get into. The only thing that I did was that I really was pretty abusive to the other kids if they teased me in class. . . . I would wait until recess or something, and I would just beat them up."

Some reported the casual, perhaps unintentional cruelty of their classmates. "I remember an instance when I wanted to die," said a girl who described an experience in a history class when she was unable to read aloud. "My girlfriend turned to me and said, 'What's wrong with you, you can't even read?' And I thought, 'You're my friend. Why did you have to embarrass me like this?' It was so hard."

In elementary school, said one participant, "I believe I didn't have friends because I was different. . . . I didn't think the way most kids thought. I didn't care about a lot of the things that they did, and I would spend a lot of time alone because I was comfortable alone, and when you would go out at recess walking alone being comfortable by yourself, people start to think you are strange. So that made the cycle even worse."

In fifth grade, Sara was identified as learning disabled and began working with a specialist. She felt, she wrote, "as if a large weight had been taken off my shoulders." On the one hand, it was clearly a relief to know what the problems were and to begin the long process of experimenting with various ways to deal with them. Like some diagnosed children, she was given certain accommodations in school, such as being allowed to take tests in a separate room from her classmates where it was easier for her to focus and where she was given more time. Nevertheless, accepting her disabilities was a painful struggle for years. She did not want to be different. She preferred not to refer to her disabilities, which became more pronounced as the workload increased. And when she did do well, she felt guilty about it: "I somehow felt I was cheating because of my accommodations. On one occasion, when I received a good science grade, a fellow student told me that the only reason I got the grade was because I had taken the test in a different room, and the adults answered everything for me. These insensitive remarks had a long lasting effect on my fragile sense of self. Each one caused my spirits to plummet."

A few obvious conclusions can be drawn from these recollections: Going through school as a gifted child who doesn't learn in the expected ways can be a miserable process without the right kinds of support. This support must take into account not only academic problems but the sensitivities and emotional vulnerabilities experienced by the youngster who feels "different."

WHAT WORKS: LESSONS LEARNED

The good news. From personal accounts and from a number of studies concerning this unique population of young people, we can sketch a picture of what is needed to help bring about a happier outcome. Briefly stated, what such children desperately require are more and more vigorously pursued opportunities to be successful.

In an ideal world, here's how that happens:

- **Strengths are emphasized over deficiencies.**

Greater attention is paid to the gifted part of the twice exceptional child equation: "Focus on developing the talent while compensating for the disability," in the words of one researcher.

The most successful schools develop a combination of support services or placements geared to individual needs. In general, the less restrictive and more flexible, the better. Small class sizes with more chances to talk, ask questions, and share information verbally are empowering to kids who have trouble reading and writing. Online courses, which have the benefit of enabling a student to control the level of difficulty or the speed, may be helpful. Accommodations can be made for a youngster's instruction style preferences — learning through doing and hands-on project-based work with peers, perhaps, instead of having to sit and listen to a teacher talk.

The lucky twice exceptional child will come to the attention of a teacher who spots his strengths and helps them come to the fore. It really is impossible to overstate the power of an insightful and supportive teacher to influence positively not only the academic performance but the emotional life of a struggling child. That, after all, has provided the fodder for more than one inspirational story or movie about a child, a class, or a school that moved from failure to success through the dynamic and unwavering efforts of one educator. For the twice exceptional youngster, hearing someone in "the system" say, "You're good at this!" can be a light in the dark.

For example, Sara remembered the law class she took in her sophomore year of high school as her saving grace. There, her outstanding verbal skills and critical thinking abilities were supported by an involved teacher who advocated for her in various ways and encouraged her to consider ways to build on her strengths. Trusting her talent for public speaking, she competed successfully on a state mock trial team. It was, as she called it, "one shining moment in this otherwise dismal high school existence."

She built on that shining moment at the end of her high school career, having transferred to a small private school, when she found the courage to join the debate team. As a last-minute replacement, she entered a tournament with a partner and won the team award and one of the two top awards for individual speaking. "After that win," Sara wrote, "my confidence soared," leading her in subsequent years to start a debate team at the small, competitive liberal arts college from which she later graduated.

Projects that grow out of personal interests can be wonderful for the twice exceptional child in school, as long as the enthusiasm is not used as the basis of a remediation intervention. When remediation is imposed, the thing that was exciting and spurred his creativity is tarnished. It becomes associated in his mind with the thing or things that are most difficult and onerous about academic work.

A young boy who loved taking nature photographs also had a disability that made writing and spelling extremely hard for him. Realizing his interest in nature subjects and then proceeding according to the deficiency approach, his teachers wanted him to write reports on the natural phenomena that intrigued him. In our view, this poor kid was already spending large amounts of his time in school trying to improve his writing skills; let's offer him an opportunity to learn that does not focus on his shortcoming. He took his photos, found a mentor in a local photographer, and went on to win a state science fair medal. Though expressing himself photographically, he was still required to prepare written descriptions of his project and he did so, stretching himself to explain a topic that was important to him. He learned in a way that enhanced his talent instead of struggling through pages of paper in which every sentence was a trial.

Mentorships and internships, advanced classes in an area in which they excel, the kinds of specialized contests and competitions described in the previous chapter — all these are also ways in which twice exceptional children might find positive reinforcement of their abilities, interests, and special talents.

Reports from the adult world bear witness to this concept of easing the laser-like focus on "fixing" learning disabilities.

In one broad-based study, adults who had struggled with learning disabilities but had also enjoyed extremely successful careers and were happy with their lives in general were asked to what they attributed their achievements and feelings of self-efficacy. They mentioned persistence, self-confidence, goal orientation, wise choices, and useful support systems in family and friends. They said that remediation aimed at correcting their disabilities did *not* play any significant role in their successes.

- **Learning disabilities are controlled through individually tailored compensation strategies.**

Disabilities, of course, do have to be "attended to," and as the successful, high-ability university students in our study discussed what worked for them, some common themes emerged. Each had developed a system unique to his needs, one that fit the characteristics of the disability or combination of disabilities, and also his personal styles or preferences. Each worked like a demon, devoting an extraordinary amount of time and energy to his learning tasks.

Individually, these students developed workable systems that let them take in information in ways that accommodated their shortcomings. They turned to books on tape as frequently as possible. They made good use of computer programs and online resources that fit their needs and relied on spell check and other self-correcting devices. Tape recorders were indispensable for many.

Some used multiple strategies to succeed at reading. Said one, "For reading, I need time, just give me time, and I can get it." He read necessary material slowly, then made extensive marginal notes summarizing important points. "And then I go back and I write a question out for what was discussed and in my own words I answer it underneath, and that way I quiz myself." Outlining and elaborately detailed note-taking procedures were common among these students.

Time management, planning and organizing, setting work priorities, and sequencing activities in an appropriate order were also critical for staying on track. "I know what I need to do and I have it in little pieces," said one. "Chunking is the term that they use. Keeping me from getting overwhelmed. . . . I have to break it up. If the chapters are really long, I do sections of chapters, stuff like that. Self-awareness, I guess that was a big thing, knowing how long I need to do something."

Sara remembered: "Taking obsessive notes forced me to stay very focused." For an art history class, "I photocopied all of the images we studied and shrunk them to half their size or less and put a copy of the image in my notes and another copy on a note card to study from. Yes, it was a lot of work, and my binder looked more like a textbook than anything else. But it was what I had to do to be successful. The pleasurable payoff for my work was that I became the 'study guru' when we were preparing for an exam. This caused other students to view me in a positive way."

These young people admired themselves for their efforts. Their capacity for hard work, they believed, was their greatest asset. Some useful tactics they figured out largely intuitively, but most benefited from the suggestions of learning specialists who provided modeling and practice in paraphrasing, highlighting text, identifying main ideas and supporting details, test preparation, and so on. Some were trained in a technique known as *SQ3R,* which stands for Survey, Question, Read, Recite, Review.

And many bitterly regretted the fact that it had taken so long — not until entering the university setting — to adopt appropriate compensation strategies for their problems. No one had told them before. "I will complain to this day about high school," said one survey participant, "and how they don't teach study skills." Said another about his school program for students with learning disabilities: "We just worked on . . . vocabulary and spelling. . . . [The idea seemed to be] they would teach you to spell better, then your disability would go away maybe."

There's been far too little attention paid to compensation strategies for kids in elementary and secondary school. But the best school-based programs for the twice exceptional focus less ferociously on the *what* (the content) is to be learned, and more on the *how,* or teaching them to think about their thinking, to learn how to learn. Even at young ages, simple learning-how-to-learn techniques can be absorbed so children can begin to compensate for their disabilities.

- **Careful consideration is given to a child's emotional and social growth.**

What may be the typical challenges of childhood and adolescence — adjusting to the rules and expectations of school, forming friendships, finding one's place within a peer group — can be exponentially harder for twice exceptional children. The fact that even in young adulthood so many easily called to mind times of excruciating embarrassment, frustration, and loneliness shows how deeply affected they were by their experiences as children.

Some were still extremely angry. Some felt sadness at what they had missed, what had been lost. "I never got my work done. You know, when you got your work done then you could go play. I think the only day I ever got to play was the last day of school and everyone did." Some had periods of serious depression. And many still found it difficult to ask for help ("It was very hard to get to the point to say, 'I need help learning to memorize things.' I wanted to be able to do it on my own") and engaged in a good deal of self-reflection and analysis to try to feel better about requesting assistance.

All of this took a toll. A number of the participants in our study sought professional counseling to reconcile some of the problems and mixed messages they encountered in their educational experiences.

The most successful young adults found the strength in college to become appropriate advocates for themselves. They learned to make use of available support services when necessary and to ask for extended test time — or to take a test in a personally less distracting setting, or extensions for assignments — without feeling self-conscious or guilty. It's unlikely, of course, that a youngster still in the earlier years of school or adolescence will have the maturity and self-awareness to accept with equanimity "being different," and then go about finding the support he needs. But the most enlightened school systems increasingly recognize the importance of early involvement of guidance counselors, teachers, or other professionals to help twice exceptional children and their parents understand the issues and develop the right kinds of support. That includes the possibility that a child's healthy emotional and social development might benefit from individual or family counseling.

PARENTS MAKING A DIFFERENCE

Getting appropriate attention for a twice exceptional child within the school system can be in large part a matter of local, state, and federal mandates and resources. But the "what works" ideas in this chapter show how parents can make vital contributions to the happier outcome:

- **Encourage a child to develop his strengths, wherever they may lie.** Most of the participants in our study had talents and abilities that were identified and nurtured by their parents at home throughout the elementary and secondary school years. They gave their kids opportunities to excel, to be successful. Out-of-school activities the young people enjoyed and were good at also often brought them into contact with peers who shared their enthusiasms, who didn't view them as "dumb" and "different."
- **Encourage home-supported dynamic learning experiences.** The kinds of independent investigative activities we've been

describing throughout this book are ideal for developing organizational and other skills in ways that are natural, comfortable, and unoppressive.

- Look for the mentor or mentors who will validate a child's
talents, and maybe open up for her a world of possibilities
outside of academic work.

STARTING FROM INTERESTS

Susan Baum — whose book *To Be Gifted and Learning Disabled,* written with Steven V. Owen, is a wonderful parent resource — described
her experiences working with several twice exceptional children who
happened to be keenly interested in building things with Lego blocks.

First, the children were taken to see the Lego Road Show, a display
of all kinds of structures designed and built by Lego engineers from
thousands of Legos. They next visited headquarters and met with one
of the engineers who explained how designs originated — a lot of creative thinking was involved, and some calculus and physics too. Most
intriguing and encouraging to the youngsters was the fact, as the engineer explained, that structures were built through experimenting
and playing around with different arrangements of the blocks.

Two boys, ten and twelve, accepted the challenge presented to
them by a Lego marketing executive: design and build original structures for the museum display the company was planning. One boy
came up with an eighteen-wheeler truck, complete with a separate
tractor and a two-foot-long trailer. Moving parts included a gate on
the trailer that could be opened and closed with a pulley. The twelve-
year-old built a three-foot-tall motorized amusement park ride in which
four miniature planes took passengers on twenty-seven revolutions
per ride.

The boys were allowed to create their projects in a resource room
at school provided they also completed their classroom assignments.

That they did, in less time and with better results than they normally exhibited.

Working on projects that interest them and completing a real product for a real audience, Baum writes, "contributes greatly to the self-esteem of the learning disabled gifted student. In the process of a real investigation, negative behaviors usually found in academic tasks seem to disappear. Long division is attempted willingly. . . . Findings are organized in some written form; spelling errors are corrected; and, in general, carelessness is replaced by attention to details in product completion. In short, learning disabled gifted students often begin to take pride in their work."

When twice exceptional children have opportunities to exercise their strengths, to do and be recognized for what they're good at, the benefits are profound. Once attention shifts from deficit reduction to talent development, children become creatively productive. They grow in self-regulation and self-confidence. They begin to find their niche, set goals that align with their gifts, and perhaps even see a future for themselves — in college and careers they would enjoy. Indeed, our research shows that the twice exceptional child starts to behave socially, emotionally, and academically more like gifted students without disabilities than like nongifted students with learning disabilities.

✳

CHAPTER 9

Performance vs. Potential

Reclaiming the "Lost Prize" Underachiever

The gifted underachiever is "one of the greatest social wastes of our culture." That statement was made by an educator over half a century ago. And today, according to a national needs assessment survey conducted by our research center, *underachievement remains the number one concern* of the professionals whose job it is to prepare a generation of children and young people for the future.

It's a complex and baffling issue. Educators do not even agree on one all-embracing meaning of the term. The simplest and most generally accepted definition of the underachiever is a child who is doing more poorly in school than would be expected. On intelligence tests, he scores in the high or superior range. He may demonstrate other characteristics of a gifted mind — curiosity, critical thinking, insight, even leadership abilities. But his school performance as measured by homework, grades, and subject tests is not in line with those capabilities and potential for academic success. Here's a shocking estimate from one of our studies: *As many as half of gifted students probably fall in the category of underachievement.*

Official efforts to reverse the pattern have not been widely successful. The educational focus typically centers on what the underachieving child isn't doing and how to make him do it. In school, young Barry may be enrolled in special classes. At home, his parents may be urging him to "just start your homework earlier," which may be a sensible tactic but not one he's likely to heed. Our research shows that "learn how to get organized" and "work harder and you will do well" messages do not produce the hoped-for results. Actually, they may discourage and alienate Barry, who then becomes further enmeshed in failure mode. For one thing, adults and child are often starting from opposing viewpoints: Parents and teachers assume that Barry *wants* to achieve. In fact, he may *not* especially want to, at least not in the ways everyone is talking about — which, at the same time, doesn't mean he feels good about himself.

But there is hardly a parenting situation more frustrating than trying to guide the smart, talented child who seems in danger of dropping off the academic map. In chapter 1, we told the story of our underachieving son, Mark, who never finished high school but whose intelligence and gifts eventually led him on to college, a brilliant career, and a happy ending. The happy ending was a long time arriving, however, and the path there was by no means smooth. For Mark, not graduating from high school was the lesser of two fates. The worse fate, in his opinion back then, was pretending to be interested in uninspiring classes taught by teachers he believed did not especially care about him.

Was he wrong about that? Or was he reacting honestly and appropriately to a dismal scene? How should we, his parents, have advised him? Should we have urged Mark to feign interest, keep up with what was required of him, and play the schoolhouse learning game? We remember being asked by several of his teachers during those difficult years why this bright kid consistently failed to complete relatively easy work. There we were, teachers and educators ourselves, and nevertheless parents who felt helpless and were made to feel responsible by these adults who were attempting to teach our "enigma" of a son.

The core of the matter is that Mark started toward his eventual happy ending once he made up his own mind that he wanted to succeed. He found the right academic program, which took a good deal of concentrated legwork, applications, and follow-through, and then he dug in. Ultimately, turning the corner of an unsuccessful early school experience was up to Mark.

If your child fits the portrait of the gifted underachiever, the power to turn things around lies in him. However, as a parent you have it in *your* power to be encouraging, and fortunately research in recent years points to some suggestions about both what doesn't seem to work very well and what *can* work in many cases to reverse a negative pattern.

"WHERE DID MY CHILD GO?"

A mother described a scene she remembered from her own youth, in her second year of high school. "There was a boy who was in several of my classes and he had a quality that was sort of dangerous or exciting. He was very smart, we all knew that, but he didn't do much work and he didn't seem to care. This one time that I recall was in a history class and he stood up and said this was all garbage, or something like that. The history teacher standing in front of the room turned bright red and told the kid to sit down. You could hear a pin drop. The boy continued to attack the teacher verbally, said who was going to make him sit down, and then he simply walked out of the room. I'd never seen anyone do that." By the end of following year, the boy had dropped out of school.

That scene and that boy had come to mind, she said, because she worried that her son was capable of similar behavior. "We have had teacher reports for two years now, starting in sixth grade, that Eric is willful, noisy, doesn't follow orders, isn't respectful. I have a terrible fear that he'll just walk out or do something really bad. His friends these days all seem to share an attitude that it's very cool to think school isn't important, the teachers are dumb." In addition to his actions in the classroom, Eric's grades were falling. Her son, she said, "doesn't seem like the same boy anymore, the boy we used to know. Where did that boy go?"

Aggressive, acting-out behaviors, according to some research, are common in some gifted underachievers. They'll talk back to the teacher, disrupt the class, come across as hostile and rebellious. They may, in a negative kind of way, be somewhat electrifying to a classroom full of young people who watch one of their own defying the norm. Other underachievers may tend to withdraw from their surroundings, appearing bored and uninterested in participating. A few go back and forth between aggressive and withdrawn behaviors.

It may not be apparent in their demeanors — recalcitrant behavior, clowning, looking bored and uncaring — but many of these young people feel down on themselves, especially if poor performance continues over a stretch of time. From the reports of professionals, teachers, and parents, we learn that such children typically suffer from low self-esteem. They perceive themselves as inadequate. And they may be highly self-critical, fearful of both failure and success. Even when they seem not to care, they can actually be anxious or nervous.

Underachievement is not difficult to spot. Obviously, school grades that are a far and dismal cry from what measures of ability indicate a child is capable of are the biggest clues that performance is not reflecting potential. The child may have many complaints about school and teachers, sometimes disliking them all. Problems frequently show up during the late elementary grades, as they did with Eric, and earlier for boys than for girls. Parents wonder, "Where did my once bright, happy child go?"

Why it is occurring is far from unclear. What to do about it is an even thornier question.

EXPLAINING UNDERACHIEVEMENT: SOME POSSIBLE CAUSES

Educators are to a large degree as baffled as parents as to why a smart youngster, perhaps one who sailed through the early elementary years as a classroom star, begins to slip. Researchers have explored a number of possible causes, including peer pressure or the influence of a rowdy crowd, self-pressure, emotional issues such as depression, a lack of internal controls, and an unwholesome or unsupportive environment that makes it difficult for the child to do well or, even, to value academic success. Certain gifted underachievers, some studies suggest, have a strong interest in an outside-of-school activity and that interest tends to keep them isolated from classmates and relatively friendless — and unhappy and distracted — during the day.

Temporary or situational underachievement is fairly common. Performance dips because of an unsympathetic teacher, or a move to a new town or new school, or passing family stresses — Dad lost a job, someone got sick. Many kids in retrospect will cite one year when the classroom atmosphere just took on a toxic tone, perhaps characterized by extreme competitiveness among students or social preoccupations. Interestingly, but maybe not surprisingly given the transition into adolescence and all that it involves, many say seventh grade was the killer, the time their academic performance noticeably went haywire. A college student — now a confident, well-adjusted girl — said seventh grade "was the worst. Aggression among the girls reached amazing heights of sheer meanness and nastiness and scapegoating. I was on the receiving end of that for a lot of the year. It's amazing that I managed to get any decent work done at all."

Not living up to potential does appear to be episodic with many young people, occurring in a certain year or only in a particular class or two. When it begins to happen consistently, over a relatively long period of time with increasing episodes, the problem is obviously a great deal more worrisome, and some research looks to the parent-child relationship for clues to understanding root causes. In this analysis, parenting styles that are either too coolly distant, indifferent, or permissive or — at the opposite extreme — too authoritarian and restrictive are both troublesome for kids. Parents who pressure their children, who are preoccupied with good grades, can inadvertently help to produce underachievement.

Occasionally parents become so overinvested in a child's success that they take command of her tasks. One teenager remembered that her mother often did her work for her: "She'd say, 'you could do this, you're plenty smart, you just don't have enough time,' and then she'd actually fill in the rest of my math problems. One year, when I was in, I think, fourth grade, she made a bunch of collages for this art project we were assigned. She told me to tell the teacher I had done them myself. I was horribly embarrassed, because the teacher was skeptical. She said, 'Well, Marianne, this is excellent, and you did this all yourself?' I said that I did. So she had to believe me, and I got a good grade. I was so ashamed." Because of such inappropriate parental involvement, Marianne believed, she "went downhill. I didn't trust that I could do anything on my own. I became very insecure about my schoolwork, and actually started to fail some things."

There is, however, no clear conclusion about exactly how parenting styles or issues interact with a child's underachievement.

More productively, we look to the school environment to understand why bright students lose their interest and drive. Minimal work may be accepted by teachers and considered perfectly satisfactory. The classroom and the school day are arranged to promote rote learning and conformity, rather than critical thinking and problem solving. Perhaps most significantly, the curriculum is unchallenging. Attempts to improve achievements across the board focus on what has been popularly called *drill and kill:* drill the basics of language arts and math, take tests to determine if everyone got it, drill some more. In these efforts to address the needs of the most disadvantaged children, and because of the ways in which policies are applied across all populations, even schools that serve the middle class are now affected by a narrow conception of what learning is all about — endless lists of standards to be covered and relentless pressure to increase test scores.

In our research, an inappropriate curriculum stands out as a major contributing factor in underachieving gifted teenagers. With colleagues, we carried out a three-year study in a large high school, comparing high-ability students who were doing well and performing as would be expected based on their intelligence with equally high-ability students who were not doing well. Our goal was to learn why these obviously talented kids were just barely getting by. The underachievers themselves believed their problems began back in early elementary school — which was "too easy," they told us. They didn't have to work, or work very hard, at daily assignments; they breezed through. Because schoolwork required so little effort from them, they failed to acquire along the way important academic skills. Work habits — such as organizing time, preparing for a test, reviewing material — and self-discipline never properly developed, neither in school nor at home. The low level of difficulty and the slow pace of learning within the regular classroom seemed to inhibit their high abilities.

In middle and high school, these youngsters encountered a tougher regime that called for more strenuous mental effort, real production, and increased homework. Breezing through wasn't easy anymore. But they did not receive opportunities to develop study skills and habits, and their weak foundation served them badly. All this, they believed, directly affected their underachieving status in high school. Like the kids with learning disabilities we talked about in the previous chapter, these young people had never adopted strategies that would help them learn. (In fact, some children with high potential do poorly in school because of undiagnosed learning disabilities. Embarrassed to admit they have trouble learning, they prefer to attribute bad grades to "boring" school or a bad teacher.)

The danger in all of these evidences of underachievement — even those produced by a seemingly temporary or situational problem — is that once the pattern starts, it can become more entrenched and difficult to reverse, in no small part because of misguided responses from both teachers and parents. Once again, the focus is on what's wrong, what the child is *not* doing, and how to fix it — the familiar story of the deficiency approach to teaching. And with perhaps mounting frustration, each "side" — home and school — looks to the other for solutions.

TRYING TO REVERSE UNDERACHIEVEMENT: OFFICIAL INTERVENTIONS

Dawn's story demonstrates a fairly common tactic in addressing the problem. Dawn had attended a relatively small school in New York City through fifth grade, where she was an outstanding student and known for her indefatigable energy and cheerfulness. Her mother said, "I remember the kindergarten teacher used to greet the kids as they arrived and said to me that Dawn came bounding off the school bus every morning with a huge smile, just full of pep and raring to go." She continued to be a popular girl who seemed to make friends with everyone. She was also a talented artist.

At the start of sixth grade, Dawn and her mother — her parents had been amicably divorced for years — moved to a town outside of the city, desirable because it was within commuting distance for the mom and was considered to have an outstanding school system. Dawn had a rocky year, largely, her parents thought, because of the adjustment to a huge student body. But her performance through the rest of middle school wasn't much better. Later she moved on to the four-year high school in their district, which also had an excellent reputation.

Dawn's increasingly chronic underachievement was noted by her teachers, and for the last two years of high school she was placed in an alternate program, an offshoot of the regular grades. "This program usually had about ten or twelve kids in it at any time," Dawn's mother said. "They met in a separate area referred to as the Annex. Two teachers were in charge, but the class seemed to run on the democratic principle. The kids could pick where they wanted to meet the next day or over the following week, so sometimes I heard from Dawn that the class was going to the park. They held several classes at the marina in town, where an instructor from the sailing school gave them talks about boats, knots, things like that. Dawn seemed to have nothing much in the way of homework. She was encouraged to use her artistic talents, and the main upshot of that was to design a very fancy web page for herself."

The end result of the whole alternate school intervention, according to this parent? "I would say that without question this program helped my daughter stay in school. Dawn graduated with some kind of degree, what they used to call in my day a *general diploma,* as opposed to an academic diploma which went to the smart kids who did well and were going on to college. As much as there are some great things about this town and the schools, there are a lot of negative influences as well. Outside of school, Dawn was hanging out with some kids who used drugs and also a couple of older dropouts. They have cars, they can get anywhere.

"Do I think the alternate program turned things around for my very smart girl? Not really, but that's probably too much to expect from a school system. She's doing better. She goes to a community college twice a week, she has a cashier's job in a discount store. But for her father and me, there's such a sad feeling that she wasted her chances. Instead of being in this little hothouse group for those years, I would loved to have seen her showing some of that energy she used to have and joining the band, gymnastics, the softball team, being around other kids who were smart and doing neat things and getting good grades."

Paul was also an underachiever. He began running into trouble toward the end of elementary school in certain subjects — mainly English and history, which didn't interest him much and called for a lot of reading, not his favorite thing. Somewhat to everyone's surprise, Paul passed the test for admission to an elite city high school. "Admission is crazy," said Paul's father, "with literally hundreds of kids competing for one slot. But it's all based on numbers. Hit the number and you're accepted, get one point lower and you're out. The test seems heavily slanted toward mathematics, and that's Paul's strength. He just aced it."

Paul's parents were elated, not least of all because they thought the new environment — the curriculum, teachers, and other students — would be exciting and demanding enough to challenge Paul to do his best work across the board. That seemed to happen the first term, when he earned straight As. Early in his second term, "he'd tuned out again," said his father. Now he didn't seem to be putting in the effort even for math. Paul and his parents had a few heated discussions. It was decided — by his parents, not him — that Paul should have some sessions with a therapist to discuss his attitudes about school. So for two months, Paul met once a week with a psychologist whom the parents had heard was "really good with teenagers." Paul was unimpressed. "This guy likes to come on like he's my buddy. He's asking me about drugs, which I have nothing to do with. Also if I'm depressed, which I'm not."

Since the therapist was pricey and no dramatic change was evident, the sessions were ended. In more talks with his parents, Paul said school wasn't that hard, he just wasn't in the mood. "He told us that eleventh grade is what counts for getting into college," his father said, "and he'll start working then, when he needs to. Maybe he's right, who knows? He's not failing anything, just not applying himself. Meanwhile, he's not doing anything else particularly constructive, just listening to his music and fooling around on the computer." But he and Paul's mother were "feeling out-maneuvered. You can't make a kid do something if he won't."

These parents' impressions of uncertainty, or lack of consensus, about the efficacy of the two standard approaches to helping gifted underachievers are reflected among professionals as well. Instructional interventions often look like Dawn's experience — a separate classroom with few students and a greater teacher-to-student ratio; less conventional activities and teaching methods; young people offered some freedom of choice about how the class proceeds. Counseling interventions may be meetings between a child and one therapist or a team of professionals assembled by the school, or may include family members, or may involve several at-risk children together. Specific counseling strategies try to explore and change some of the causes contributing to poor performance, help a youngster decide whether or not succeeding in school is a desirable goal, and then discuss how to change counterproductive habits.

The verdict is still out on whether or not these efforts are effective. And of course, alternate classes and guidance counselors or therapists are not all created equal in terms of quality. Many professionals now believe that some interventions will produce immediate desirable results — Dawn's mother may have been right that the alternate program kept her daughter in school — but show little long-term success.

WHAT WORKS (OR HELPS) TO PREVENT OR REVERSE UNDERACHIEVEMENT

Reclaiming a "lost prize" gifted underachiever — how do you do it? As the discussion so far indicates, there is no guaranteed formula because of the many different reasons that children underachieve. To a large extent, the reclaiming is up to the young person himself.

Marina, a graduate student working for a doctorate in clinical psychology, told this story: "I was such a slacker. I was recently looking through a box where my mom keeps all my old elementary school report cards and records. The teachers wrote their comments. Here are some of them:

> 'With a little more application, Marina could do much better; with a bit more attention to the details in her work, she would do very well indeed.'
>
> 'Marina tests very quickly. I'd like to see her spend more time rereading and editing her work. Her work often contains errors that could be fixed if she did proofread more carefully.'
>
> 'Marina fell behind mostly because of badly done homework. As she develops better reviewing skills and more attention to homework, she will do better.'
>
> 'Marina has very creative ideas that are not always fully developed in her papers and assignments. She has a habit of turning her work in late because she says she left it at home.'
>
> 'Marina is doing acceptably well. It remains for her to focus attention, while reviewing at home on a regular basis (a must at this point).'

"Well, they go on in that vein. My poor parents! They did their best, but not much changed. I went away to college, and one day midway through my first semester I was sitting by myself on the steps outside the student center and I suddenly thought, 'This is my education. This is it. It's up to me.' I have no idea why this dawned on me just then, but from that day, I started working. I graduated cum laude and Phi Beta Kappa."

Dawning — the lightbulb switching on — is not uncommon. Maybe often it's synergy, with emotional maturation, greater independence, a new environment coming together to reorient a mind-set. Which is not to say that the parent of an academically drifting youngster might as well just wait it out and hope for the best. Our research findings and those of other professionals underscore several factors that play a role in this whole matter of gifted young people who aren't performing according to their potential, and these are factors parents can influence throughout a child's early education.

- *Studies should be enjoyable and challenging, at least a lot of the time, from the earliest school years.* **Since the beginnings of underachievement often appear in elementary school, that's the time to pay attention to possible causes, including work that is too easy for a high-ability youngster. The child who can breeze through is clearly in danger of being bored *and* of failing to acquire good work habits, or learning how to learn. But in addition, some researchers believe that not putting out effort can actually affect a child's mental ability, causing it to decline over time.**

In the following chapter about parents working with schools, we talk further about a critical component of our enrichment approaches — curriculum compacting. Simply put, the child who demonstrates that he can do simple addition problems with ease should not be required to continue filling out pages and pages of simple addition problems. Our own research has shown that up to *50 percent of the regular curriculum for high-achieving students can be eliminated* without causing declines in their test scores. But little effort is made to get the standard stuff off the backs of those students who have already mastered, or could quickly and easily master, the material. Even in "good" schools, with well-established enrichment programs, the mismatch between gifted youth and the curriculum they are forced to follow most of the time is nothing short of a tragedy. We know that gifted underachievers can respond extremely well when offered appropriate educational opportunities. Of course, curriculum compacting relates to school procedures, but parents can voice concerns and offer tactful suggestions regarding their child.

At the same time, helping a young gifted child develop regular patterns of work and practice seems to be highly beneficial. A clearly defined schedule (which can be flexible) of school time, a piano or dance lesson once a week, twenty minutes of piano practice each evening, homework time, and quiet private reading time before bed will help a child get used to organizing his day and his efforts.

- *The peer group matters.* **Several of the parents who talked about their underachieving children expressed concerns about the company they were keeping. Those are legitimate concerns. Hanging out with kids who "have the attitude that it's cool to think school isn't important" is not good. Being with a group of friends who take school seriously can make a huge difference.**

In our study of high-ability high school students, we discovered that if a previously good student — one who'd been doing well the previous year or semester — began to slide, he could be supported by a network of high-achieving peers who refused to let their friend falter. To these students, achievement was like walking up a crowded staircase. If one started to do poorly and tried to turn and walk down the staircase, other students pushed him back in the right direction. That might have meant studying for a test together, sharing class notes, picking him up at home to leave for school together, insisting they put off going to the mall or a party until work was finished, and otherwise sticking to the program.

For some kids, underachieving seems to be a way to gain popularity, to fit in with the "cool" crowd. In one study, an eighth grader and her friends were proud of their negative attitude toward school. When this extremely bright girl, at the suggestion of her teacher and school counselor, began spending time in the enrichment resource room and gradually became intensely involved in an environmental project with other girls, her self-perception changed and her grades began to pull up. The new peer group valued academic achievement and admired her for her contributions to the project. She got attention and popularity in another, better way.

You can't pick your child's friends for him. But there's usually a lot of opportunity, especially during the elementary and even middle school years, for parents to encourage "good" peer connections — through arranging playdates, coaching a team, or making one's home a welcoming and inviting place for kids to gather.

- **Extracurricular activities make a positive difference. Much research suggests that young people who are involved in clubs, plays or musical productions, 4-H programs, science fairs, sports, and so on are less likely to underachieve in school. These activities take commitment and time. By having too much time on his hands, a child is more apt to develop poor self-regulation strategies.**

But these kinds of activities are significantly different from what happens in the formal classroom; they operate by a different set of rules. The major goal is to produce a high-quality product or service. There are no tests and grades. The adult leaders tend to be more like guides and compatriots than teachers. Consequently, a qualitatively different kind of relationship develops between the young people and the adults. For the youngster who is resisting or rejecting the importance of tests, grades, teachers, and schoolwork, this can feel like a breath of fresh air.

- **Using his strengths and interests empowers a child to do better. The higher-end learning projects we've been describ-**

ing in this book are invariably fun for kids. Their attention is engaged. They're inspired to stretch themselves and do well at what they've chosen to do. Of great relevance to this argument about the "lost prize" in school, child-centered approaches that emphasize personal strengths and value personal interests help to turn the tide from academic failure toward academic success.

In a study focused on our enrichment models, seventeen students with high potential and low performance were encouraged to develop projects based on their individual strengths and interests. Over the course of a year or more, these youngsters — ranging in age from eight to thirteen — worked separately on various ambitious activities, including doing set designs for drama club, teaching a computer class, creating a series of relief and topographic maps, constructing a planetarium, and building a rocket for actual launch.

The most compelling finding of the study was that involvement in creative productivity reversed the cycle of underachievement. Fourteen of those students improved during that year and the following. One boy, an eighth grader, had been receiving Cs and Ds in seventh grade. Following up on his interest in science and technology subjects, an enrichment specialist helped him pursue a current passion, solar-powered vehicles. Over the course of many weeks, the boy and the specialist, helped by an outside expert in the community, met daily to design and construct a model solar-powered car to enter in a contest. The project was completed. The boy demonstrated a renewed sense of purpose. By tenth grade, he was earning As and Bs.

Just as revealing as those accomplishments were the attitude and actions of the successful teachers who steered the kids throughout the process. These teachers typically ignored the fact that their students were underachievers and focused on helping them develop their original investigations. They provided resources and made suggestions when a project seemed to be stuck, without assuming control. They "got" the idea that a child's work should have a real-world purpose and a real-world audience, rather than being something to be graded and taken home. And they had faith! When a child became discouraged and felt he was getting nowhere, a teacher demonstrated belief and patience — and, eventually, shared in the excitement of the student's achievement.

- *Many children want to feel useful in the world.*

Justin, a very smart ten-year-old who was getting mediocre grades, was asked by his parents if a problem existed and if there was anything they could do about it. The problem, he told them, was that school was "childish." They pointed out that since he *was* a child, perhaps that was unavoidable. Anyway, Justin said, he thought it would be more interesting being a grownup and "doing real stuff."

Following our Interest-a-Lyzer model, his mother engaged him in some lively conversations. There were a number of activities that interested him, mostly having to do with sports, nature, and the outdoors, but what Justin really wanted was money. He wasn't talking about an increase in his weekly allowance. "I want to make my own money," he said, "and I'll use it to save the trees." He was referring to vanishing rain forests, an issue he'd been studying and worrying about.

This started the family on a yearlong series of activities, which included helping Justin set up a small business trading and selling sports memorabilia along with researching environmental conservation organizations to find appropriate ones for his involvement. He raised a good sum of money to donate to his cause and also came in contact with a number of activists who inspired him further. "He was so excited about this," his mother said, "and it absolutely carried over. He started doing a lot better in school. I think he just saw himself now as a capable person, a person who could do something important."

Many youngsters, like Justin, need to feel usefully challenged. This, in fact, may be the most positive contribution a concerned parent can make: allow a child to put his gifted assets to work toward a socially constructive goal, the opportunity to act as a change agent and do "real stuff" in the world outside the classroom.

※

CHAPTER 10

Cooperative Alliances

Partnering with Teachers and Schools

O ur work has convinced us that the best way to develop gifts and talents in young people is to provide them with what we call *ORE* — Opportunities, Resources, and Encouragement — within areas of self-selected interests. Our book has, thus far, focused largely on ORE-on-the-home-front, or the ways parents can support a youngster's higher-end learning and creative-productive activities. At the interface of home and school it's not always so clear when and how parents can be just as effective and participatory.

The mother of a son and daughter in elementary and middle school shared these reflections that may sound familiar: "I meet with my children's teachers twice a year. We go over their test grades, their workbooks. We talk about what the kids are doing well, what needs improvement. I hope I'm not going to hear anything too terrible, and I don't. My kids are pretty good all-around students. There haven't been any red flags."

She was pleased about the good reports, but not entirely pleased about her children's experience. "I have no complaints about their teachers. They do a good job and it's a hard job. But maybe because my kids are presenting no problems, doing okay, their teachers' involvement stops there. I don't know how much personal attention my children get. I don't know if they're being challenged. I want the best education for them, but I feel kind of disconnected from what happens in this huge area of their lives, other than that I review their homework every day and show up for those couple of meetings a year. It sometimes seems that the school and I are kind of on opposite sides of the fence."

The truth is, school and parents are not really on opposite sides of any fence. The vast majority of teachers teach because they want to make a positive difference in the lives of young people. But what does happen so often is that the school and the parent are running on parallel tracks, both hoping and striving in their separate worlds to give a child "the best education."

Parents do want to play a role. And how to involve them meaningfully in the school system has, of course, been the subject of much discussion and many plans and programs — some targeted to special needs populations, some working well, some a source of contention. To bring the issue down to the personal and the particular, to the singular child, we would start by asking: What are the very best things you know about this young person? What are her strengths? How can they be coaxed out and built up within a classroom ideally designed to pay at least as much attention to encouraging what's "right" as to fixing what's "wrong"? And what can you, the parents, do to help make that happen?

Every involved parent can answer the first two questions about her child. The answers to the last two are tougher, but in the course of introducing enrichment programs in schools throughout the country we have learned that parents absolutely can be integrated in lively and dynamic ways, rather than simply being summoned twice a year for progress reports.

So this chapter is about forging a cooperative alliance, home and school, parent and teachers. Some of the suggestions we present may sound as if they will require time and effort. They will — but a manageable amount of each. And some may give you a new idea or two about how your own talents and strengths — as an interesting, informed human being, not just a parent — can be put to good use in this "huge area" of your child's life, the daily classroom.

ROOTING OUT REPETITION

As young teachers of mathematics and science years ago, we were assigned to teach highly heterogeneous classes, especially in math. Everybody's equal, was the thinking. Consequently, in the same room were children who literally could not add or subtract and a few others who probably could solve calculus problems better than we could. In an effort to do something about this alarming discrepancy, we instituted the practice of allowing students to work backward up the workbook page, if they so chose. (Typically, problems become more difficult as one moves down the page.) So if a youngster started on and completed the last row, then came up to the front desk and checked his answers and the answers were all correct, that student was finished with math for the day.

We later extended the process to science classes. In that school, students shared textbooks. One day, a boy turned his book in two or three days before it was scheduled to be passed along to another youngster in another section. "You finished the chapter already?" we asked. "No," he said, "I finished the whole book. Go ahead, ask me anything." So we put our minds to dreaming up some special projects to which he could apply himself, almost as a defense mechanism on our part: we realized intuitively that if we were not able to point him in the direction of an intriguing and engaging activity, we would be embarrassed to teach a child who in fact already knew what we were teaching.

All this evolved into what we later called *curriculum compacting.* The know-how or the sophistication to take pen in hand and start writing about these ideas came later, after advanced degrees and all that goes along on a road toward defined scholarship and supportive research. But the core discovery remains: the biggest frustration for so many children in school is being required to plow through material they have already mastered, or could easily master quickly, and thus buy time for more creative endeavors. We still, in this day and age, see whole-group instruction in the majority of classrooms we visit across the country. But to suggest that a child does not actually need to go through half the workbook or textbook, that he can skip the things he already knows, that's radical.

We remember working once with a class at one of our local Connecticut schools. Both the classroom teacher and the principal joined in the discussion regarding one child's progress through a spelling workbook. We all agreed Susie knew the material and didn't really need to fill in the many pages in question, and the principal then and there tore them out. That work was already completed. After our session, the principal retrieved the torn pages from the trash basket, folded them up, and took them away with her — because she suspected the teacher would pull them out later and still use them with this youngster! Here was an example of a principal getting into the act and doing the right thing. Her teacher, she thought, might not have been quite as enlightened.

Candidates for compacting are usually found by means of a test administered to the whole class in a particular subject such as reading, spelling, mathematics, or writing. Those who can comfortably skip material that will be covered over the following few weeks may be offered the option of doing independent reading or spending time in the enrichment center. Or they may stay, quietly, in the classroom working on a project of their choosing. Of course, this presents a time-consuming, difficult challenge for a classroom teacher who has, perhaps, twenty students to attend to and the regular curriculum to cover. Some schools have been successful at compacting curriculum for selected students by asking volunteer parents or community mentors to come in for brief periods to help youngsters pursue independent studies.

Care is taken, or should be taken, to provide a child with appropriately challenging substitutes that are in some area that engages his interest. Just offering a youngster who's good in math — but perhaps not especially in love with the subject — a sheet of harder math problems may give him the idea that he might as well not get his work finished so speedily. In curriculum compacting we're saying to a child, we realize that going through drill-and-kill exercises on material you have already got down pat is boring and turning you off. And we respect your advanced abilities and care about you enough that we're willing to provide you with time to pursue more interesting and meaningful things.

Not all schools or teachers are willing or able to get on board with this concept. Maybe you are aware that your child is spending a lot of class time on repetitive work with no gain to his learning. Maybe you observe that he is required to complete pages of homework every evening and for the most part it's routine and tedious stuff. (The amount of time kids spend on homework has increased 51 percent from a generation ago. According to recent research, however, there is almost no correlation between homework and achievement during the elementary years. In high school, more than two hours of homework a day actually was associated with *lower* scores on standardized tests.)

It's worth discussing the possibility — at the parent/teacher conference or even in unscheduled contact with the teacher — that substitute work might be put in place for a while. Is your child currently caught up in a fascination with how the ancient pyramids were built? Could he bring a book on that subject and be allowed to read quietly until the class moves on to the next study set? Is there some way to reduce the assigned homework on material he already knows? These are legitimate issues to raise.

CHALLENGING THE ACCEPTED WISDOM

A talented, able child can get placed on a track for slow learners because of one or another of the difficulties we've discussed. And she might be unable to get off that track from year to year. Parents can speak up.

For example, Frank was a boy who had trouble with reading. By the end of seventh grade he was still reading two years below his grade level. Frank was also a creatively productive child when left to his own devices; over a summer he became intrigued with the abstract concepts of geometry. That fall, his parents insisted he be put in the math class offered to the brightest students in eighth grade. They were met with resistance. But school officials did reluctantly consent and Frank not only did excellent work in math but made the honor roll that year. These parents challenged the official belief that because their son was not a top-notch reader he was not capable of top-notch learning in other areas.

Speaking up isn't necessarily easy or pleasant. It might feel a little like bearding the lion in his own den, as you're making suggestions about a child's path that educators claim as their territory. But though some educators do rely on measures of achievement across all content areas when deciding where a child will be placed, many others make truly concerted efforts to take into account a child's interests and unique strengths.

TOOTING A LITTLE HORN FOR A CHILD'S TALENTS

Young people don't necessarily let themselves be known in school for what they're good at or what they love. And in school, nobody asks. In chapter 1, we told the story of Ross, a boy with a passion for railroads who was doing poorly in his subjects — in fact, he was falling asleep regularly at his desk! When given the opportunity to "do something" about his passion, he immediately had a plan, which was to produce a video about the rail system in his town, and he came to life. Not only did he accomplish his specific goal, he pulled up his grades in all areas. But before that time his teachers and counselors had no awareness of his enthusiasm or his ability to be creatively productive. As Ross told us, "No one ever asked me what I like to do."

A scheduled parent-teacher conference or an open house evening can be an excellent opportunity to mention that your child reads everything he can about the stock market. Or that he's built a replica of a nineteenth-century printing press. Or that your preteen organizes imaginative birthday parties for youngsters in the neighborhood.

One parent said that her son and two of his friends had become skilled jugglers and provided entertainment at little kids' parties. They were such a hit that word spread in the community and they were often booked weeks in advance, earning some nice pocket money. When asked if his school was aware of her son's alternate life as a juggler, this mother said she didn't think he had brought it up there, and she herself had not: "It's not an academic thing. It doesn't have anything to do with his schoolwork, and the kids do it mostly for fun."

Mentioning his juggling talents and entertainment business to his teacher wouldn't necessarily lead to his being invited to perform in the school assembly. But knowing about them might help shed a new, improved light on his student. Here was a boy who had a serious interest, who obviously was capable of a high level of task commitment in learning difficult skills, who demonstrated leadership and determination by using his talents to bring enjoyment to other people, and who made a little spending money for himself and his friends. Here was a creatively productive boy.

THE PARENT AS ENRICHMENT FACILITATOR

Our Schoolwide Enrichment Model promotes the concept of *enrichment clusters*. Several of the projects we have described here in earlier chapters — the youngsters of the Environmentally Friendly Construction Company who built birdhouses, for example — were developed in an enrichment cluster at school. A cluster bears some similarity to the chess club, the chemistry club, or those other post–3 p.m. groups some of us remember joining in our school days. But there are significant differences. Enrichment clusters have students creating an end product or service, or several, depending on the style and expression preferences of the kids. In one cluster on puppetry, for example, some students became puppeteers and developed a traveling show; others chose to teach the art of puppetry and making puppets to primary students; and yet another group published a book that chronicled the history of puppets. Throughout, there was a focus on creating a professional level of work.

A cluster usually gets going with a teacher finding out what students would like to learn through a simple survey (asking kids to select ten topics they might like to explore from a list of the general areas of science, social studies, art, and so on) or through a more in-depth assessment procedure such as the Interest-a-Lyzer. They might also be asked about their favorite after-school activities. Upon compiling this information, it may come to light that a group of children would love to explore what causes hurricanes or they'd like to create a TV show. Those who share this interest will meet each week in a regularly scheduled block of time, usually at least one hour, to pursue a creative, challenging, enjoyable project that involves authentic learning applied to real-world problems and real-world audiences. A cluster typically lasts for eight to ten weeks. In a number of schools across the country, educators have found a way to squeeze out enough time for such student-driven learning.

Who will guide them?

In programs based on our models, the first and most obvious candidates are discovered among teachers and other staff members. And in fact, some enrichment clusters have formed when teachers reveal their own outside enthusiasms. One teacher mentioned that she enjoyed playing in a handbell choir at her church; she teamed up with the school nurse and the choir director to create the Chimers: A Handbell Choir. Other staff members may get in the game. In one school, a secretary, an award-winning watercolor painter, organized Young Artists. In another, middle school students learned how their building worked — by studying blueprints and engineering diagrams and using resource materials from the fields of architecture, heating and ventilation, and landscape planning — under the guidance of the school custodian.

Often, however, there are interest areas that cannot be comfortably supported by a teacher or staff member. Parent volunteers can step in.

Schools that institute enrichment clusters typically reach out to possible parent-volunteer facilitators by sending letters home with an invitation to join the program or contacting them through PTA groups or phone calls. Often, parents are given a list of students' ideas or interests to choose from. One mother said she thought the program was a great idea, she'd like to be involved, but didn't think she had any particularly useful talents. But the list of student interests she received noted a number of kids who enjoyed math games and puzzles. A puzzle enthusiast and a math lover herself, she was inspired to develop the Mathematics and Puzzle Guild. The participants explored different types of games they could create and, with this mother's help, developed their own puzzle books and board games that were then given to teachers to use in enrichment centers in their classrooms.

If your child's school does not have enrichment clusters, can you raise the issue? Could you perhaps take a leading role in locating other parents or community members who might join in? There are various ways to set up a cluster. Sometimes a parent will not be the main facilitator but will be willing and available to play a support role — helping in the classroom during cluster time each week, serving as a guest speaker, making phone calls, providing transportation. For inspiration and to illustrate the great diversity and liveliness of the possibilities, we have listed in the box below a number of clusters that schools and parents have developed. In almost all of these examples, appropriate outlets — those real-world audiences — for student products were discovered. You might also enjoy checking out our SEM Web site (www.gifted.uconn/sem), where you will find a link (www.gifted.uconn.edu/clusters) to our enrichment cluster database.

Parents who elect to take part in these student-driven, project-oriented learning situations are usually excited and energized by what they see going on. One parent talked about her involvement in her child's school and drew a comparison with an experience from her own youth: "When I was in high school, my mother, who did some semi-professional acting, organized a show for the students. It was called *Circus Daze,* the rough theme being that there were a series of performances by different kids. It was a pretty ragtag affair, with one kid coming out on the stage and doing a tumbling act, one kid doing a ballet dance, a couple of boys who did a kind of Marx Brothers slapstick skit. The stage was decorated to look like a circus tent. My grandfather, a commercial illustrator, painted large, cartoonlike posters of a clown, an acrobat, and so on to hang around the stage. My mom got lots of other people involved. She was the director, one boy's father was the master of ceremonies. Somebody else's father printed up programs, and the big show was put on one Friday evening in the school auditorium. The band teacher volunteered his time and got a few of the band kids to join up, so we had this kind of brassy music in between every act.

"It wasn't exactly what you'd call a polished production! But I remember this was huge fun, with a lot of my friends and their parents taking part."

As a parent now herself, her activities at her child's school felt more pro forma and less interesting. "The school does encourage parents to participate. I've been along on some field trips. There's a once-a-year holiday fair organized by the parents' organization where we sell things to raise money for the school. Part of this has involved going around soliciting contributions from stores and services in the community, so for example we'll have a free dinner at a nice restaurant to offer in the auction part of the fair. One year I ran the plant booth, where we sold poinsettias donated by a local plant nursery."

She believed these efforts were unquestionably worthwhile, though

A Few Very Neat Enrichment Projects

These are just some of the enrichment clusters, their titles and descriptions, that have taken place in schools involved in our research studies on the Schoolwide Enrichment Model.

The Poets' Workshop

What is it like to be a poet? Explore the poetry of some of America's greatest poets, including Robert Frost, Langston Hughes, Emily Dickinson, and others. Write, illustrate, and perform original poems or interpret others' work.

Voices from Olympus

Step back into the lives of an ancient civilization and explore the world of the ancient Greeks. Was the world held on the shoulders of a giant? Did monsters lurk in the depths of a maze? Was the world controlled from a mountaintop?

Invention Convention

Are you an inventive thinker? Would you like to be? Come to this cluster to brainstorm a problem, try to identify many solutions, and design an invention to solve the problem. You may share your final product at the Young Inventors Fair, a statewide, daylong celebration of creativity.

Printing with Panache

Explore printmaking by creating your own print blocks. Use different printing techniques, such as the "rainbow roll," to create your own art. Take a look at early printmaking techniques, body prints, vegetable prints, and monoprints.

personally they were vaguely unsatisfying. They had the feel of "busy-work." She said, "I'd like to get involved in a more substantial way and more directly with the kids." Bitten with a little theatrical bug herself, she was exploring the possibility of organizing a show with her daughter and friends — *Circus Daze* revisited.

Children's Rights' Institute

"That's not fair!" Have these words ever come out of your mouth? What is the difference between whining and real problems? Explore laws that define how you live and how they may be different from the laws that determine how other kids live. Develop a plan for action.

Survey Said . . .

Do you want to find out what people think about things? Survey your friends, your family, or the community about something you want to know: How much TV should kids be allowed to watch? Does the town need a new park? Organize their responses in a creative way. Decide how to share this information.

Video Production

Become a moviemaker and produce a video for a box office audience. Show your creativity and moviemaking talents through the camera lens and on the big screen. Learn the tricks and techniques of the trade while developing your movie.

Cultural Stompers Institute

Design an interactive process to showcase cultural diversity and rhythmic stomping movements. You can use your skills to design costumes or develop different and unique steps. Create community performances, workshops, and more.

CALLING ALL VOLUNTEERS

A number of schools have successfully established Enrichment Committees. Here's how it works: A small group of individuals — one or two parents, one or two teachers, perhaps an enrichment specialist or a librarian, and even one or two students — meets to brainstorm and work toward bringing a class or a selected group of youngsters in contact with dynamic community resources. The Enrichment Committee arranges for a speaker, a demonstration, an artistic performance, or other activities. It asks, what professionals do we know who can convey the passion they feel for their work? A veterinarian, a designer of theater sets, or a choreographer — any of them can explain the real-world problems they focus on and the real-world methods they use to solve them. The goal is to expose young people to a subject or area of learning that is outside or above and beyond the regular curriculum and that is based on their expressed interests.

Such a unique individual might be invited to give a one-time talk to students, something more than the "career day" or "show and tell" presentation with which many kids have become familiar. There is nothing *wrong* with show and tell, but to light up youngsters' minds, visiting speakers should be those "turned-on" professionals who can convey the excitement of a field and who can show kids how to do things by sharing high-level methods of inquiry.

This individual may be invited into the enrichment cluster program as a facilitator. Volunteering to facilitate a cluster is often a win-win situation for both parties. In one of our pilot sites, a local park provided a biologist to facilitate a cluster on forest and wildlife biology. The students gained the benefit of firsthand experience with a wildlife biologist and the resources and materials he brought, while the park benefited from the chance to set up some youth programs.

Sometimes, this person may be willing to act as a mentor, working on a systematic basis with one or more kids who want to pursue an interest at a semiprofessional level. The mentor performs the roles of adviser, consultant, specialist, and critic, seeing the student through to the achievement of her goals and objectives.

Almost surely, you live in a community rich with adult "talent" and experience, men and women with vocations and avocations that young people would like to hear about. Many of these talented, experienced adults would likely be delighted to be invited to contribute to a school's enrichment project. (We can say that with some confidence based on our own success rate: For every ten phone calls we have made extending such an invitation, nine people have graciously and enthusiastically volunteered their services. Many have agreed to return time and time again after talking to groups of obviously attentive and interested students.)

If you volunteer to ferret out other volunteers, you will likely recognize a huge untapped resource of options. Public agencies, youth services staff, police precincts, fire departments, local businesses, local universities, senior centers, community theater groups, neighborhood newspapers, and professional and service organizations, leagues, and clubs — all of these groups and many more may have people willing to become involved in a good educational cause.

Then there are all those other parents in your child's school, probably 95 percent of whom you know nothing about. Program leaders in some of our enrichment pilot projects have sent out blanket surveys — such as the Community Talent Miner questionnaire on pages 273–274 — to learn more about the parent population and extend a general invitation to contribute time, know-how, and enthusiasm for the good of the children.

As educational institutions ideally provide students with ORE — Opportunities, Resources, and Encouragement — within areas of self-selected interests, parents can also be involved. They *should* be involved. They *must* be, not only so that one child receives the "best education," but so that schools become the best they can be. When parents and teachers work together, students will be successful, schools will be successful, and the well-being of the nation as a whole will improve.

Over the previous chapters, we have outlined many ways to help your youngster build on her strengths and talents. These strategies all derive from a few simple but powerful ideas:

- **Each child learns in her own way. And the best, most motivationally rich learning opportunities take into account a child's unique abilities, interests, and styles.**
- **Learning is more effective when kids enjoy what they're doing and feel passionate about it. Enjoyment — having fun, getting excited and carried away by the process — is a goal as important as any other.**
- **Knowledge and thinking skills are greatly enhanced when a child applies her efforts to a real and present problem, a "something" that is personally meaningful and important.**

Among the benefits your child will derive from involvement in such higher-end learning experiences, this is perhaps the best of all: She will grow in the self-confidence and self-knowledge that will propel her into a happy, healthy, successful life.

Afterword

The good we secure for ourselves is precarious and uncertain until it is secured for all of us and incorporated into our common life.

—Jane Addams

This book has centered on the personal and the individual, on what your child needs and how you can help provide it. We'll end with an observation on the broader scale of what society needs.

Perhaps more than ever, we must bring up children who in time will be committed to making the lives of all people more rewarding, more joyful, environmentally safe, peaceful, and politically free. We need creatively productive young people who will become the adults who change things for the better, who make positive contributions to the sciences, arts, and humanities. And so we need to think about what we can provide today for those children who will shape both the values and the actions of this new century.

It is intriguing to realize that the men and women who will be future political leaders and corporate CEOs — and perhaps a Ludwig van Beethoven, a Louis Pasteur, or a Georgia O'Keeffe — are the boys and girls in our classrooms today. If we are not conscious of ways to help our children pursue their creative productivity, we must consider the consequences — the great American novel not written, the poem not conceived, the cure not developed, and the war not averted.

It starts early, with the kinds of enlightened attention we've been advocating — in the school, in the home — to help children believe in their strengths and value their unique selves.

✳

Renzulli's Best Resources

On the following pages, you will find the names and descriptions of a slew of how-to books, Web sites, and contests and competitions that are ideal for youngsters who are digging into topics that intrigue them. We call them *Renzulli's Best* because we have used them, we like them, and we have watched them light up young minds and give kids hours of enjoyment along with higher-end learning. In fact, they are really just the tip of a very large iceberg, the literally thousands of excellent resources available with a trip to the library or bookstore or a click of the computer mouse. For example, the Web sites named here were chosen from more than 35,000 sites accessible through Renzulli Learning (www.renzullilearning.com), our online interactive learning program that is used by many schools. The program is now available for individual purchase for use in the home and can be accessed through a separate Web site (www.renzullihome.com/home/splash.aspx).

Where possible, we have included general age categories, but *general* is the operative word. Youngsters who become deeply engaged in an area of study or a project are often capable of going above and beyond the abilities suggested by their age or grade level in school. Interest and excitement can propel a child to read additional — and more difficult — materials, or to follow through on more complicated virtual online investigations, than might be expected.

Our mentors-in-print are arranged by subject category. Web sites and contests are listed more randomly, as these resources often cross borders into various activities and enthusiasms.

Of course, any such listings are subject to change. As of this writing, all Web sites and contests are active. All how-to books are available; most can be purchased through Creative Learning Press (www .creativelearningpress.com).

You and your child can look over these lists and see what sounds appealing, appropriate, and worth checking out. There is, indeed, something for everyone in this wide world of knowledge and creative exploration.

RENZULLI'S BEST MENTORS-IN-PRINT

Art

- **American Folk Art for Kids**
  by Richard Panchyk
  (grade level: 4–12)

"Folk art is all about taking something ordinary and making it extraordinary," says Panchyk. Twenty-one activities show youngsters how to put their imaginations together with everyday items — bottle caps, gum wrappers, glass, wood — to create something beautiful. Projects include making a rag doll, painting a folk portrait, designing a trade sign, and creating a button collage. Engaging text on the development of folk art in America and full-color photographs draw youngsters into the history of everyday America made extraordinary.

- **Awesome Alphabets**
  by Mike Artell
  (grade level: K–6)

Although there are plenty of interesting computer fonts, hand lettering is always unique and can be molded to fit particular needs, convey moods, and add humor. This book is written especially for young authors and illustrators creating their own books, posters, banners, or signs, providing guidance and inspiration for making all sorts of fanciful alphabets. Suggestions for how and where to use particular alphabets are also included.

- **Classroom Cartooning**
  by Mike Artell
  (grade level: 1–8)

Even the artistically challenged can learn how to draw people, animals, and holiday items with this collection of step-by-step instructions and illustrations. Activities and puzzles are interspersed throughout.

- **Drawing Cartoons**
  by Anna Milbourne
  (grade level: 2–8)

Packed with lively ideas and examples, the book gives kids the tools they need to develop great cartoons. Step-by-step instructions and illustrations show how to create characters, make bodies move, add dramatic lighting, activate superheroes, animate a flip book, and more. Throughout are links to Web sites that provide additional examples, tips, and ideas.

- **The Elements of Pop-Up**
  by David A. Carter and James Diaz
  (grade level: 3–12)

This fun book covers all the techniques used in making pop-up books and cards — parallel folds, angle folds, wheels, and pull tabs. There's also a working example of each technique and a history of this fascinating process.

- **Making Masks**
  by Renee Schwarz
  (grade level: 2–5)

Let your child step into character by donning an eye-catching mask: thirteen unique projects invite youngsters to turn themselves into grumpy gargoyles, jolly jesters, ferocious fish, lonely aliens, and more. Each project uses easy-to-find materials and includes illustrated step-by-step instructions.

- **Origami Activities**
  by Michael G. LaFosse
  (grade level: 3–8)

With instructions on cutting paper to size as well as explanations of each kind of fold, LaFosse makes origami truly kid-friendly. Each of the fifteen projects (Chinese good luck bat, lotus blossom, dollar bill dragon, and more) includes a brief explanation of what the project symbolizes and clear step-by-step instructions and diagrams.

- **Origami Animals**
  by Michael G. LaFosse
  (grade level: 4–12)

Forty-five easy-to-follow projects show young artists how to make a zoo full of animals, from jumping frogs and cobras to penguins and skunks. Also included are ninety-eight sheets of paper to start students off.

- **Storybook Art**
  by MaryAnn F. Kohl and Jean Potter
  (grade level: K–6)

Using great picture book art and artists as inspiration, Kohl and Potter offer a hundred engaging activities. Each activity introduces a picture book illustrator (Eric Carle, Chris Van Allsburg, Shel Silverstein, Tomie dePaola, and others) and technique, lists step-by-step instructions, and provides variations for kids who would like to do more.

Artwork produced by children ages five through twelve is featured throughout.

- **Using Color in Your Art**
  by Sandi Henry
  (grade level: 2–5)

Finally, a book for children that explains how to use color to express ideas and emotions in art. Thirty-six easy-to-follow projects explore the color wheel, warm and cool colors, complementary colors, color values, neutral colors, and intermediate and analogous colors. Clear explanations of techniques are illustrated with student artwork, and quotes from famous artists explain how and why they used color in their work. Henry also suggests paintings to look at, questions to ponder, and additional ideas for projects.

Drama

- **Break a Leg!**
  by Lise Friedman
  (grade level: 4–8)

Young performers learn warm-ups, stretches, and breathing exercises to hone body and voice; discover theater games and improvisations; and develop essential skills like clowning. There's information about costumes and makeup; a backstage tour of props, drops, pits, and rigging; plus advice on going professional.

- **Let's Put on a Show!**
  by Adrea Gibbs
  (grade level: 2–6)

From drafting and script to final curtain, Gibbs shows youngsters all aspects of play production. Written for young children, the book covers playwriting, casting, acting, set design, lighting, costume design, and more. Step-by-step instructions and simple drawings show children how to set up a stage, construct props, make costumes, and apply makeup. A glossary lists all the important theater terms.

- **Make Your Own Puppets & Puppet Theaters**
  by Carolyn Carreiro
  (grade level: 4–6)

Thirty-three puppet projects, three theaters to create, and tips on puppet operation, scripting a show, setting the scene, and lighting, sound, and special effects keep young puppeteers busy bringing stories to life. Using easy-to-find materials and following step-by-step instructions, youngsters can make paper puppets, stick puppets, painted-hand puppets, shadow puppets, and more.

- **On Stage**
  by Lisa Bany-Winters
  (grade level: 1–6)

Young thespians learn by doing as they construct props, design sets, and act in and direct plays. The book offers activities; ideas for improvisational games; ready-to-use monologues, scenes, and short plays; instructions for making props; and more. Most activities require only an imagination and a few household materials.

Social Studies, History, Explorations

- **Ancient Greece**
  by Avery Hart and Paul Mantell
  (grade level: 2–6)

Travel back in time to ancient Greece and hold a pentathlon, participate in a symposium with Socrates, write an epic poem, and create a Greek sculpture. Probing questions prod children to think about slavery, language, the definition of a hero, and much more. Each chapter covers a period or aspect of ancient Greek culture such as philosophy, mythology, and the dawn of the Golden Age.

- **Ancient Rome**
  by Avery Hart and Sandra Gallagher
  (grade level: 2–6)

Young children can join a parade of history and march into the world of enlightenment, regulation, and engineering that was ancient Rome. Readers learn everything about the ancient Roman way of life, from politics to paths, wisdom to waterworks. Meet the great Roman emperors, explore the empire's engineering marvels, examine popular forms of entertainment (are they so different from today?), and more. Along with discovering the amazing achievements of the Roman Empire, the authors encourage youngsters to discuss the events and attitudes that led to its downfall and compare ancient history with modern times.

- **Ancient Science**
  by Jim Weise
  (grade level: 3–8)

Kids are engaged in history and science through forty "time-traveling, world-exploring, history-making" activities. Divided into civilizations (Egyptian, Roman, Greek, Mayan and Aztec, Chinese, and Middle Eastern), projects explore scientific contributions from each culture such as a clepsydra (water clock) from Greece, a sled kite from China, glue from Egypt, and sunglasses from the Thule culture. Projects require only easy-to-find materials and include step-by-step instructions. The "More Fun Stuff to Do" section offers variations for students to try.

- **Archaeology for Kids**
  by Richard Panchyk
  (grade level: 3–8)

Twenty-five projects — including making a surface survey and building a screen for sifting dirt and debris — teach kids the techniques that unearthed Neanderthal caves and the ancient city of Pompeii. Children learn to "read" objects excavated in their own backyards.

- **The Art of the Catapult**
  by William Gurstelle
  (grade level: 6–12)

Students combine math, science, and history to build English trebuchets, Greek ballistae, Roman onagers, and more ancient artillery. Children follow the history of catapult warfare from the Vikings to Alexander the Great to the Crusades up until gunpowder was invented and catapults lost favor as the weapon of choice. Each project includes a list of materials, step-by-step instructions, and diagrams. Most projects require some adult supervision.

- **Climbing Your Family Tree**
  by Ira Wolfman
  (grade level: 4–9)

Filled with comprehensive information on using the Internet, this how-to book shows children how to dig up family documents, ships' manifests, naturalization papers, and more genealogical raw data. Readers also learn how to create oral histories, detail a family tree, and make a scrapbook of family lore.

- **Frank Lloyd Wright for Kids**
  by Kathleen Thorne-Thomsen
  (grade level: 3–8)

A narrative of Frank Lloyd Wright's life combined with photographs of his designs and the nature that inspired him introduce youngsters to the architect's world. Activities such as making paper flowers, baking geometric cookies, and designing cities invite children to experience life from Wright's perspective.

- **Going West**
  by Carol A. Johmann and Elizabeth Rieth
  (grade level: 2–8)

Thought-provoking questions and hands-on activities transport twentieth-century kids on an unforgettable journey through westward expansion. Youngsters can travel the Erie Canal, build a paddle boat to take down the Ohio River, build a prairie schooner and stock it for the trip, revisit the Trail of Tears, and hold a frolic with new neighbors in Oregon Country. It's "Wagons Ho" as children make true-to-life choices and use their ingenuity to discover the American frontier.

- **The Kid's Guide to Social Action**
  by Barbara A. Lewis
  (grade level: 4–12)

Along with a collection of stories about real kids who are making a difference, this book explains and gives examples of social action power skills, such as letter writing, interviewing, speech making, and fund raising.

- **Knights & Castles**
  by Avery Hart and Paul Mantell
  (grade level: 1–6)

Readers explore the feudal system, life as a peasant, medieval merry-making, and more. Youngsters can compose ballads, put on a medieval feast, and design a castle. Thought-provoking questions establish a relationship between life in the past and life today: Who writes history? Is the "simple" lifestyle in medieval Europe better than life today? How and why have table manners evolved?

- **Pyramids!**
  by Avery Hart and Paul Mantell
  (grade level: 1–6)

Youngsters get to know the wonders of ancient Egypt by exploring King Tut's tomb, creating pyramids, learning hieroglyphics, and going on an archaeological dig. Questions challenge kids to think about history and culture: Were ancient Egyptians on the right track when they created a society without money? Why were Egyptians so peaceful? Could people today learn from them?

- **The Underground Railroad for Kids**
  by Mary Kay Carson
  (grade level: 4–12)

Eighty firsthand narratives, thirty biographies, and twenty-one activities help students understand the experiences of slaves and the quest for freedom. Activities invite youngsters to create an antislavery handbill, write and decode underground railroad messages, design quilts that signal safe houses, sing songs, tell their family history griot-style, and much more. Photographs, newspaper clippings, and a resource section round out this book.

- **Understanding History: A Primer of Historical Method**
  by Louis Gottschalk
  (grade level: 6–10)

Detailed guidelines lead the reader from start to finish of a project in the field of history, with practical advice on refining a topic, locating unusual sources of data, and presenting findings in a polished and professional written form.

Language Arts

- **Haiku**
  by Patricia Donegan
  (grade level: 3–8)

Haiku is a beautiful and powerful form of poetry that is easily accessible to children. Donegan explains the seven keys to writing haiku (form, image, "season word," here and now, feeling, surprise, and compassion) and provides step-by-step instructions for expressing the world through "haiku eyes." Projects invite kids to create a *haibun* (story with haiku), *haiga* (drawing and haiku), *renga* (linked poetry), and much more. This versatile and insightful resource will change how youngsters think about poetry.

- **In Print!**
  by Joe Rhatigan
  (grade level: 4–10)

Instead of publishing in old-fashioned black and white, this book encourages kids to think beyond paper and ink. Forty publishing projects invite youngsters to stamp their words on an umbrella, create a curtain of poems, chisel idioms on stepping stones, make a haiku T-shirt, and much more. Also included are secret ideas for improving writing, tips from young writers, ideas for starting a writer's workshop, and guidelines for getting published in the traditional way.

- **Kindle the Fire**
  by Shelley Tucker
  (grade level: 4–8)

Help middle school kids warm up their inner poet! Shelley Tucker's engaging writing exercises show students how to create relevant and exciting free verse poetry from everyday thoughts, experiences, and language. Young poets can experiment with using parts of speech in new ways, developing ideas through sound and imagery, assigning human traits to objects, establishing mood with consonance and assonance, and more. Inspiring examples of student writing appear throughout.

- **Once Upon a Time**
  by Annie Buckley and Kathleen Coyle
  (grade level: 3–8)

Getting started on a great story can be as easy as dealing a hand from this deck of cards. Activities in seven categories help youngsters with genre, character, setting, action, feeling, object, and the important "how-to" of putting it all together. The introduction to the cards explains how to use them to develop ideas, practice different elements of a story, map out a plot, and much more. Also included are literature selections that provide good examples of story elements.

- **Some of My Best Friends Are Books**
  by Judith Wynn Halsted
  (grade level: K–12)

Finding a good reading list for bright students is not easy, but this second edition details nearly 300 titles and materials to support gifted children. Indexes by grade level, author, title, and theme make finding appropriate titles easy, and discussion topics are provided for most titles. In addition, Halsted describes how to use the books to support emotional and intellectual development.

- **Word Weavings**
  by Shelley Tucker
  (grade level: K–2)

Young children learn a deep appreciation of the relevance, humor, rhythm, and beauty of poetry by using the natural flow of speech and language. Using the poetic elements from everyday conversation, children compose their own poems. Art activities extend and enhance poetic expression, and writing suggestions and exercises throughout stimulate thought and creativity.

- **Yoga for the Brain**
  by Dawn DiPrince and Cheryl Miller Thurston
  (grade level: 5–12)

Over 300 prompts stretch brain muscles and help young writers become strong and nimble. Ideas are fun, fascinating, and creative. Idea 181 reads "Start a story with, 'You are nothing to me but a smear on the sports page of the morning paper.' End the story with 'Don't you want dessert?'" Fifty writing projects give writers real-world outlets.

Science

- **Bridges!**
  by Carol A. Johmann and Elizabeth J. Rieth
  (grade level: 2–6)

Youngsters can explore the nuts and bolts of bridges as they build a cofferdam, design a bridge to cross wide expanses, test the strength of triangles versus squares, hang a suspension bridge, and more. *Bridges!* also includes anecdotes about famous bridges, engineers, architects, and inventors, ideas to think about, and problems to solve.

- **The Complete Handbook of Science Fair Projects**
  by Julianne Blair Bochinski
  (grade level: 7–12)

Bochinski presents every aspect of creating a successful science fair project, from choosing a topic and preparing experiments to presenting findings. Also included are guidelines for fifty award-winning projects from actual science fairs, a list of 500 science fair topics, information on state and regional science fair listings, and more.

- **Fizz, Bubble & Flash**
  by Anita Brandolini
  (grade level: 3–8)

Finally, someone can explain the Periodic Table of Elements in a way that makes sense and relate it to the average person's everyday world. Did you know that bismuth (Bi) gives lipstick and eye shadow a lustrous sheen and helps cure acid indigestion? Or that zirconium oxide (ZrO_2) is used to make fake diamonds and artificial joints? Or that you can actually move the iron (Fe) in your fortified cereal with a magnet? Straightforward explanations, engaging activities, and brief anecdotes bring the elements into the realm of mere mortals.

- **Flying Things**
  by Michael DiSpezio
  (grade level: 3–8)

Eighteen projects guide young aviators in making a paper copter, an osprey, a balloon rocket, a dragonfly, and more. Each project includes a list of materials, step-by-step building instructions, flying guidelines, fun facts, and prompts to get kids to think about how the craft performs and what modifications to the design would do. Linking science, design, and fun, these projects are sure to engage and inspire youngsters.

- **Geology Rocks!**
  by Cindy Blobaum
  (grade level: 2–6)

Dig into geology and what makes the earth rock with engaging activities that measure an earthquake, create a mini–coal mine, find out the effects of acid rain, and more. Throughout are fascinating facts, short biographies, and helpful Web site addresses. Insightful questions inspire kids to think about mining practices, beach erosion, the best building materials, and more.

- **Janice VanCleave's Scientists Through the Ages**
  by Janice VanCleave
  (grade level: 4–8)

Travel the world and through time to meet twenty-five influential thinkers in astronomy, biology, chemistry, earth science, and physics. Each section includes a short biography of a scientist such as Archimedes, Thomas Edison, Maria Mitchell, and Alhazen; an experiment that examines each scientist's most important contributions and an explanation of the results; extension ideas; and a bibliography for further reading. This resource offers a wonderful opportunity for putting a human face on science.

- **The Kids' Book of Weather Forecasting**
  by Mark Breen and Kathleen Friestad
  (grade level: 2–7)

This guide takes the fascinating science of meteorology from mystery to meaningful as children discover what creates weather and learn how to predict what the weather will do next. They can build a weather station from scratch, keep a weather log to record observations, create graphs and charts to spot weather trends, and explore how hurricane, tornado, blizzard, and flood predictions are becoming more accurate.

- **Insectigations**
  by Cindy Blobaum
  (grade level: 2–5)

Experiments, art projects, and games help kids get up close and personal with bugs of all kinds. Activities include making a terrarium for observation, raising mealworms, measuring bug strength, and examining exoskeletons. Fascinating information, such as the medicinal use of maggots and the allowable insect parts per cup of food, are sure to intrigue and inspire youngsters to give the world of creepy-crawlies a second look.

- **Machines**
  by David Glover
  (grade level: 4–8)

Gears, levers, engines, and pulleys all make our lives easier. Kids learn how to use them to build machines such as clocks, steam engines, airplanes, windmills, and more. Projects provide a list of easy-to-find materials and step-by-step instructions.

- **Partners in Crime**
  by E. K. Hein
  (grade level: 5–8)

Ready-to-use lesson plans, activities, and exercises focus on real-world applications of critical thinking, problem solving, science, and nonfiction. In addition to activities on hair and fiber analysis, toxicology, blood typing, interrogation, and more, Hein provides information on further research opportunities through the community and careers in forensic science. This comprehensive resource can be used in a range of applications, from a single activity to a full unit.

- **Skyscrapers!**
  by Carol A. Johmann
  (grade level: 3–8)

Kids plan a model city and try out the roles of architect, engineer, soil expert, and city planner as they learn about local zoning laws, make towering decisions, and solve problems about design, materials, costs, worker safety, and how a building will affect and be affected by the community and environment. Construction activities include building a tower crane, sinking pilings in the soil, bolting together columns and girders, and laying a concrete marble cladding. Amusing illustrations, fabulous photographs, and exciting schematic drawings will have youngsters bulldozing for more.

Thinking Skills, Math, and Business

- **Brain Food**
  by Paul Fleisher
  (grade level: 4–12)

Over a hundred classroom-tested strategy, math, word, and logic games from around the world ask players to analyze situations, develop and evaluate strategies, manipulate patterns, use their imaginations, and more. Games such as Cows and Leopards from Sri Lanka, Nine-Man Morris from England, and Achi from West Africa encourage high-order thinking skills as well as exploration of other cultures. Most games require only pencil and paper.

- **The Media-Savvy Student**
  by Guofang Wan and Hong Cheng
  (grade level: 2–6)

With media around every corner, students need to develop strong skills in analyzing, evaluating, and communicating information. Activities include writing local TV stations or program directors about programming, developing print or television ads, and calculating instances of violence in a minute of television.

- **Mind Benders: Warm Up**
  by Anita Harnadek
  (grade level: K–2)

Fun, challenging activities sharpen children's deductive reasoning skills in all academic areas and enhance real-life problem solving. Exercises encourage them to recognize and organize sets of clues, deduce logical conclusions, match up attributes, and apply information to a matrix in order to solve the puzzles.

- **Stories to Solve Series**
  by George Shannon
  (grade level: 2–12)

Each illustrated story in this collection of folktales from around the world offers a riddle to solve. The stories challenge readers to pay attention to detail as they figure out how characters escape danger, catch thieves, or inherit kingdoms and discover who is telling the truth, who is lying, and more. Titles in the series include *Stories to Solve, More Stories to Solve, Still More Stories to Solve,* and *True Lies.*

- **Exploring Statistics in the Elementary Grades**
  by Carolyn Bereska, Cyrilla Bolster, L. Carey Bolster, and
  Richard Schaeffer
  (grade level: K–6)

Leery of leaf plots? Puzzled by probability? Scared of statistics? Classroom teachers joined hands with a research statistician to make statistics accessible. This book presents activities that introduce statistical concepts (such as finding meaningful patterns in data) using authentic vocabulary. Each activity includes an overview of the lesson, teaching tips, and reproducible student pages. Help kids overcome the odds and explore statistics in an original, enjoyable way.

- **Math Games & Activities from Around the World**
  by Claudia Zaslavsky
  (grade level: 2–6)

Math, history, art, and world cultures come together in more than seventy games, puzzles, and projects that encourage youngsters to exercise their math skills. They can use geometry to design a board game, probability to analyze the outcomes of a game of chance, and logical thinking to devise strategies.

- **The Secret Life of Math**
  by Ann McCallum
  (grade level: 3–8)

To answer the question "What will we use this for?" McCallum looks at the history of math and why it has developed. Activities that invite youngsters to make Chinese counting rods, solve an ancient Egyptian math problem, and add Roman numerals help put math into a historical (read: human) perspective.

- **Philosophy for Kids**

  by David A. White

  (grade level: 4–12)

Forty fun questions help children wonder about things: Can computers think? Can you think about nothing? Suggested activities organized around the topics of values, knowledge, and reality encourage kids to reason and think critically and introduce them to Confucius, Aristotle, Locke, and other legendary philosophers.

- **Kid Cash**

  by Joe Lamancusa

  (grade level: 6–9)

Written by an enterprising teenager, this how-to gives the reader information on all sorts of money-making enterprises, from lawn mowing and snow shoveling to more sophisticated ventures. Included are job descriptions, start-up costs, tips on finding customers, suggested fees, and information on record keeping.

- **Better Than a Lemonade Stand**

  by Daryl Bernstein

  (grade level: 4–12)

Written by an ambitious teenager, this book offers business ideas ranging from cleaning things to profiting from a special talent, with many tips on keeping customers happy, setting a selling price, and handling loans.

- **The Kids' Business Book**

  by Arlene Erlbach

  (grade level: 2–6)

This book shows how youngsters can turn their interests and talents into profitable businesses that fit their schedules and lifestyles. There's some good advice on handling the growth of a personal business or, when tough times hit, knowing when to stop.

- **Competitions for Talented Kids**
  by Frances A. Karnes and Tracy L. Riley
  (grade level: K–12)

With more than 140 competitions in areas such as journalism, leadership, philosophy, and technology, children are sure to find a competition that fits their interests and talents. Part I contains listings with sponsor, contact information, deadlines, judging criteria, awards, and more. Most competitions are free to enter and all are open to children nationwide. Part II includes a competitions journal to help kids get organized, thank those who have helped, and assess their learning.

RENZULLI'S BEST WEB SITE ENRICHMENT ACTIVITIES

- **Let's Build a City in the Solar System**
  (www.oncampus.richmond.edu/academics/education/
  projects/webquests/space)

Kids who have dreamt of traveling in outer space or think it would be cool to live on another planet are invited to build the first human city in the solar system. They will describe the site of the city, what people will eat, how they will dress, the kinds of buildings, and what people will do for fun.

- **Make-a-Flake**
  (www.snowflake.lookandfeel.com)

Visitors click and drag scissors to make cuts in a folded-up snowflake and then see what it looks like in this fun Web site for wintertime. Snowflakes other people have made are also shown, and visitors can try to figure out how to duplicate them.

- **Weather Extreme: Tornado**
  (www.dsc.discovery.com/convergence/tornado/tornado.html)

Kids who are fascinated by storms will love this site. Children create their own tornadoes to learn about the different levels and see what kinds of damage each level causes. They can also discover how a tornado starts and ends.

- **Cartoonster**
  (www.kidzdom.com)

Here's a step-by-step tutorial for young artists interested in learning how to make their own cartoons. Colorful illustrations and animated clips make it easy for beginners to explore the process of animation and discover concepts like perspective and exaggeration.

- **Ben's Guide to U.S. Government for Kids**
  (www.bensguide.gpo.gov)

Benjamin Franklin, one of our Founding Fathers, teaches kids about the U.S. government. Visitors find a grade range to begin, then pick topics to learn about, everything from the branches of government to how laws are made to the election process.

- **NASA Space Place**
  (www.spaceplace.nasa.gov)

On this site children can explore some really cool science projects — learning how a tortilla chip is like a spaceship, trying their luck at the robot puzzle, working on a puzzle with a billion possible wrong solutions, and even designing a planet.

- **Go West Across America with Lewis and Clark**
  (www.nationalgeographic.com/west)

It is 1804. President Thomas Jefferson has asked Meriwether Lewis to lead an expedition across western North America — unknown territory to all but Native Americans. The goals: map the rivers, make friends with natives, open the West to trade, and look for a Northwest Passage. Lewis and his colleague William Clark have chosen a special team for the journey, and visitors to the site are invited along.

- **Secrets @ Sea**

  (www.secretsatsea.org)

  Take an interactive trip to discover why all the killer whales in a certain part of the ocean have been getting sick. There are plenty of clues to put together, and if you ever get lost, you can always consult your field guide. Collect notes in your notebook along the way and you're sure to solve the mystery.

- **Inequity!**

  (www.pbskids.org/wayback/fair)

  What is fair and what is not? The visitor can take this quiz challenge with a pal and see who has the quickest response and the best understanding of what is fair and what is not.

- **Secrets of the Dead: Murder at Stonehenge**

  (www.pbs.org/wnet/secrets/case_stonehenge)

  Kids can learn the story of Stonehenge here. The purpose of the stone circle in Salisbury, England, has long been a mystery. Now, thanks to archaeologists, we are able to see not only the stages in which the circle was built, but understand more about the skeletons that have been discovered there.

- **Secrets of the Dead: Day of the Zulu**

  (www.pbs.org/wnet/secrets/case_zulu)

  On January 12, 1879, Zulu warriors handed the British the worst defeat in their colonial history. While the victory ultimately led to the destruction of Zululand, the Africans' superior tactics, native weapons, and traditional medicines won the day. How did the underdog Zulus defeat the British army? Catch all the details here.

- **Secrets of the Dead: Bridge on the River Kwai**

  (www.pbs.org/wnet/secrets/case_kwai)

  While the Thailand-Burma Railway, begun in September 1942, was not an innovative engineering venture, its construction was an amazing feat. Completed in just eighteen months by more than a quarter of a million laborers, 61,000 of whom were Allied prisoners of war, the railway spanned 257 miles of treacherous terrain. How were the Japanese able to accomplish their goal three and a half years ahead of schedule? Find out here.

- **Secrets of the Dead: Search for the First Human**
  (www.pbs.org/wnet/secrets/case_firsthuman)

Paleontologists believe that humanity split from our ape relatives approximately six million years ago. In 2000, teams of scientists from the Collège de France and the Community Museums of Kenya discovered fragments of a skeleton they believe to be the earliest known human ancestor. What methods did the scientists use to examine their discovery and what does it mean if their theories are true? Dig here for the answers.

- **Secrets of the Dead: Mystery of the Black Death**
  (www.pbs.org/wnet/secrets/case_plague)

The bubonic plague — its origins unknown — killed more than 25 million people within five years of appearing on the European continent. In 1665, the entire English village of Eyam was quarantined in an attempt to halt the spread of the illness. It was assumed that the entire village would die and yet, a year later, half the town had survived. What did scientists discover in Eyam and what has it meant in the fight against a modern plague? Uncover the secret of life after the Black Death.

- **Secrets of the Dead: The Great Fire of Rome**
  (www.pbs.org/wnet/secrets/case_rome)

In 64 AD, the great fire of Rome destroyed two-thirds of the city. At the time, recorded opinion claimed that Emperor Nero had purposely set the blaze in order to make room for his own building projects. Using modern technology, archaeologists, historians, and fire investigators have tried to determine the true cause of this historic conflagration. Check out this hot mystery and discover some cool answers here.

- **Secrets of the Dead: Tragedy at the Pole**
  (www.pbs.org/wnet/secrets/case_southpole)

In late March 1911, Captain Robert F. Scott and his teammates lost their lives in an attempt to become the first expedition to reach the South Pole. While popular sentiment at the time labeled Scott a hero, history has branded him incompetent. Critics point to the team's poor equipment and late start, as well as Scott's ill-advised decision to take an additional team member. Check out the cold, hard facts here and decide for yourself if Robert Scott was really inept or simply the victim of unusually cold weather.

- **Secrets of the Dead: Titanic's Ghosts**
  (www.pbs.org/wnet/secrets/case_titanic)

When the Titanic sank on April 14, 1912, more than 1,500 passengers lost their lives. Among those now buried in Fairview Lawn cemetery in Halifax, Scotland, was an anonymous two-year-old boy. Check out how scientists and historians use modern DNA analysis to attempt to identify this lost child and other Titanic victims.

- **Enemy Pie**
  (www.storylineonline.net)

Actress Camryn Manheim reads the story, by Derek Munson, of when Jeremy Ross moves into a new neighborhood and the grassy yard in front of his house quickly turns into a battlefield. The kids who live nearby are not seen by Jeremy as friends to play with, but as enemies. When Jeremy's father sees what is happening, he reveals a special recipe that somehow manages to turn enemies into friends.

- **Science of Music**
  (www.exploratorium.edu/music)

Kids can explore the science of music through online exhibits, movies, and musical experiments at this amazing Web site.

- **Windows to the Universe**
  (www.windows.ucar.edu/windows.html)

Choose "Our Planet," "Our Solar System," or "Astronomy and the Universe," then pick from dozens of specific topics to learn about the universe. There are also games and other fun activities, scientists' blogs, and an online journal to store the most interesting Web addresses or pictures from Windows to the Universe.

- **From Cave Art to Your Art**
  (www.alifetimeofcolor.com/play/caveart)

Explore the history of art and art techniques by watching short video clips with examples from almost 30,000 years of media. Kids can upload some of their own art and create a movie featuring their work.

- **Who Wants to Win a Million Dollars?**
  (www.education.jlab.org/million)

In this science game, kids test their math and science knowledge with questions about chemistry, physics, biology, astronomy, and math. If they're stuck on a question, they can eliminate two of the answer choices, poll the "audience," or ask an expert, but they can do each of those things only once, so they're advised to save that option for the hardest questions.

- **Simple Machines**
  (www.edheads.org/activities/simple-machines)

This site shows how simple mechanical devices, such as the lid on a toilet, dominate our everyday life. By inspecting items in a home, garage, and tool shed, visitors discover levers, gears, axles, inclined planes, and other simple mechanics. Which simple principle is behind the toilet lid?

- **The Compound Machine**
  (www.edheads.org/activities/odd_machine)

Learn how forces and simple machines can work together to create the Compound Machine. Click the green "Start" button to begin and answer the questions to get points.

- **Virtual Labs**
  (www.hhmi.org/biointeractive/vlabs)

At this site, the visitor has the opportunity to work in five different labs: the Transgenic Fly Virtual Lab, the Bacterial Identification Lab, the Cardiology Lab, the Neurophysiology Lab, and the Immunology Lab. The labs teach various skills, like identifying bacteria, how to dissect organisms to learn about their organs, the use and function of antibodies, and much more.

- **Collapse: Why Do Civilizations Fall?**
  (www.learner.org/interactives/collapse)

The history of humankind has been marked by patterns of growth and decline. Take a look and see how four civilizations collapsed. Some declines have been gradual, occurring over centuries. Others have been rapid, occurring over the course of a few years. War, drought, natural disaster, disease, overpopulation, and economic disruption: any of these can bring about the collapse of a civilization.

- **Virtual Hip Surgery**
  (www.edheads.org/activities/hip)

Welcome to Edheads Virtual Hospital. Take on the role of the surgeon throughout a hip replacement surgery.

- **Virtual Hip Resurfacing**
  (www.edheads.org/activities/hip2)

More virtual surgery for the doctor-to-be. The visitor performs the duties of the surgeon throughout a hip resurfacing surgery.

- **Virtual Knee Surgery**
  (www.edheads.org/activities/knee)

In this interactive virtual tour through a knee surgery, the visitor makes choices during the procedure that will change the outcome. In addition, as a surgical resident he will help prepare five patients for different knee surgeries.

- **Jamestown Live!**
  (www.jamestownjourney.org/jlive.htm)

This one-hour, fast-paced interactive program delivers key historic information on the founding and significance of Jamestown in an engaging format. Three of Jamestown's enduring legacies — exploration, cultural diversity, and democracy — are explored. Each theme is presented by education experts, historians, and authors through informative interviews conducted by student reporters.

- **Harvest of History**
  (www.harvestofhistory.org)

This is for the child who loves history and wants to be a filmmaker but doesn't have a video camera. Students can explore a historic colonial village to find out how and where food was grown and compare life in 1845 with our modern world, then produce an original movie with the Village Videomaker.

- **ABC Sign Language**
  (www.starfall.com/n/level-k/sign-abcs/load.htm?f)

This fun activity site teaches kids sign language for the letters A through Z.

- **Clifford the Big Red Dog: Interactive Storybooks**
  (www.teacher.scholastic.com/clifford1)

This site is for all youngsters who love Clifford. With these great interactive storybooks, beginning readers build reading and phonics proficiency in both English and Spanish by playing along with Clifford and learning letter and sound matching as well as other reading skills.

- **Virtual Cell**
  (www.ibiblio.org/virtualcell/tour/cell/cell.htm)

This interactive Web site lets kids explore a biological cell. Roll the mouse over the animation and click on any part to learn more about what the different parts of a cell do.

- **Virtual Dinosaur Dig**
  (www.paleobiology.si.edu/dinosaurs/interactives/dig/dinodig .html)

Join the Smithsonian National Museum of Natural History on an archaeological dig in Wyoming for dinosaur fossils. The visitor to this site uncovers fossils, prepares them, transports them, and puts them back together.

- **Nab the Aquatic Invader!**
  (www.sgnis.org/kids)

Be a Sea Grant Super Sleuth at this fun, interactive Web site. Join Detective ID, Detective Thumb-a-Ride, Detective EcoFriend, Detective Dollars and Sense, or Detective Barrier as each investigates invading aquatic plants and animals.

- **The Amazing Human Body**
  (www.harcourtschool.com/activity/bodyintro_34)

Kids can check out this site to learn all about the human body and play interactive games to test what they know. First, "drain the brain" and indicate what parts are coordinated with certain activities. Build the digestive system and see how different foods are broken down once they are ingested. Help put a skeleton back together with all the bones in their proper places. Color-code different parts of the tooth, such as the crown. In addition, get in touch with all the five senses.

- **Dental Space Odyssey**
  (www.ada.org/public/games/space.asp)

Journey through space to help the kids of Smileyville. Use the ToothShuttle Spaceship to collect good foods, floss, and other objects that promote healthy teeth.

- **Recording Artist**
  (www.tvokids.com/framesets/play.html?game=94)

Kids can record their own music here. They choose their instruments, adjust volume and balance, and start recording.

- **Virginia Trivia Challenge**
  (www.solpass.org/PenaltyGame/Penalty%20Game.htm)

Visitors can test their knowledge of Virginia's history with this cool online soccer game. First you need to decide who will be goalkeeper and what color the team jersey should be. Then play the game by answering questions about Virginia history.

- **Professor Garfield**
  (www.professorgarfield.org)

This Web site catches your eye with brightly colored animations that move and talk. Step into Professor Garfield's lab and learn about a wide range of subjects, from music to reading to drawing to sculpture, and more.

- **Rhyme Rodeo**
  (www.tvokids.com/framesets/play.html?game=71)

Who's the fastest rhymer in the West? The cowpokes at the Rhyme Rodeo need your help.

- **Crossword Puzzler**
  (www.tvokids.com/framesets/play.html?game=72)

Life in Docville is mighty strange. Saddle up and help the cowpokes keep the title as the best book-slinging, word-wrangling town around. There's lots of ground to cover.

- **The Presidential Time Line of the Twentieth Century**
  (www.presidentialtimeline.org)

This interactive site features a multimedia exhibit of key events and decisions that U.S. presidents faced in the twentieth century: the stock market crash, Pearl Harbor, the atomic bomb, Little Rock school integration, Gulf of Tonkin, trip to China, Berlin Wall, and more. Visitors can explore the time line, examine the exhibits, and search through the gallery of hundreds of presidential records.

- **Kids' Corner (Ancient Egypt)**
  (www.oi.uchicago.edu/OI/MUS/ED/kids.html)

This amazing interactive Web site helps kids explore ancient Egyptian culture. Prepare a mummy for burial and learn all that had to be done to each body, decipher images left on a tomb, learn more about the artwork of ancient Egypt, or study a time line of ancient Egypt.

- **National Zoo — Just for Kids**
  (www.nationalzoo.si.edu and click on "Kids")

The National Zoo's Web pages for kids are loaded with information about animals, a Conservation Kids' Club, and things we can all do to make a cleaner planet. There are also many fun games on this page: a bird bill matching game, a panda quiz, and the Beaver Valley Trivia Challenge. You can also take a virtual tour of the zoo.

- **Bones and the Badge**
  (www.projects.edtech.sandi.net/kearny/forensic)

For kids who like a good mystery, here's a chance to become part of a team of forensic investigators. After collecting and analyzing evidence from a crime scene, the visitor must use logic and scientific inquiry skills to trace the steps of the crime and determine whether or not the science accurately explains the crime.

- **Donate Blood!**
  (www.biologycorner.com/quests/bloodquest/blood.html)

In this creative activity kids are in charge of a blood drive at school. The task is to design a flier that explains the process and importance of blood donation to the community.

- **The Alamo**
  (www.thealamo.org)

This intriguing site relates the story of the Alamo, originally named Misión San Antonio de Valero. It served as home to missionaries and their local Native American converts for nearly seventy years beginning in 1724. In 1793, Spanish officials secularized San Antonio's five missions and distributed their lands to the remaining Native American residents. These men and women continued to farm the fields, once the mission's but now their own, and participated in the growing community of San Antonio.

- **The Moon and the Sun**
  (www.teacher.scholastic.com/researchtools/researchstarters/space)

Learn why scientists study the sun and the moon through this Web site's recommended research ideas and articles to help in developing ideas.

- **Explore the States**
  (www.americaslibrary.gov and click on "Explore the States")

Click on any one of the states on the colored map to begin exploring the fifty United States of America. You can also go on a Treasure Hunt to find pictures among the states.

- **300 Women Who Changed the World**
  (www.search.eb.com/women)

Get inspired by influential women from all over the world! Encyclopædia Britannica introduces kids to important women from antiquity to modern times, complete with audio clips and photos.

- **Inventor's Toolbox**
  (www.mos.org/sln/Leonardo/InventorsToolbox.html)

Check out this site with pictures and descriptions of simple machines, inventions, and so much more.

- **Space Camp and Space Academy**
  (www.spacecamp.com)

The weeklong Space Camp is a program designed to excite and educate children ages nine through eleven in areas of math, science, and technology. Teamwork, self-confidence, and communication are achieved through state-of-the-art simulations, missions, rocket building, and robotics. This site describes the camp, where kids try out space food, learn to sleep in space, and even learn how to go to the bathroom in space — plus everything else there is to know about the Space Shuttle systems and life aboard the Orbiter and International Space Station.

Space Academy is an increased-intensity program of astronaut and mission training and academics for twelve- to fourteen-year-olds. Simulated missions to a space station and crew rotation highlight the week. Participants have three fields of specialized study to choose from: aviation, space, and robotics.

- **Road Trip! Through SC Civil Rights History**
  (www.knowitall.org/roadtrip)

Go on the road without ever leaving the house. Learn about the civil rights movement in South Carolina. Take a virtual trip back in time and find out what really happened.

- **E-Quarium**
  (www.mbayaq.org/efc/cam_menu.asp)

This virtual tour of underwater exhibits at the Monterey Bay Aquarium lets kids watch different animals — penguins, sharks, otters, and more — live on Web cams. Visitors can click on the species they want to look at and fun and interesting facts appear along with the Web cam.

- **The Cave of Lascaux**
  (www.culture.gouv.fr/culture/arcnat/lascaux/en)

In September 1940, Marcel Ravidat, Jacques Marsal, Georges Agnel, and Simon Coencas discovered paintings on the walls of the ancient cave of Lascaux in France. The cave was closed in 1963 because the carbon dioxide from visitors' breath was destroying the paintings, but visitors can now explore this ancient cave virtually and learn about the meaning of the beautiful paintings.

- **Virtual Tours of the Louvre Museum**
  (www.louvre.fr/and click on "Museum")

Take virtual tours of one of the greatest art museums in the world, the Louvre in Paris. Online exhibitions include Egyptian Antiquities; Greek, Etruscan, and Roman Antiquities; Islamic Art; Sculptures; Paintings; and much more.

- **The ~~Nine~~ 8 Planets — For Kids!**
  (www.kids.nineplanets.org)

Explore the solar system on this terrific site: watch a solar eclipse, find out what you would weigh if you lived on Mars, look at photographs of the planets and stars, and learn all about our home, the Milky Way.

- **Ology**
  (www.amnh.org/ology)

The American Museum of Natural History's Web site for children invites the visitor to explore archaeology, astronomy, biodiversity, Earth, Einstein, genetics, marine biology, paleontology, and other "ologies." Among the many topics: the Incas, the ancient city of Petra, gravity, Mars, the Milky Way, tree of life, saving species, tectonic plates, rocks, deep-sea vents, matter and energy, space and time, a genetic journey, a nature and nurture walk, the quest for the perfect tomato, ocean creatures, and fighting dinosaurs.

- **Girls Are I.T.**
  (www.girlsareit.org)

Calling all tech girls! Visitors can discover all the amazing careers for women in the information technology world at this Web site. Girl Scouts have a chance to earn the "Girls Are I.T." patch.

- **Art and Culture**
  (www.artandculture.com)

Information on the visual arts, performing arts, design, literature, music, and film is presented using the Web's first interconnected guide to the arts. Kids will find an explanation of each expression of art, along with biographies of some of the leading artists of that genre.

- **Low Life Labs**
  (www.robotsandus.org)

In this incredibly interesting Web site, children get to see how robots work. The robot's actions are divided into four groups: moving, sensing, thinking, and being. There's fun with many different activities.

- **Owen & Mzee**
  (www.owenandmzee.com)

In December 2004, a frightened young hippo, separated from his family by a devastating tsunami, bonded with an Aldabra tortoise named Mzee. The 130-year-old tortoise accepted Owen as his own and an inseparable bond was forged. This heartwarming story teaches kids about hope, friendship, and more.

- **Phases of the Moon**
  (www.wonderville.ca/v1/activities/phases/phases.html)
What is the moon? Why do we see the moon? Why does the moon look different on certain nights? Kids will find the answers to these questions by checking out this exciting interactive video.

RENZULLI'S BEST CONTESTS AND COMPETITIONS

The descriptions below provide brief overviews of contests and competitions for children. Fuller information can be found at the sites, including submission deadlines and entry fees, if any. Some contests and competitions are designed for student teams and some must be originated and coached by teachers or research specialists in a child's school.

- **Amazing Kids! Contests**
  (www.amazing-kids.org/contests.htm)
This Web site describes a selection of art, music, video, and writing contests for children.

- **American Kennel Club — Kids' Corner Contest**
  (www.akc.org/kids_juniors)
For dog-loving youngsters, the AKC invites entrants to draw a picture of any breed of dog. Winners receive a variety of doggie-related prizes.

- **Animation Station!**
  (www.amazing-kids.org/anistation1.htm)
Children create and send in their animations to be featured in the online Animation Showcase on the Amazing Kids Web site.

- **Arts and Kids Open Art Contest**
  (www.artsandkids.com and click on "Art Contest")
Open to all kids seventeen and under, this contest awards a money grant to the grand-prize-winner's school for art education, art supplies, or art-related technology. Entries are featured on the Web site.

- **Arts Olympiad**

  (www.icaf.org/programs)

The Arts Olympiad, held every four years for children ages eight through twelve, arranges art competitions in which students often serve as judges. Involvement in this competition can lead to national exhibitions and celebrations and, for finalists, a trip to Washington, D.C.

- **ASPCA Animaland: Pet of the Week**

  (www.aspca.org/kids_home)

Youngsters enter this contest by sending in a photo of their pets and a brief explanation of why they love them so much.

- **Best Robotics Competition**

  (www.bestinc.org)

For middle and high school kids, this competition aims to inspire students to pursue careers in engineering, science, and technology. Entrants participate in a sports-like, engineering-based robotics-building effort.

- **Chicago International Children's Film Festival**

  (www.cicff.org)

This is described as the largest and most celebrated film festival devoted to films for and by kids.

- **Comic Strip Drawing Contest!**

  (www.amazing-kids.org/comicscontest.html#top1)

From the Amazing Kids Web site, this is a contest for kids who love to draw comics. Entries are displayed in the AK Comics section and a grand prize is awarded.

- **Courage in Student Journalism Awards**

  (www.splc.org/csjaward.asp)

Middle or high school student journalists who have shown determination in exercising their First Amendment rights to freedom of speech can submit a brief essay, along with clippings and letters of support. Two winners and their school administrators receive cash awards.

- **Department of Energy Contests & Competitions**
  (www.energy.gov/contests&competitions.htm)

This site describes several contests related to new ideas for alternative energy sources, including Rube Goldberg Machine Contests, the Junior Solar Sprint, and the Solar Decathalon.

- **Earth Artists**
  (www.epa.gov/region1/students/poem.html)

Students in kindergarten through sixth grade from New England are invited to create posters and poems suggesting actions that everyone can take to increase awareness and protect the environment.

- **eCybermission**
  (www.ecybermission.com)

A Web-based science, math, and technology competition for teams of students in sixth through ninth grades. Teams compete for regional and national awards by proposing a solution to a real problem in their community.

- **ExploraVision Awards**
  (www.exploravision.org)

Designed for kindergarten through twelfth-grade students of all interest, skill, and ability levels, this competition encourages kids to create and explore a vision of future technology by combining their imaginations with the tools of science.

- **First Lego League**
  (www.usfirst.org/what/fll)

This is a global robotics program for kids ages nine through fourteen. Youngsters work in teams with the help of an adult coach to research, design, build, and program an autonomous robot that will compete in friendly, sports-like tournaments.

- **Future Problem Solving Program**
  (www.fpsp.org)

Teams of students in grades four through twelve apply creative problem solving in competitive and noncompetitive activities to develop a vision for the future. Students from around the world take part.

- **Gutenberg Awards**
  (www.igaea.org)

These competitions for students in middle school through college recognize exceptional achievement in the field of graphic arts, with competitions for print, Web publishing, and photography.

- **Igniting Creative Energy Challenge**
  (www.ignitingcreativeenergy.org)

Children from kindergarten through twelfth grade use their creative energy in this competition to demonstrate what can be done in the home, school, or community about the growing energy crisis.

- **International Student Media Festival**
  (www.ismf.net)

Kindergarten through college students demonstrate artistic talent in instructional, informational, documentary, persuasive, narrative, or entertainment categories by presenting live action, animation, podcasts, or other mixed-media productions.

- **International Young Eco-Hero Awards**
  (www.actionfornature.org)

For young people ages eight to sixteen, this competition awards cash prizes to kids who have completed creative environmental projects.

- **Jostens Photo Contest**
(www.jostens.com/yearbook/show_contest.asp)

Take fabulous photos that tell a story relevant to the middle school, junior high, or high school experience and get a chance to win amazing prizes.

- **Junior Duck Stamp Design Contest**
(www.fws.gov/juniorduck)

Derived from a program that teaches wetlands habitat and waterfowl conservation to students in kindergarten through high school, entrants submit drawings, paintings, and sketches of waterfowl species.

- **Kids Philosophy Slam**
(www.philosophyslam.org)

This is an annual program designed to make philosophy fun and accessible to all children, from kindergarten through high school. Entrants can express themselves in words, artwork, poetry, or song.

- **Letters About Literature**
(www.loc.gov/loc/cfbook/letters)

A national reading-writing contest for fourth through twelfth graders. Participants write a personal letter to an author, living or dead, explaining how that author's work changed their way of thinking about the world.

- **Math League Contests**
(www.mathleague.com)

Entrants in four age levels problem-solve questions from different areas of mathematics.

- **National Geographic Bee**
(www.nationalgeographic.com/geographybee)

Schools can enter kids in grades four through eight in this annual contest that tests geographic knowledge.

- **National History Day Contest**
  (www.nationalhistoryday.org/contest.htm)

Kids engage in discovery and interpretation of historical topics related to an annual theme, producing projects in the form of exhibits, documentaries, historical papers, and performances.

- **National Schools Project**
  (www.youngpoets.org)

This poetry contest is open to all students who compete to have their work published in the *Young American Poetry Digest.*

- **National Science Bowl**
  (www.scied.science.doe.gov/nsb/index.html)

The Science Bowl is an academic competition that tests students' knowledge of all areas of science in a fast-paced question-and-answer format. Middle school students also have an opportunity to design, build, and race a model hydrogen fuel cell car.

- **NCTE Promising Young Writers Program**
  (www.ncte.org/about/awards/student/pyw)

Eighth-grade students are nominated by their teachers and submit a sample of their best writing and an essay on a theme topic.

- **NewsCurrents Student Editorial Cartoon Contest**
  (www.newscurrents.com and click on "Cartoon of the Week")

Entrants submit original cartoons on any subject of national or international interest. Winning cartoons are featured on the Web site weekly.

- **Poetry.com Open Amateur Poetry Contest**
  (www.poetry.com)

Cash prizes are awarded to amateur poets who submit original poems on any subject, in any style.

- **President's Environmental Youth Awards**
  (www.epa.gov/enviroed/peya)

Students are invited to describe projects they have created that demonstrate their commitment to the environment. Winning projects have included tree planting, constructing nature preserves, writing newsletters, and more.

- **Prudential Spirit of Community Awards**
  (www.prudential.com/spirit)

Youngsters from middle school and up are honored for outstanding volunteer service to their communities.

- **Rube Goldberg Machine Contests**
  (www.rubegoldberg.com)

A good Rube Goldberg machine incorporates everyday machines and connects them in weird and ingenious ways. Entrants are asked to construct a machine that uses at least twenty individual steps to complete an assigned task, which varies from year to year.

- **Scholastic Art & Writing Awards**
  (www.artandwriting.org)

This long-running awards program identifies and documents outstanding achievement from young artists and writers in the visual and literary arts.

- **Scholastic's Kids Are Authors Contest**
  (www.scholastic.com/bookfairs/contest/kaa)

Kids in kindergarten through eighth grade work in small groups using their artistic and writing skills to create a picture book. The two grand-prize-winning books will be published.

- **State-Fish Art Contest**
  (www.statefishart.com)

Children in grades four through twelve draw an official state fish in its natural habitat and write a one-page composition about that fish.

- **Stone Soup**
  (www.stonesoup.com/send-work)

Stone Soup is the only magazine made up entirely of the creative work of children. Kids from all over the world contribute stories, poems, book reviews, and artwork.

- **Tattered Cover Scary Story Contest**
  (www.tatteredcover.com and click on "Young Readers")

Write your own scary story. Prizes are awarded for age groups ranging from kindergarten through grade six.

- **TOYchallenge**
  (www.sallyridescience.com/toychallenge)

Form a team, sign up, and build your own toy or game. Kids in grades five through eight use design principles and problem-solving skills; a team consists of three to six members, at least half of whom must be girls.

✳

The Community Talent Miner

This questionnaire can be adapted to be used with different audiences and to meet particular information-gathering goals.

In filling out this questionnaire, please keep in mind:

Be as original as you like in your replies.

Take as much space as you need; use the back of the sheet if necessary.

If there are sections or questions you'd rather not answer, simply skip them.

Professional Experiences

What do you do for a living? _____

_____

How long has it been your career? _____

_____

What other career(s) have you explored? How? _____

_____

How did you select your current career? _____

_____

_____

What unique or creative aspects of your profession would you like to communicate to a young person who might be interested in entering your field (for example, skills you have had to learn "the hard way")?

_____

_____

Academic Experiences

If you attended college, business school, or had technical training, what subject was your major emphasis? _____

_____

Did it have any unusual aspects (for example, an interdisciplinary major or involvement in original research, publications or presentations)?

_____

Trips, Safaris, and Excursions

Have you traveled to any unusual or out-of-the-way places? Where and when? _____

_____

What sorts of records do you have of your travels (for example, photographs, local products, or other artifacts)? _____

_____

Intercultural Experiences

Have you lived in another culture? If so, where? _____

_____

For how long and under what circumstances did you live in the culture? _____

_____

Can you describe one meaningful experience you had during your time in another culture? _____

_____

Hobbies, Collections, and Competitions

What are your hobbies? _____

_____

Are you a collector? If so, what do you collect? _____

_____

How did you become involved with your hobby or collection? _____

_____

Do you belong to an organized group of people with like interests (for example, American Philatelic Society, Flat Earth Society)? _____

_____

Have you entered in a competition related to your collection or hobby? _____

_____

Have you entered any other unusual competitions or contests (for example, a frog jumping contest, limerick competition, model sailboat race)? What sort? Is this something in which you participate on a regular basis? _____

_____

_____

Esoteric Interests

Most of us know people who describe themselves as history buffs, ecology enthusiasts, science fiction freaks, health food nuts, or Sherlock Holmes addicts. Do you have a special interest for which you'd give yourself a similar label? Please include areas of interest and labels. _____

_____

_____

In what ways have you followed up on your interests? _____

_____

Do you meet with other people who have similar interests (include group names, any "organized" activities)? _____

_____

Community-Related Activities

For each activity, please include group names, positions held, dates of involvement, and how you became involved.

Have you ever:

Lobbied for something? _____

Belonged to an interest group? _____

Campaigned for a cause or a person? _____

Been involved in a religious group? _____

Joined a community action group? _____

Donated time to a charitable organization? _____

Of those areas explored in this questionnaire, the following are ones about which I am especially enthusiastic: _____

_____

I would be willing for the teacher of _____ to contact me regarding possible applications of some of my interests and talents with students in the program.

Acknowledgments

We acknowledge, with gratitude and humility, our many colleagues and collaborators over the years who have helped to extend our work and expand our ideas. They include:

Linda H. Smith, Susan Baum, Terry W. Neu, Joan M. McGuire, Alane J. Starko, Gina D. Schack, Deborah Burns, Jeanne Purcell, Marcia Gentry, Jann Leppien, Thomas Hayes, Thomas Hébert, Marcy Delcourt, Gara Field, Rachel Reed, Mary Rizza, Ken McCluskey, Del Siegle, E. Jean Gubbins, Kristina Morgan, and Rachel Knox.

We want to acknowledge our more recent colleagues at Renzulli Learning Systems who have helped us translate our lifetime of work into an online opportunity that can engage and challenge all children:

Mike Daversa, Paul Rector, Jim Howe, Jenny Halter, David Hodges, and Wendy Bernardo.

We extend our appreciation to the thousands of parents and teachers who have attended our seminars, worked with us, written to us, and shared the stories of their children with us. The students we have worked with over the decades are depicted in many of the case studies in this book. We thank them and hope they know how they have changed our lives.

Our thanks to our agent, Linda Loewenthal, for her encouragement and support, and to our Little, Brown editor, Tracy Behar, for her careful attention and great enthusiasm for our ideas.

Finally, to our children, Mark, Scott, Sara, and Liza Renzulli, our thanks for their love and inspiration. Being parents has given us our greatest gifts, provided us with some of our best lessons in life, and, most important, taught us most about patience and love.

Index

About the Authors

Dr. Joseph S. Renzulli is a professor of educational psychology at the University of Connecticut, where he also serves as director of the National Research Center on the Gifted and Talented. His research has focused on the identification and development of creativity and giftedness in young people, and on organizational models and curricular strategies for differentiated learning environments that contribute to total school improvement. A focus of his work has been on applying the pedagogy of gifted education to the improvement of learning for all students.

His most recent books include the second edition of *The Schoolwide Enrichment Model, The Multiple Menu Model for Developing Differentiated Curriculum, The Parallel Curriculum Model,* and the second edition of *Enriching Curriculum for All Students.* His 1978 article titled "What Makes Giftedness" has been cited as the most frequently referenced article in the field. Dr. Renzulli is the author of more than 380 articles in professional journals, books, chapters in books, and numerous technical reports. He has been awarded more than $35 million in research grants, $1.3 million in personnel training grants, and $3.7 million in grants and endowments to support direct service programs for students and teachers.

Dr. Renzulli is a Fellow in the American Psychological Association and a former president of the Association for the Gifted, and he has served on the editorial boards of *Learning Magazine,* the *Journal of Law and Education, Exceptionality,* and most of the national and international journals dealing with gifted education. He was a consultant to the White House Task Force on Education of the Gifted and Talented and has worked with numerous schools and ministries of education throughout the United States and abroad. His work has been translated into several languages and is widely used around the world. His most recent work is a computer-based assessment of student strengths integrated with an Internet-based search engine that matches enrichment activities and resources with individual student profiles (www.renzullilearning.com).

Dr. Renzulli was designated a Board of Trustees Distinguished Professor at the University of Connecticut in 2000, and in 2003 he was awarded an Honorary Doctor of Laws Degree from McGill University in Montreal, Canada. The American Psychological Association's *Monitor on Psychology* named Dr. Renzulli among the 25 most influential psychologists in the world. He lists as his proudest professional accomplishment being the founder of the summer Confratute program at UConn, which began in 1978, and has served approximately twenty-five thousand teachers and administrators from around the world.

Dr. Sally M. Reis is a professor and a past department head of the Educational Psychology Department at the University of Connecticut where she also serves as a principal investigator for the National Research Center on the Gifted and Talented. She was a teacher for fifteen years, eleven of which were spent working with gifted students on the elementary, junior high, and high school levels. She has authored or coauthored more than 140 articles, 14 books, 50 book chapters, and numerous monographs and technical reports. Her most recent work is a computer-based assessment of student strengths integrated with an Internet-based search engine that matches enrichment activities and resources with individual student profiles (www.renzullilearning.com).

Dr. Reis's research interests are related to special populations of gifted and talented students, including students with learning disabilities, gifted females, and diverse groups of talented students. She is also interested in extensions of the Schoolwide Enrichment Model for both gifted and talented students and as a way to expand offerings and provide general enrichment to identify talents and potentials in students who have not been previously identified as gifted. She is the codirector of Confratute, the longest-running summer institute in the development of gifts and talents. She has been a consultant to numerous schools and ministries of education throughout the U.S. and abroad and her work has been translated into several languages and is widely used around the world. She is coauthor of *The Schoolwide Enrichment Model, The Secondary Triad Model, Dilemmas in Talent Development in the Middle Grades,* and a book published in 1998 about women's talent development entitled *Work Left Undone.* Dr. Reis serves on several editorial boards, including the *Gifted Child Quarterly,* and is a past president of the National Association for Gifted Children. She recently was honored with the highest award in her field, the Distinguished Scholar of the National Association for Gifted Children, and named a Board of Trustees Distinguished Professor at the University of Connecticut.

Renzulli Learning
Proven Differentiation™   A University of Connecticut Research & Development Corporation Company

The Renzulli Learning Family Edition is an exciting new technology-based program that helps you capitalize on your child's interests, learning styles, and preferred mode of expression. Your child first completes a series of questions about his or her interests, learning styles, and expression style. This inventory takes about 30 to 40 minutes to complete and results in an individualized strength-based profile. A computer program then uses the profile to match your child's strengths with high-interest enrichment resources and exciting learning activities.

The activities your child receives are selected from a large collection of enrichment learning resources that have been carefully reviewed by curriculum specialists to ensure that they are educationally sound and promote both engagement and enjoyment in learning. Thousands of activities from the world's best museums, libraries, and scientific organizations are included in the databases from which your child's activities are selected. The activities are in highly engaging areas such as virtual field trips, e-books, projects, creativity training, critical-thinking activities, independent study, and interactive online programs that promote the application of knowledge rather than mere memorization of information.

Your child can also complete high-interest projects using Renzulli's Wizard Project Maker and can store his or her favorite sites and topics in an electronic portfolio for further investigation or future projects.

The Renzulli Learning Family Edition is currently being used by families all over the world. Renzulli Learning can help you better understand how your child learns and provide innovative and exciting ways to promote learning and to light up your child's mind.